D1521135

Democratic Reform in Yugoslavia

Democratic Reform in Yugoslavia

The Changing Role of the Party

April Carter

Princeton University Press
Princeton, New Jersey

Published by Princeton University Press, Princeton, New Jersey

LCC 81-47910
ISBN 0-691-09397-0

This book has been composed in Aldine Roman

Clothbound editions of Princeton University Press books
are printed on acid-free paper, and binding materials are
chosen for strength and durability

Printed in the United States of America by
Maple Vail Press, Binghamton, New York

CONTENTS

List of Abbreviations

Periodicals

NIN	*Nedeljne Informativne Novine*; a weekly published in Belgrade
VUS	*Vjesnik u Srijedu*; a weekly published in Zagreb
RFE	*Radio Free Europe*

Organizations

EB	Executive Bureau
EC	Executive Committee
FEC	Federal Executive Council – the Government of Yugoslavia.
LCY	League of Communists of Yugoslavia.
SAWPY	Socialist Alliance of the Working People of Yugoslavia (sometimes abbreviated to SA or SAWP)
YF	Youth Federation

Organizations (Serbo-Croat)

CK	Centralni Komitet (Central Committee)
IB	Izvršni Buro (Executive Bureau)
IK	Izvršni Komitet (Executive Committee)
SKJ	Savez Komunista Jugoslavije (League of Communists of Yugoslavia)
SK B i H	Savez Komunista Bosnie i Hercogovine (League of Communists of Bosnia and Herzogovina)
SK C.G.	Savez Komunista Crne Gore (League of Communists of Montenegro)
SKH	Savez Komunista Hrvatske (League of Communists of Croatia)
SKM	Savez Komunista Makedonie (League of Communists of Macedonia)
SKS	Savez Komunista Serbije (League of Communists of Serbia)
SKS	Savez Komunista Slovenije (League of Communists of Slovenia)

Acknowledgements

Whilst doing early research for this book I was received with great kindness by a number of people in Yugoslavia who made helpful suggestions. It would however be invidious to imply that any of them has any responsibility at all for the contents of this book. I am also indebted to a number of colleagues for useful comments on some of the theoretical considerations raised in this book. But by far my most substantial debt is to Richard Kindersley, who gave me valuable advice on research, read two earlier drafts, and made detailed suggestions about both major and minor issues of interpretation and presentation. He is certainly responsible for reducing the number of errors in this book, but in no way responsible for any that remain.

Introduction

Eastern Europe has, in the years since Stalin's death, seen a number of popular movements for democratic reform: Poland and Hungary in 1956, Czechoslovakia in 1968 and Poland again in 1980. There has been a lively intellectual debate about the possibilities of reform associated with these movements, a debate pursued in the last decade by disaffected intellectuals in many parts of Eastern Europe. There have also been more cautious attempts by some Communist Party leaders to promote reform from above. The Polish experiment, symbolised by the creation of the independent Solidarity Trade Union, is the most dramatic so far, but still unpredictable.

The most sustained attempt to promote a model of socialist democracy radically diverging from the Soviet prototype has, however, taken place in Yugoslavia. The Yugoslav party under Tito broke with Stalin in 1948, and by 1950 had begun a searching critique of what was wrong with the internal politics of Stalinism. Reform in Yugoslavia has been initiated primarily from above — though workers and students exerted some influence on politics from below in the period 1968–71. The predominant role of the party leadership in designing experiments in reform meant that change was less rapid and far reaching than in the Prague Spring, and despite the speculations of intellectuals round *Praxis* and other theoretical journals the intellectual debate was less intensive than in Czechoslovakia. But the fact that reforms have been tested in practice, that the Yugoslavs have shown a continuing willingness to innovate, and that in the 1960s a lively and independent minded set of party leaders were prepared to talk openly about the difficulties of reform, means that Yugoslavia provides the best case study available so far of the real possibilities and limits of democratic reform within a communist-party state. An additional advantage in studying Yugoslavia is that, although sensitivity to Soviet reactions did sometimes influence party attitudes, Yugoslavia's established independence of Moscow ensured that the most important limitation on other East European regimes — the threat of direct Soviet intervention — has not imposed an arbitrary external check on democratic change.

Yugoslavia's 30-year experiment in socialist democracy has run a varied course. There were two periods of intense debate at the top of the party, relative freedom and rapid reform, in 1952–3 and 1966–71, both followed by a reaction towards stricter party control. But there have in addition been longer-term and more consistent commitments to some aspects of the independent Yugoslav model of socialism. The 1952–3 period stressed restoration of true Marxist–Leninist principles, in particular the 'withering away' of the state, and gave priority to dismantling both state and party bureaucracy, decentralizing government power and replacing the party's 'leading role' by a more limited and less autocratic 'guiding role'. The idea most central to the concept of socialist democracy in the 1950s, heralded in 1950 when Tito announced the principle of 'factories to the workers', was that workers should participate directly in running their own enterprises. This approach held out the possibility of genuine working class democratic control and of undermining the bureaucratic power of the state in economic allocation and regulation. It also made popular participation a touchstone of democracy.

The discussion and experiment in the early fifties was marked by ideological fervour and a degree of utopianism, which encouraged even Tito to speak in terms of the (ultimate) withering away of the party as well as the state, and which encouraged Milovan Djilas to go too far, too fast, for his more pragmatic colleagues, and to speculate publicly about the party dissolving itself immediately in the broad popular front body, the Socialist Alliance. Djilas was formally denounced and expelled from the party early in 1954, and the period of radical debate was temporarily brought to a halt, while the party reverted in practice towards its old commanding role. Reforms continued, however, under the control of the party leadership, at the level of local government, in the systematic extension of worker participation in management to all types of enterprise, and in further devolution of economic power to enterprises. The party Programme adopted at the Seventh Congress set out the Yugoslav ideal of participatory democracy in the work place and in the local commune, characterized as 'self management', and also maintained in theory the purely 'guiding' role of the party adopted at the Sixth Congress in 1952, when the party had been symbolically renamed the League of Communists (LCY).

The Yugoslav party which emerged victorious from the partisan war against the Axis powers and confronted Stalin in 1948 was a party marked by crusading zeal and fierce pride in its achievements, attributes which precipitated the conflict with Moscow and which the leadership carried over into the initial attempt to create a new form of socialist democracy, to overcome the extreme poverty of their society, and to triumph over the economic blockade and political campaign conducted against them by the Soviet bloc. At lower levels party officials had often been corrupted by their new found power and acted very arbitrarily. The party had not at any level been accustomed to showing tolerance towards its critics or opponents, nor to displaying any sympathy with liberal values and principles. But a rather more tolerant and liberal spirit did begin to characterize Yugoslav politics in the 1960s and influenced the new movement towards reform.

One of the precipitating factors making for reform was the need to improve the economic performance of the country. After achieving impressive growth rates in the 1950s the indices of economic growth were slowing by the early 1960s. Debate about reform was therefore often marked by concern for economic efficiency, and was less utopian in vision than in the early fifties, although attempts to create a market economy were arguably very radical in their political and social implications. A number of reform leaders did, however, have a genuine commitment to promoting a greater degree of democratic choice and effective participation inside the party and in society as a whole, welcomed greater freedom of debate, and accepted a degree of dissent. The period of Yugoslavia's 'second reform movement', which gathered momentum in mid 1966 and ended in December 1971, saw very interesting and wide ranging political experimentation. It also established an atmosphere of considerable freedom for Yugoslav citizens in their private capacity, much greater than that enjoyed in other East European countries, let alone the Soviet Union.

The latest phase of Yugoslav politics has seen a marked decrease in political liberalism, though at a personal level Yugoslavs still enjoy considerable latitude, and there is greater stress on central control inside the party and an orthodox party role. But the League has not repudiated all the institutional changes of the sixties. The 1974 state Constitution has maintained a considerable devolution of power to the republics, and the market economy created in 1965 still operates. Moreover the cornerstone of the Yugoslav system, self-management, was stressed in ideological formulations in 1972 and received further support and elaboration in a law of 1976 increasing the powers of shop floor units inside large enterprises.

Reflection on the course of the Yugoslav experiment suggests that there are two contrasting models of democratic reform which can logically be pursued by a communist party committed to significant change: a participatory model drawing on the Rousseauist and Marxist theoretical tradition of democracy, and a liberal model freely adapted to the circumstances of a socialist one-party state. The participatory model was implicit

in the reforms of the 1950s, the liberal model dominant in the aims of
the party reformers in the 1960s, although its nature was obscured by the
obligatory rhetoric of 'self management', and the model itself was opposed
by an intellectual and student new left movement. These conflicting
concepts of reform were also apparent in the Czechoslovak reform movement, but the conflict was clearer in Yugoslavia as the liberals put their
ideas into practice. Reflection on the Yugoslav experience, and comparison
with other communist regimes, also suggests that party reformers will
normally, from habit, training and self interest, tend to avoid following
either model too far towards its logical conclusion, and will fall back
on a concept of party reform which might be construed as a return to
Lenin.

A participatory model of democracy stems most naturally from the
Marxist commitments of a communist party committed to reform. Even
official Soviet ideology extols the virtues of participation as a central
element in a Marxist theory of democracy, though Soviet style regimes
generally manipulate popular participation. Marx's pamphlet on the
Paris Commune, which the Yugoslavs celebrate as a vital landmark in their
revolutionary tradition, is usually read as an endorsement of the institutional forms of the Commune government and of worker control of
factories.[1] The participatory model grows out of a republican theory
of citizenship which stresses political commitment and duty rather than
individual rights and freedoms, and which accepts the need for democratic
political control of education and culture. It is also in principle a strongly
egalitarian model opposed to institutionalizing group interests and seeks
a consensus of ideas and values which will promote a 'general will'.[2]

The model, as interpreted by the Yugoslavs in the 1950s and early
1960s, implied in principle a radical decentralization of political power
to local government, the 'commune'; extension of democratic control
to the sphere of work; elements of direct democracy through ward level
voters' meetings and workers' assemblies, and frequent use of referenda;
electoral choice of delegates mandated to their electorates and measures
to avoid any professionalization of politics, for example frequent rotation
of all elected delegates and officials. This model was consistent with the
goal of a 'withering away' of the state and with Marx's comments on the
Paris Commune.

The most obvious question which arises is whether this model can be
more than a participatory façade if the whole system is organized and
directed by a centralized and hierarchical communist party. There is
a general theoretical issue as to whether there is in principle an intrinsic
contradiction between a decentralized, participatory model and any party

system, whether single or multi-party.[3] If it is assumed that mass political parties tend to be fairly centralized and committed to specific policy goals, then it does seem likely that they will undermine the independence of workers' councils or local assemblies. A multi-party system may produce ideological divisions which preclude a local unity of purpose, but a one-party system has ample opportunity to manipulate a declared common will.

There is in addition a very specific conflict between an orthodox communist-party interpretation of its role and the standard requirements of party discipline on the one hand, and the autonomy of local participatory bodies on the other. These issues were openly debated in Yugoslavia in the late 1960s. The problems facing the party were:

1 should the party meet in advance of workers councils or commune assemblies to agree on preferred policies;
2 could the party allow representative bodies to pursue policies opposed to the party line;
3 were individual communists on these bodies obliged to speak and vote for party policies? (If they did this implied an abdication of their individual judgement and political rights, if they did not it implied an abdication of party discipline.)

Yugoslav theorists disagreed in their answers to these questions, though they tended to propose a distinction between basic policy guidelines and decisions on detail, assigning the party responsibility for the former, but not the latter.

Yugoslav theorists did not wholly evade these issues when they developed their participatory model in the early fifties. The Sixth Congress resolution to alter the party role recognized the need for a change in the position of the party. But they confronted them more openly and in more detail in the sixties, when it was clear that self management would only be infused with political life if steps were taken to loosen party control and to make effective popular activity possible. The elaboration of self management in the 1963 Constitution made evident the need for a corresponding change in the internal and external mode of operation of the party.

The liberal model of reform which evolved in the 1960s was promoted largely by the requirements of economic reform, but was also a response to a genuine desire to promote political democracy and to extend the power of self managing bodies. One of the most obvious requirements for giving workers' councils real decision-making power, for example, was to dismantle the state controls over the economy and in particular over investment decisions. Thus the Yugoslavs quite logically embarked on the creation of a market economy in the name of self-management. But a competitive market system stressing economic incentives and criteria of efficiency, and requiring industrial mergers and increasing technological sophistication, has also proved antagonistic to worker equality and democratic control of enterprises and enhanced managerial and technocratic power.

Liberal economic reforms in communist states have entailed an ideological shift of emphasis, abandoning explicitly the ideal of economic equality and reducing security of employment for market freedoms and inequality of rewards, while openly recognizing a diversity of interests which may conflict. The existence of a market economy may therefore increase the independence not only of managers, but also of trade unions, since workers will be brought into sharper conflict with management and the party will recognize the legitimacy of workers' interests whilst accepting less direct responsibility for safeguarding their welfare. Legalizing strikes may therefore be more acceptable in a market context, and the Yugoslav Draft Self-Managers' Code of 1971 included the right to strike.

A liberal model drawing implicitly or explicitly on Western liberal theory places a positive value on social diversity, unlike the pure participatory ideal or Soviet Marxism, which have both espoused the goal of a uniform social interest. Liberal reform therefore implies recognition of some form of pluralism, an issue which was a source of debate and some confusion in Yugoslavia in the sixties. Official theory defined some economic interest groups as illegitimate, if they sought economic power through monopoly and exerted political pressure to strengthen their own economic interests, at the expense of weaker sectors of the economy and the social interest. Legitimate pluralism suggested as a minimum greater influence for social groups already granted organizational status, and hence more autonomy for trade unions, student unions and other mass organizations. Liberal reform also implies respect for individual freedom in family life, work, travel and recreation; for the freedom of individual belief, speech and association; and for the freedom of science, learning and culture. It therefore requires legal safeguards of personal and group freedom and respect for the due process of law. In contrast with the participatory model it may value political activism less highly than the ability to express diverse interests and opinions, and concentrate on providing a choice of qualified representatives to ruling bodies rather than maximizing the opportunity of all social groups to participate in assemblies. The liberal reform model also implies the desirability of parliamentary curbs on government and judicial checks on government power. The greater independence of the Yugoslav parliament in the legislative and budgetary sphere and its willingness to vote against the government on specific issues in the sixties suggested a shift towards a parliamentary concept of democracy, though officially the Yugoslavs denied the existence of a division and balance of powers on the Western pattern and insisted on the orthodox Marxist unity of the executive and legislature. The Constitutional Court set up under the 1963 Constitution also implied a move towards the American concept of constitutionalism, though in practice the role of the Court has been limited to disentangling conflicts of jurisdiction at various levels of government rather than challenging the scope of government.

When considering how far the participatory and liberal models of reform conflict in their values and in their institutional results, it is important to note the ambiguities involved in a 'liberal' approach. In a communist reform movement there may well be two conflicting strands: an economic liberalism stressing economic efficiency as a means to social progress and the role of economic incentives; and a humanist ideal drawing on the libertarian elements in the Marxist tradition and stressing individual autonomy and the intellectual, cultural and political values of a free society. Both were represented in Yugoslavia, where the virtues of a free market were sometimes extolled with an Adam Smith-like enthusiasm, and where the 'humanist intelligentsia' represented by the *Praxis* group upheld a humanist and liberal interpretation of Marx. This latter ideal meshes with belief in political activity as a form of necessary self expression and upholds social and political equality against technocratic and elitist tendencies. It is therefore possible to interpret liberal reform so that its values coincide rather than conflict with the participatory model.

It is arguable that in practice there is some overlap between the liberal and participatory programmes of reform: that both require respect for freedom of speech, of the press and of association if they are to achieve their goals; and that the principle of the autonomy of self-managing institutions may strengthen for example the academic freedom of universities. In some circumstances, however, the institutional requirements of the two models come into conflict. Selection of effective political representatives to workers councils, local or national assemblies, may not square with rotation and an end to political professionalism; it may be necessary to choose between elitist but effective representative bodies and an egalitarian participatory ideal. This dilemma emerged in the Yugoslav elections of 1967 and 1969. There is also a conflict between a participatory ideal of worker self-management and the alternative of defending worker interests through strong trade unions. Consultative forms of participation may supplement weak trade unions, but in practice participatory forms may undermine unionism both in principle and in terms of organizational effectiveness. It is certainly arguable that participatory institutions are more easily manipulated by the party, so that participatory theory may be invoked against liberal gains. For example the adoption since 1974 of a 'delegate' system for all elections has in practice undermined the degree of electoral choice that existed briefly in the late 1960s and strengthened party control over delegates in the assemblies, under the guise of eliminating political elitism.

The liberal model of reform, much more obviously than the participatory model, is in conflict with the commonly accepted values of Marxist theory and the political practice of ruling communist parties. It tests the extent to which the party is prepared to relax control over society more directly, for example by promoting trade union autonomy and asserting the right of dissent. A consistent policy of liberal reform requires recognition of organized opposition and opposition programmes, which implies legalizing factions inside the party and allowing opposition candidates in parliamentary elections. It is arguable that the natural tendency for a liberal model is to evolve towards a pluralism of political parties, a tendency illustrated by the Czechoslovak reform movement.

If the ultimate logic of liberal reform is a multi-party system and of participatory democracy a non-party system, then combining either approach with maintenance of the dominant role of the Communist Party clearly requires a delicate balancing act. Alternatively communist reformers may opt for a less radical conception of liberalization and democratization. In practice this is what many party leaders espousing reform have tried to do, either consciously seeking to 'return' to Leninism, or pragmatically adapting existing structures to allow for a greater degree of genuine consultation and rather more opportunity to express different interests and views.

This approach might be compatible either with a fully planned economy or market socialism. What it does imply is insistence on internal party discipline and continued party dominance, whilst the leadership encourages greater debate and rank and file participation inside the party, and removes the party from involvement in detailed administration in government and the economy. One obvious facet of this theory of reform is to end the purely subordinate status of mass organizations and grant them limited autonomy. Lenin's answer to the problem of the correct status of the trade unions, adopted at the Tenth Congress of the Bolshevik Party in 1921, which rejected both the claims of the Workers' Opposition to trade-union independence and power, and Trotsky's proposed total subordination of the unions, suggests an ideal solution and a neat dialectical argument of the kind which trips off the tongue of party theorists. The other obvious measure, stressed by Yugoslav reformers in the sixties, is to create some separation between party and government by ensuring different people hold top posts in each; some differentiation between party and government was supported by both Lenin and Trotsky in principle in the 1920s.

The majority of Yugoslav party leaders implicitly held to a conception of limited reform, which they periodically made explicit by stressing the need for democratic centralism in the party, by asserting the importance of party control over the conduct of elections, by reacting strongly to signs of popular 'spontaneity' or independent organization, and by suppressing advocacy of a multi-party system. The comparative consistency of their position was, however, obscured by the formal party commitment to the ideal of participatory democracy, by the implied radicalism of some of the popular slogans of the reform — for example 'separating the party from power' — and the ambiguities of the Sixth Congress commitment to the party's 'guiding' and 'educational' role. The stance of the Yugoslav party on reform was also complicated by the fact that party leaders were divided in their assessments of what was either desirable or permissible, and some leaned quite far towards a liberal reform model.

This book concentrates on the period of the 'second reform movement' which may be dated 1961–71. This was the most interesting period of Yugoslav politics from the standpoint of attempts to achieve reform, and illustrates some of the dilemmas of trying to reconcile a limited 'Leninist' conception of party reform with more radical commitments to self management or liberal freedoms, and also some of the potential conflicts between a participatory and liberal model. Because it was a comparatively free and tolerant period it is also well documented, with the press reporting disagreements inside the party and dissent outside, and party spokesmen themselves airing their personal views and collective difficulties in public.

The main focus of this study is the party itself. As a result it covers the main political development in Yugoslav society in the 1960s, but since the emphasis is on party reform detailed analysis starts in 1964, the year of the Eighth Congress. Concentration on the party results naturally in an examination of most of the aspects of the reform, and gives due weight to the central questions of inner-party democracy and of how the party interpreted its role in various spheres.

This focus on the party does, however, also result in omission of issues of considerable importance in the politics of the period: economic problems and debates receive minimum attention; so does the extensive decentralization of government powers to the republics in the period 1967–71; and there is no comprehensive account of the nationalist problem or the complexities of nationalist politics, though it is essential to take account of nationalism as it affected party organization, promoted reform in the early sixties and undermined it later.

There are also certain omissions which are relevant when assessing the degree of liberalism achieved in the sixties. This study does not cover the surprisingly vigorous parliamentary activity in the mid-sixties, the relations between the party and the various churches, or the important issues of academic and cultural freedom (except where these overlap with freedom of the press).

The other gaps in this account stem not from the focus chosen but from the nature of the evidence. The main sources used are party materials and the party press, Yugoslav newspapers and periodicals, and the findings of Yugoslav social scientists. These sources, even when supplemented by the excellent work of some Western researchers and commentators, do not provide equally full information on all aspects of internal party reform or of the role of the party. As a result some intrinsically important questions, in particular the independence of the judicial process, get less coverage than they deserve. Despite these limitations, however, the comparative openness of the Yugoslav political system does allow for the amassing of a fair degree of information on many significant issues, and in most cases there is enough evidence to assess with reasonable confidence how far the League of Communists did put its declared goals into effect, and to analyse the reasons for the gap that remained between theory and practice.

Notes

1. Karl Marx, 'The civil war in France', in K. Marx and F. Engels, *Selected Works*, Progress Publishers, Moscow, 1935.
2. Jean-Jacques Rousseau, *The Social Contract*, Penguin, Harmondsworth, 1968.
3. See Hannah Arendt, *On Revolution*, Penguin, Harmondsworth, 1973; for the alternative argument that parties are compatible with local participatory bodies see: C. B. Macpherson, *The Life and Times of Liberal Democracy*, Oxford University Press, Oxford, 1977.

PART I

WHAT KIND OF PARTY?

1 The Politics of Reform in the Party

Introduction

A history of the League of Communists between 1964 and 1972 is primarily the history of a reform movement: its legitimation at the Eighth Party Congress in 1964; its victory in 1966; its subsequent evolution and its partial defeat after 1971. The reformers represented a coalition of interests pressing for a more decentralized economy reliant on market mechanisms, for greater republican independence and for more democracy in the party and in society. The reformers were united up to July 1966 by their struggle against the opposition, headed and symbolized by Aleksandar Ranković, Vice-President of Yugoslavia since 1963, who was responsible for the secret police. As a Serb Ranković represented the interests of the less developed republics opposed to the economic reforms and stood for economic and political centralism. The relative unity of the reformers was due not only to tactical considerations, but to the logical interconnection between support for economic reforms in the richer republics of Slovenia and Croatia and demands for greater independence from Belgrade, and between belief in economic independence for enterprises and reducing the powers of local party bureaucrats. But after the reformers were free to implement their economic and political measures the implications of market socialism, of devolution of powers to the republics and of modifying the old-style party role and discipline became more apparent, and divergences in the political and ideological commitments of the reformers became more significant.

Before examining the struggle between factions within the party leading to 1966, it is necessary to sketch in how the League was organized up to 1964. Since the end of 1948 the structure of the League had reflected the political and administrative divisions of the country: a federation with six republics and two provinces, which had been created by the Yugoslav Constitution of 1946 in recognition of the claims of diverse nationalities and in an attempt to avoid the nationalist conflicts, especially between

Serbs and Croats, which had dogged the pre-war Yugoslavia, which had
been a Serb dominated unitary state. The heritage of distrust by other
nationalities of Serbian hegemony was a major factor in the politics of
the 1960s. The party regularized its structure at the Fifth Congress of 1948
held soon after the break with Moscow, when Stalin had accused the
Yugoslav party of hiding its political activities, which were never publicized,
and of failing to maintain internal democracy, for example in electing the
Central Committee. The Congress met Soviet accusations of lack of
openness about the internal organization of the party and of failure to
honour proper electoral procedures. The republican parties also formalized
their position: the Serbian, Croatian, Slovenian and Macedonian parties,
which had been created to allow representation of national interests in the
Yugoslav party itself, held follow-up congresses; and the party bodies in
Bosnia and Montenegro (where there had previously been no political
necessity to placate national pride by creating nominally separate parties)
obeyed instructions given by Ranković at the Fifth Congress to elevate
themselves to republican-party status. The provinces of Vojvodina and
Kosovo were represented within the Serbian republican party by their own
provincial conferences and committees.[1] Below each republican central
committee there was a hierarchy extending through the district (srez) or
city committee, responsible for a number of communes, to the commune
committee, which in turn had jurisdiction over the basic organizations
in its area.[2]

Since the Sixth Congress of 1952, policy on where to form basic
organizations had varied. After the Sixth Congress the party had dissolved
its organizations in the administration and in social and cultural bodies
as part of its newly declared policy of abandoning its controlling role
for a guiding role within Yugoslav society. The Sixth Congress Statute
only provided for basic organizations in economic enterprises and on
a territorial basis, although it also envisaged the possibility of setting
up aktivs in other institutions. During the mid-fifties, when the leadership
tried to reactivate and strengthen the party, the aktivs were created in
all spheres of work. There were, however, some spheres, in particular
universities and secondary schools, where an official party organization
was thought necessary. At the end of 1958 there were over 1000 basic
organizations in higher education and 1200 in unspecified 'institutions'.[3]
After the March 1962 Executive Committee Plenum and the Executive
Committee Letter which demanded much stricter discipline within the
party, the process of winding up aktivs, which often met infrequently and
did little, and replacing them by basic organizations was accelerated, so
that by mid-1964 there were 1890 basic organizations in social service

institutions. There was also an increase in the number of party organizations in schools and universities due in part to the expansion of the
universities.[4]

By 1964 party organizations had been set up in some ministries: in
the Secretariats for Foreign Affairs and for Foreign Trade, whose party
bodies merged during 1964; and in the Secretariat for Internal Affairs.[5]

One of the most important sections of the party had existed ever since
1945: in the armed services. The League of Communists within the Yugoslav
People's Army had since 1949 been associated with the Central Committee
through a special Central Committee bureau. Although it held its own
annual conference its leading organs were not formally elected, but
appointed.[6] The party organization was represented on Central Committee
bodies in the same way as the republics.

Evolution of Reform

The reform movement within the party can reasonably be dated from the
passing of the economic reforms of 1961, which were designed to reduce
state control, by making prices more responsive to market forces and giving
banks greater control over distribution of credit, and to improve Yugoslavia's
competitive position in international trade by devaluation of the dinar.

During 1962 the Ranković opposition blocked the realization of the
economic reforms, which were eroded by a series of specific economic
measures taken in that year. There was also a purge within the party
designed to strengthen internal party discipline, and Tito made a speech
in Split which signalled new intolerance of expressions of dissent in
intellectual and cultural spheres. This swing towards a less liberal style in
Yugoslav politics coincided with Tito's *rapprochement* with Moscow in
the same year. It is at least plausible that Tito decided to back the Ranković
group partly because he knew that this would be more acceptable to the
Soviet leaders and because he saw wider foreign-policy gains from ending
the breach with the Soviet Union.[7] Since the success of the economic
reforms was linked to gaining further large Western credits it is also probable
that the party leaders were divided in their assessment of the *rapprochement*
with Moscow.[8]

The crucial meeting in 1962 which apparently ended in Tito giving
temporary support to Ranković, and which was the scene of violent
polemics between the opposed groups in the top leadership, was an enlarged
session of the Executive Committee of the LCY held in March. Rumours
circulated that Serbs and Macedonians had drawn guns on one another
during the session. The debate and conclusions reached at this meeting,

however, were never published and are still shrouded in mystery. The revelations made after Ranković had been deposed in July 1966 stopped short of explaining in detail what happened at the March Executive Committee meeting. A reporter from *VUS* put the question to Miko Tripalo, one of the younger generation of Croatian reformers who rose to the top in the mid-sixties and who was a member of the party commission investigating abuses of power by the Security Service. The reporter noted that one question being widely asked at meetings in Croatia was: 'what did really happen at the 1962 EC Plenum?' Tripalo, who had not been at the meeting, answered initially in general terms that differences between the supporters and opponents of reform 'were brought to the surface' and that it became obvious that there were two contradictory concepts about the best policy for the future. He did, however, disclose that Ranković had arranged for the meeting to be secretly taped and that later it was transferred to a 'special durable tape which was kept at the State Security Service in four copies where they were discovered by our Commission'. Tripalo went on to comment:

> There is no doubt that eventually, when the question of the succession would have been raised, the group led by Ranković, which planned in the meantime to occupy decisive positions, would have used these materials as well to 'expose' certain comrades who might appear as 'opposition'.[9]

It seems probable that one of the targets of Ranković's attacks was the Slovene, Edvard Kardelj, chief theoretician of the party and recognized as a leading advocate of reforms. Kardelj had been one of Tito's closest aides since 1937 and was Ranković's main rival.[10] However, some observers credit the canny Vladimir Bakarić, head of the Croatian party until 1966, who was given to periods of strategic withdrawal into illness and to a delphic mode of public speech, with being the main architect of the reforms.[11]

By the time of the Eighth Congress in December 1964 the reformers were in a relatively strong position, though it is difficult to pin-point when they began to take the initiative. There had apparently been a slight shift as early as the Fourth Central Committee Plenum in July 1962, which initiated one important strand of the reformers' policy, rotation of cadres to displace the grip of the partisan generation; though it is not clear that Ranković, who had considerable control over cadre policy, necessarily opposed this move. It is certainly reasonable to see the 1963 Constitution, sponsored by Kardelj, with its emphasis on extending self-management and its introduction of rotation of offices in government, as a reform document.

Three events during 1964 were crucial in the struggle for economic reforms: the Fifth Congress of the Trade Unions in April, the Resolution adopted by the Federal Assembly on further economic development in May, and the Eighth Congress of the League in December.[12] The Congress was vitally important to the reformers, who could later draw on Congress Resolutions to prove the legitimacy of their policies; and they were clearly active in promoting their views in Congress documents, especially in elaborating the principles of economic policy incorporated in Congress materials.[13] Krste Crvenkovski, a prominent reformer who became Political Secretary of the Macedonian party in 1963, told *Politika* in 1966 about the role of the reformers in influencing the drafting of the 1964 Statute. The first draft took account of strong criticisms which had been made of the work of the LCY Central Committee, but as the Congress drew near 'other tendencies' gained in influence, 'so that the platform for wider democracy in the League and the concept of its new role in the coming period were reduced to a minimum'. This minimum was preserved, however, and the Statute itself was 'a kind of compromise'.[14] The reformers were prepared to proclaim publicly their expectations. Tripalo said in a newspaper interview that he expected 'a lot' from the Congress, including the conclusive authorization by the party of more democracy, more self-management and more favourable conditions for enterprises.[15]

At the first Central Committee meeting immediately after the Eighth Congress Ranković announced a number of changes in the structure of the Central Committee commissions, apparently designed to focus the energies of members on the problem of the economy and society, rather than purely on inner-party matters.[16] The Committee also endorsed the decision to create one unified secretariat in place of the existing Executive Committee Secretariat and the 'Organizational-Political Secretariat' of the Central Committee. The latter incorporated the Organizational Secretaries of the Republican Committees and appears to have been dominated by Ranković's supporters. The dissolution of this body, and the abandonment of the formal title Organizational Secretary at the same time, both look like an attempt to erode Ranković's organizational base and status. Svetozar Vukmanović, who is usually known by his nickname 'Tempo', and who as head of the Trade Union Federation in the early sixties played an important role in the struggle for reform, observed later that, from an organizational point of view, Ranković practically 'had the entire party in his hands'. He also spoke of the Organizational-Political Secretariat, of which he had been a member, and noted that though formed for political work the Secretariat had confined itself to discussing membership, expulsions and discipline, and that Ranković had personally vetoed attempts to discuss issues like the standard of living, which he said were not matters for the Central Committee.[17]

Despite the stated intention of the new Statute to subordinate the Executive Committee to the wider body of the Central Committee, no real change appears to have occurred until after the fall of Ranković; although there was an indication, made in a brief aside at the Fifth Plenum in October 1966, that attempts had been made earlier to invigorate the Central Committee through reorganization, presumably as part of the reformers' struggle to limit Ranković's influence, but that these measures had been blocked.[18]

During 1965 the reformers succeeded in pushing through a further package of economic measures intended to enable enterprises to dispose of 70 per cent of their income and to have a decisive say over the credit policy of banks. There was, however, continued obstruction of the actual implementation of the agreed measures, especially in Serbia and Montenegro. Bakarić said in a speech to the Croatian Executive Committee in December 1965 that the battle must be waged for the proper implementation of the decisions passed at the Eighth Congress, and claimed pointedly that the Croatian party had carried out these decisions more consistently than some other republican parties. He also used the occasion to make a specific plea for more republican autonomy, noting that nationalist sentiments and the relations between Serbia and Croatia could best be resolved by looking to the future development of socialism and of the federation. 'It is quite clear that the federation itself ought to be more "federalised", that it must be more flexible, because what is introduced at one time cannot remain valid for good.'[19]

The struggle between the reformers and their opponents was brought fully into the open at the Third Plenum of the Central Committee in 1966. The Plenum opened on 25–6 February, but was then adjourned whilst the Serbian Executive Committee met to discuss problems of the reform and of nationalism in the republic. The Plenum reconvened on 11 March. The proceedings of this Plenum were very fully reported in the Yugoslav press and revealed the rifts in the Committee. Tito sided with the reformers, and in his opening speech bitterly attacked lack of discipline in implementing agreed policy. He said *inter alia* that one of the main obstacles to reform lay in 'the top circles of our League of Communists . . . certain communists who spoke in favour of the reform did nothing in reality, or acted in the opposite direction', and observed that criticism of this obstruction had so far been too generalized.[20] According to Tempo's memoirs, Tito admitted that relations between Ranković and himself were bad and took Tempo's advice to talk to Ranković in advance of the Third Plenum. Tempo notes that 'at the Plenum Ranković spoke well'.[21] The Conclusions of the Plenum duly called for the agreed measures to be implemented rapidly.

The conflict at the top of the League was not resolved, however, and came to a head in June 1966. The sequence of events is still partially obscure, but Tito was apparently persuaded to act when Army Intelligence demonstrated that Ranković had been bugging Tito's own offices and residences.[22] An Executive Committee meeting held on 16 June set up an investigatory commission to report on Ranković's activities, and its findings were publicized at the Brioni Central Committee meeting on 1–2 July, when Ranković was denounced for abuse of his police powers and for factional activity. The director of the security service throughout most of the post-war period, and Ranković's ally, Svetislav Stefanović-Ćeća, was condemned at the same time.

It has been suggested that Ranković had moved on to the offensive and planned to organize a *coup d'état* when Tito went abroad.[23] Whether or not this interpretation is correct — Tripalo gave it as his opinion that Ranković was planning to seize power in the long term and not immediately[24] — there is convincing evidence that Ranković was, as Tito claimed, engaged in 'a factional group struggle, a struggle for power'.[25] During the Central Committee discussion one member commented: 'all the materials seemed to point to the fact that there was taking shape a policy different from that of the League of Communists, on both the internal and international plane'.[26] Ranković had apparently established close contacts with Soviet intelligence and often visited the Soviet Ambassador.[27] He had clearly established effective control over the Secretariat for Foreign Affairs, where the Deputy Foreign Minister, Bosko Vidaković, was one of Ranković's key men, and his supporters on the party Committee were able to influence personnel policy, including the appointment of ambassadors.[28]

One well publicized example of the power wielded by the pro-Ranković faction inside the foreign service was the Predrag Ajtić case. Ajtić had been a prominent and popular party official in Kosovo and was appointed ambassador to Bulgaria in June 1962, where he was approached by a member of the foreign service who suggested to him that there were two 'parties' in the League and that he should decide for the one led by Ranković. *Politika Ekspres* later speculated that Ranković's strategy had been to attract key men representing various parts of the country.[29] When Ajtić refused to side with Ranković's party he was dismissed from his post and expelled from the League on the evidence of two of his subordinates that he had criticized Yugoslav foreign policy. An attaché who refused to testify against Ajtić was also fired.[30]

Republican Reactions to Brioni

The revelations made at Brioni and at the subsequent republican central committee meetings indicated that Ranković built up his power base by using his dual position as Organizational Secretary of the party, and effective head of the Security Service, to control cadre appointments. As Organizational Secretary he could rely on an established habit of subservience by officials in some republics to the centre on cadre issues. Several speakers at the Montenegrin Central Committee meeting said they had known for years that all Montenegrin cadre lists were checked with Ranković and it had been accepted as a matter of course.[31] As head of the police he used police records to influence choice of personnel and the careers of individuals in the party and in the Federal Government.

The republican meetings were concerned with three main questions: how far sections of their own party and security service had been involved in Ranković's factional activity; how far Ranković had directly controlled cadre policy in the republic; and the degree to which the security service in the republic had abused its powers. Not surprisingly the Serbian party, which had been dominated directly by Ranković, admitted that all these charges could be brought against them — although even in the Serbian Central Committee there was a liberal opposition.[32] It was also clear that the Ranković group had been active in Montenegro, the 'second Serbian republic'. The Montenegrin leaders, who were compromised by their association with Ranković, tried to minimize their admissions of guilt, but came under fierce attack from members of the Montenegrin Central Committee, who criticized the Executive Committee Report and exposed the extent of republican subservience to Ranković and abuses of the security service. The critics — in an unprecedented display of democratic power by the Central Committee over its executive — forced the resignation of the main target of their attacks: a former republican Secretary for Internal Affairs and Organizational Secretary of the Montenegrin party.

The Croatian and Slovenian party meetings by contrast denied that Ranković had exercised any direct control over their republics, though the Croats admitted that they had been indirectly hampered by Ranković and that he had damaged the career of Croats in federal organs.[33] Both the Croatian and Slovenian party Executives also made strong claims for the independence of the security service in their republics from Belgrade; the Croats claimed to have curbed political abuses by their service, and the Slovenes said there was no evidence their security service had been used for political purposes. Two members of the Slovene Executive Committee were, however, highly critical of the official report and suggested that the Slovene service had bugged political officials and tried to discredit progressives, and that the republican Secretariat for Internal Affairs had only resisted the centre over 'administrative competences'.[34] Despite an element of official self congratulation by the Croatian and Slovenian leaders, the evidence does suggest that they were comparatively independent of Belgrade.

The picture so far appears to support the most popular interpretation of the conflict between Ranković and the reformers, as a natural coalition of the two most developed and Western-orientated republics, Slovenia and Croatia, against the backward republics led by Serbia, who had a vested interest in retaining a centralized economic system which supported less developed areas and subsidized non-competitive enterprises. According to this interpretation the division between the economically progressive 'north-west' and the underdeveloped 'south-east' is enhanced by the historical national antagonism between Croatian and Slovene aspirations to autonomy and the centralist tendencies of Belgrade. This interpretation overlooks the possible conflict between apparent economic interest and republican nationalism in some of the poorer republics, however, and also ignores the role of different attitudes and beliefs among party leaders within a republic. Both considerations are relevant in examining where Macedonia and Bosnia stood in relation to the conflict between Ranković and the reformers. In Macedonia, although there is some evidence of a tendency to side with Serbia on opposition to the economic reforms, there is also ample evidence that the Macedonian party under Crvenkovski led the way in demanding and partially implementing political reforms.[35] The position of Bosnia is particularly difficult to determine. There is evidence that it was under Ranković's influence – until 1965 Djuro Pucar, head of the Veterans' Association which backed centralist and conservative policies, and a personal supporter of Ranković, was head of the Bosnian party – and that the security service was subservient to Belgrade. On the other hand reformers inside the Bosnian party seem to have had some success in promoting personnel changes and reform policies at the 1965 Republican Congress.[36] Moslem members of the Bosnian party might also be expected to want republican autonomy to protect their cultural differences and ward off the ambitions of both Serbs and Croats to influence internal republican affairs. So like Macedonia its republican political aspirations were not directly related to its economic position.

Generalizations about republican parties tend to obscure the various shades of reformist or anti-reform opinion which existed in all the republics. The chief opposition to the reform appears to have been mounted by party officials at district and commune level. The Croatian economist and

advocate of reform, Rudolf Bićanić, noted that the partial decentralization
of the 1950s had created 'a middle layer of state and party officials . . .
who became pillars of dogmatism and the establishment. As a rule more
liberal opinions and critical attitudes were found at higher levels.'[37]
Hostility to reform among middle-level officials was undoubtedly based
on the threat posed to their power and privileges, but it also sprang from
fear of the political consequences of loosening party control and from
ideological commitment to economic centralism and old-style party
discipline. The Yugoslav contemporary historian Bilandžić comments
that this section of the party 'saw in the process of decentralization,
democratization, and especially in the "restoration" of a freer market type
economy and the establishment of several centres of decision making, the
road to anarchy and chaos . . . '.[38] This middle-level opposition to reform
existed in all republics, though it was stronger in Serbia than in most
other republics.

The Reform Coalition

Two economic groups sided with the party reformers in promoting
economic reforms. One group was the trade union officials representing
the more competitive industries, backed by Tempo at the head of the
Trade Union Federation. The other was the new group of managers of the
more successful enterprises, who wished to reduce governmental intervention and to be free to maximize profits. Dennison Rusinow suggests
that this class of 'successful socialist entrepreneurs' was strongly represented
in the economic chambers of the parliamentary assemblies and quotes a
pro-reform communist who confided privately: 'When we realised we would
never be able to count on the Party machinery, we put our boys into the
assemblies.'[39] Explicit support for the managers' desire for greater freedom
was written into the 'Basic Outlines for Pre-Congress Activity' adopted at
the Central Committee Plenum of March 1964. This document called for
greater independence and responsibility for 'direct producers' and managers
in making decisions on all matters concerning production, distribution and
'expanded reproduction' as the first prerequisite for improving productivity
and living standards. 'De-etatization' (reduction of state control) and
'depoliticization' (reduction of party control over the economy) became
key phrases in the reformers' vocabulary in the mid-sixties.

As in any reform movement there was also an ideological and idealistic
dimension, represented in particular by a group of intellectuals who voiced
fairly radical demands for greater democracy in the party and in society.
These demands were expressed openly at an academic conference held

in June 1964 to debate themes arising under the topic of 'Marx and Contemporary Reality'. The 1964 Conference inaugurated a series of annual academic gatherings and clearly reflected a belief that much freer and more critical debate had become possible. The discussion included analysis of the position reached by the LCY and a number of fairly concrete proposals for reform. Demands for the party to adopt fully democratic forms of organization compatible with the principles of self-management in government and the economy led the Ideological Secretary of the League, Vlahović, to condemn the idea of extending self-management to the party both at the Conference and later at the Eighth Party Congress.[40] Two of the most radical contributions were made by Besim Ibrahimpašić (from Sarajevo University) who compared the Leninist theory of the party unfavourably with Marx's original conception of the role of the Communist Party, and by Svetozar Stojanović (from Belgrade University) who spelt out the measures required to increase democracy in the Yugoslav League, including the right of minorities to disseminate opinions opposed to adopted policy decisions. Both these papers were printed in the Sarajevo theoretical journal *Pregled* together with the discussion which arose out of contributions to the Conference.[41] *Pregled* was one of a number of theoretical journals which expressed the views of the radical party academics based primarily in the philosophy faculties of the universities. The editorial boards of these journals, which included *Gledišta* in Belgrade and *Praxis* published in Zagreb, tended to overlap. Until the Brioni Plenum of July 1966 the radical academics can be seen as one wing of the reform movement in the party. Although their views were naturally criticized by more orthodox colleagues, and although a prominent reformer like Bakarić felt it was desirable to dissociate himself from advocacy of 'minority rights'[42] — that is of legalized factions in the party — their demands were on the whole in harmony with those of leading reformist spokesmen.[43] It was only after July 1966, and more especially after the student demonstrations of June 1968, that the radical academics became a prime target for attack by the liberal reformers who now dominated the League.

The Coalition Disintegrates

There were a number of reasons why, after the overthrow of Ranković, the radical theorists who had been allies of the party reformers began to coalesce into a dissident opposition group. One was that party officials, whilst being genuinely committed to democratize the organization and methods of the League, were also concerned to set limits to this process in order not to endanger the position of the party. The denunciation of

secret police powers which accompanied the victory over Ranković, and
the consequent encouragement of a much greater degree of freedom,
carried with it the danger of encouraging groups opposed to the party,
and of the disintegration of party discipline. Fejtö is probably correct in
concluding that:

> It was no coincidence that Bakarić, who up to the summer of 1966 had
> shown himself very indulgent towards the group of revisionist intellec-
> tuals in Zagreb gathered around the magazine *Praxis*, chose this particu-
> lar moment to penalize the magazine's contributors and to suspend its
> publication, although it reappeared eight months later.[44]

Miko Tripalo, speaking as Secretary of the Croatian League to the Croatian
Central Committee in February 1967, spelt out the limits to democracy
within the party from the standpoint of the now triumphant reformers.

> Finally, I would like to say that the democratization of the League of
> Communists does not mean that it can be organized on the principle
> of self-management, which is another thing about which there has been
> considerable talk recently, and that all principles which are effective in
> a body of self-management can be transferred to the League of Com-
> munists too, which in the final analysis must rest on the principle of
> democratic centralism, though with greater emphasis on democratiza-
> tion, and less emphasis on centralism. We are a political organization,
> not a debating club in which views are discussed; we are an organization
> which wishes to realise its views and see them implemented in life.[45]

Their heretical views on the extent of democracy desirable in the party,
however, were not the most important division between the radical
intellectuals and the leading party liberals. It was even more alarming when
the radicals began to criticize the effects of the economic reforms, in
particular the high level of unemployment and the inequalities of wealth.
These issues became politically explosive in June and July 1968, when the
Trade Union Congress revealed the strength of worker discontent, which
had manifested itself in numerous brief strikes but had not previously
expressed itself through official trade-union channels, and when a wave
of student protests originating in Belgrade took up demands for ending
unemployment and for economic equality. Whilst the party leaders were
prepared to condemn extremes of wealth and managerial corruption, the
logic of the economic reforms, designed to improve the efficiency of
enterprises through competition and economic incentives, and to eliminate
non-competitive 'political' factories, meant they had to oppose egalitarian
demands. In the rhetoric of the liberal reformers support for economic

'levelling' was practically identified with Stalinism, or its Yugoslav equivalent, 'Rankovićism'. By 1968 the managers of enterprises, the 'technocratic elite', were becoming the target of attacks by their erstwhile allies among intellectuals, and were in the early seventies to be blamed by the party leadership for undesirable repercussions of the reforms.

The nervousness felt by the leading party liberals in 1968 was due not only to the strength of the worker and student forces, who espoused demands for greater economic equality, but also to the continued existence of an opposition within the League hostile to the economic reforms. The new leftist views of the 1968 student movement and of the university lecturers who supported them could be seen as playing into the hands of the old guard in the party. This opposition had an organizational base in the Veteran's Association, as became clear in the 1967 elections to the parliamentary assemblies when a number of partisan heroes stood as candidates opposed to the officially sponsored candidates. As the elections also showed, this opposition was most active in Serbia, though it is reasonable to assume that there was still strong resistance to the reforms in Montenegro, where the Executive Committee had tried to minimize the repercussions of the overthrow of Ranković, and that there was still middle-level resistance to reformed leaderships in other republics.

Awareness of this opposition was indicated in various speeches and articles. Srecko Bijelić, Croatian member of the LCY Executive Committee, spoke in May 1968 about 'dilemmas, doubts, suspicion and resistance' by some individuals and groups. He went on to note that there was at that time 'a very sharp clash between the old and the new', that the old forces were trying to discredit the results of self-management and reform, and these must be the standpoints from which to attack 'all that is conservative, bureaucratic, etatist, or suspicious'. He condemned compromises being made in the League and referred especially to resistance at the level of commune conferences and committees.[46] *Borba* hailed the new economic Guidelines adopted by the LCY Executive Committee in June 1968 as 'a declaration of war on coexistence of different ideological concepts in the League of Communists itself and a call for liquidation of that coexistence'. The article went on to attack leading politicians who had refused to state their views openly, and whose prolonged silence played into the hand of the 'political underground' who interpreted this silence in their own favour. 'Those who keep silent make it possible for that underworld to spread rumours about disunity in the leaderships to such an extent that the authority of the League of Communists' organs is seriously endangered.'[47] The 'political underground' was the term coined in this period to denote what was assumed to be a coalition of oddly assorted political

bedfellows — supporters of Ranković, Cominformists who had opposed
the break with Moscow in 1948 and aspired to closer links with the USSR,
and former Chetniks — linked only by sympathy for Greater Serbian
nationalism. This underworld was accused of promoting a number of
'opposition' candidates in Serbia in the 1967 elections.

The struggle waged by the liberal reformers in the party against the old
guard and the dissident intellectuals was to be complicated by the growing
strength of nationalism. The nationalism which had caused disquiet during
the period 1961–6 had expressed itself primarily in economic terms,
although the issue of 'Yugoslavism' — the eventual creation of a unifying
socialist Yugoslav culture — led to polemical debate in 1961–2 and later
reassurance by party leaders that there was no intention of 'assimilating'
the existing nationalities, and the party press was by the beginning of 1966
attacking the renewal of old-style Serbian 'café nationalism'.[48]

During 1967 cultural nationalism manifested itself in provocative
statements by Croatian and Serbian intellectuals on the language issue.
During 1967 and 1968 republican leaders agreed on amendments to the
Constitution, which strengthened the role of the republics in the Federal
Assembly by greatly enhancing the powers of the Chamber of Nationalities,
and extended the governmental powers of the republics. From 1970
nationalist feelings grew in intensity in all republics, and in particular
mutual distrust between Belgrade and Zagreb increased; newspapers in
each republic indulged in bitter attacks on each other, and Serbs increasingly
argued that the Croatian nationalist demands reflected the influence of
emigré Ustashi forces,[49] whilst the Croats attacked indications of Serbian
centralism as a product of pro-Moscow Cominformist forces.

In this context the new Serbian leaders Marko Nikezić and Latinka
Perović, elected at the 1968 Congress, acted to restrain Serbian nationalism
and maintained a carefully non-nationalist policy until deposed in 1972 for
excessive liberalism. Their stand on the national question was at least
partly a reflection of the fact that the liberals had come to power in
Serbia in opposition to the Greater Serbian nationalism associated with
Ranković. The only charge which could be brought against the Serbian
leaders in connection with nationalism was that their liberalism gave scope
for the expression of nationalist attitudes, for example by the Serbian
Orthodox Church and in the press. A discussion by the Serbian party's
Commission on Internationality Relations in October 1969 noted with
concern increased nationalist activity by the Church and a series of articles
on 'Yugoslavism' in NIN.[50] The Croat leaders on the other hand had, ever
since 1961, espoused what they regarded as legitimate Croatian economic
and political aspirations, and the younger leaders elected in 1968 continued

to pursue this policy. As a result they became increasingly committed to the developing nationalist movement inside Croatia. The Croatian reformers remained united in this policy until early 1971, when a number of them, including Bakarić, became alarmed at the implications of the nationalist movement, and its repercussions on relations between Croats and Serbs inside the republic. The movement, centred on the historic cultural association the Matica Hrvatska, by 1971 posed a direct political threat to the party as an alternative political organization, gaining rapidly in membership and publishing its own newspapers. It was able to challenge the party successfully for control of the student union in Croatia, and was also winning over to its own policies sections of the party itself. When Tito stepped in to demand the resignation of the top Croatian officials in December 1971 the more moderate reformers took over, and subsequent purges in the Croatian party were directed against those who had worked with the nationalists organized in the cultural organ the Matica Hrvatska rather than reformers as such — though often the categories overlapped. In the other republics, however, the liberal reformers were the chief victims of extensive purges in 1972-3, since Tito and the new dominant group in the party set out in 1972 to re-establish old-fashioned party discipline and a much more orthodox style of party rule.

The complexities of the factional struggles inside the League after 1966 will emerge in much more detail in subsequent chapters. The reorganization of the party at local level was closely linked to the republican leaders' desire to reduce the powers of the commune party bosses. The redrafting of the party Statute for the Ninth Congress and the debate about changes in the League after Brioni clarified the limits which divided the liberal reformers in power from the radical democrats. Divisions in the League also became apparent in the elections of 1967 and 1969, in reactions to student protests, and especially in disagreements about the best policy to adopt towards rising nationalism.

Notes

1. Kosovo Metohija previously had 'oblast' or regional status, but was upgraded to a province in the 1963 Constitution and 1964 Party Statute.
2. District committees had been abolished in Montenegro by 1963. There were forty in all in the other five republican parties. See Zvonko Štaubringer, *SKJ izmedju VII i VIII Kongresa*, Sedma Sila, Beograd, 1964, p. 51.
3. *Yugoslav Survey*, July–September 1966, p. 164.
4. Details about basic organizations are given in the Central Committee Report on the work of the Committee between the Seventh and Eighth Congresses printed in *Yugoslav Survey*, October–December 1964, pp. 2721-36.
5. *Komunist*, 2 July 1964 and *Politika*, 27 June 1964.

6. *Narodna Armija*, 4 December 1964.
7. After the *rapprochement* between Moscow and Belgrade in 1955 there was a second breach after the suppression of the Hungarian uprising in 1956, because the Yugoslavs had not supported the first intervention by Soviet troops.
8. See Andrija Kresić, 'Principi Rukovodjenja u Savezu Komunista', *Gledišta*, January 1967, p. 33.
9. *VUS*, 7 September 1966.
10. Francois Fejtö, *A History of the People's Democracies*, Penguin, Harmondsworth, 1974, pp. 200-1, gives one interpretation of Kardelj's role in blocking Ranković's ambitions to replace Tito as General Secretary of the party just before the Eighth Congress.
11. See Paul Lendvai, *Eagles in Cobwebs*, Macdonald, London, 1970, pp. 155-7.
12. These events are cited by Dušan Bilandžić, *Ideje i Praksa Društvenog Razvoja Jugoslavije 1945-1973*, Kommunist, Beograd, 1973, p. 229.
13. Ibid. p. 230. Bilandžić stresses the role of the group led by Kardelj.
14. *Politika*, 23 October 1966.
15. *VUS*, 14 October 1964.
16. The Organizational, Cadre and Ideological Commissions were dissolved, and replaced by a more flexible arrangement in which the three joint secretaries of the LCY — Ranković, Vlahović and Kardelj — each had overall responsibility for an area of work: party organization, ideology and socio-economic problems respectively. There were several specialized commissions in each grouping. Full details in *Komunist*, 14 December 1964.
17. See extracts from discussion at the Fourth Plenum of the LCY, Central Committee, July 1966, printed in *Socialist Thought and Practice*, July-September 1966, p. 119.
18. *Yugoslav Survey*, February 1967, pp. 46-7, speech by Mijalko Todorović.
19. *Borba*, 24 December 1965.
20. *Borba*, 26 February 1966.
21. Svetozar Vukmanović Tempo, *Revolucija Koja Teče, Memoari*, Komunist, Beograd, 1971, p. 487.
22. Ivan Mišković, head of armed forces security, partly confirmed this in an interview with *VUS*, 19 April 1972. His brother, Milan Mišković, became Secretary of Internal Affairs in 1965, but found himself bypassed. It is assumed that the brothers, who were Croats, collaborated to deal with the Serbian Mafia at the top of UDBA. It is also possible they fabricated some of the evidence, in particular the bugging of Tito.
23. Fejtö, op. cit. p. 202.
24. *VUS*, 7 September 1966.
25. *Yugoslav Survey*, October-December 1966. Report on IV Plenum, p. 3918.
26. *Socialist Thought and Practice*, July-September 1966, p. 131.
27. Lendvai, op. cit. pp. 160-1.
28. See *Komunist*, 28 July 1966.
29. *Politika Ekspres*, 6-7 November 1966.
30. *Komunist*, 3 November 1966.
31. *Stenografske Bełješke, VI Plenum, CK, SKCG*, 20. IX. 1966, pp. 38, 77 and 313, cited in Risto T. Kilibarda, *Socijalna Otvorenost Rukovodstva Saveza Komunista*, Magistarski Rad, Beograd, 1973. The Plenum was fairly fully reported in *Borba*, 21 and 22 September 1966.
32. Mijalko Todorović, who was appointed Secretary of the LCY Central Committee after Brioni, and Milentije Popović, who later became President of the Federal Assembly, were two leading Serbian liberals. Ranković's chief agent in the Serbian party, appointed a Secretary of the Serbian Central Committee in 1965 and previously Federal Secretary for Internal Affairs, Vojin Lukić, was expelled

by the Serbian Central Committee meeting, whose proceedings were reported in *Borba*, 16-19 September 1966.

33. See the report of the Croatian Central Committee meeting in *Borba*, 23 and 24 September 1966.

34. See the report of the Slovene Central Committee meeting in *Borba*, 1 and 2 October 1966.

35. For the Macedonian Central Committee Plenum see *Borba*, 27 and 29 September 1966. For evidence of Crvenkovski's public pressure for democratic reform in the party see his speeches published in *Borba*, 25 March and 19 October 1964. For evidence that the Macedonian party leadership was collaborating with the Serbian party to avoid implementation of the 1965 economic reforms see Paul Shoup, *Communism and the National Question*, Columbia University Press, New York, 1968, pp. 256-7, who cites *Komunist*, 3 and 24 March and 28 April 1966.

36. See Bosnian Executive Committee report in *Borba*, 30 July 1966; the report of the Bosnian Central Committee meeting in *Borba*, 25 September 1966; and report of speech by Osman Karabegović in favour of economic and political reforms at the Republican Congress of 1965 published in *Pregled*, January 1965, pp. 221-7. Djuro Pucar was replaced as Political Secretary in 1965 by Cvijetin Mijatović, who became established in the new reform leadership after 1966.

37. Rudolf Bićanić, *Economic Policy in Socialist Yugoslavia*, Cambridge University Press, Cambridge, 1973, p. 69.

38. Bilandžić, op. cit. p. 215.

39. Dennison Rusinow, 'Understanding the Yugoslav Reforms', *World Today*, February 1967, p. 78.

40. See Gerson S. Sher, *Praxis: Marxist Criticism and Dissent in Socialist Yugoslavia*, Indiana University Press, Bloomington, 1977, for a discussion of the development of the *Praxis* position, especially pp. 40-4. This account stresses the gap between the *Praxis* group and the official party position and ignores differences between party leaders. The conference proceedings were published as *Marks i Savremenost*, Beograd, 1964.

41. *Pregled*, June 1964.

42. *Borba*, 19 May 1966; reproduced in *Socialist Thought and Practice*, July-September 1966.

43. The fate of the Slovenian intellectual periodical *Perspektive* which was closed down in mid-1964 might be seen as evidence that the radical intellectuals were not tolerated at this time as part of the reform movement. It appears, however, that liberal reformers in Slovenia supported the journal until the editors of *Perspektive* stepped outside the Marxist framework of argument maintained by the other periodicals. *Komunist* quoted indignantly the statement printed in the paper that the spread of Marxism was 'a forcible and clumsy introduction of concepts, criteria and values which are unknown to the traditions of Slovene culture'. *Komunist* also quoted an article by Veljko Rus which suggested that if abolition of antagonism through socialization is unrealistic, genuine democracy is only possible 'through the institutionalisation of opposition tension' which it interpreted as a call for a multi-party democracy (*Komunist*, 19 July 1964).

44. Fejtö op. cit. p. 205.

45. *Vjesnik*, 8 February 1967.

46. *VUS*, 15 May 1968.

47. *Borba*, 5 July 1968.

48. *Komunist*, 13 January 1966, cited by Shoup, op. cit. p. 216.

49. The Ustashi were the extreme Croatian nationalists who flourished in the

quisling Croatian State created by the Axis powers during the Second World
War. The Ustashi were primarily responsible for the massacre of about 350 000
Serbs during the war.
50. *Politika*, 9 October 1969.

2 The Nature of the Party

The nature of the membership of a party is of considerable ideological and political importance. Whether it is a strictly vanguard party or a more open mass party depends on its size; its social composition reflects its claim to represent the working class and other social groups; the nature of admissions and expulsions policy will affect the degree of political unity and internal discipline; and the general quality of its members will determine political effectiveness and the respect in which that party is held by the wider population.

The size of a party reflects both the nature of its recruitment policy and the degree of enthusiasm for its policies among various groups. The Yugoslav party grew very rapidly from the end of the Second World War until the Sixth Congress in 1952: from 141 066 in May 1945 to 772 920 by the end of 1952. The party clearly welcomed new recruits in this period, and in the early years after liberation was able to capitalize on the loyalty of former partisans among the peasantry, to mobilize the enthusiasm of young people in building a new socialist society and to win support in the growing working class. If the party alienated some people through its impatience and ruthlessness in the early years, the break with Stalin appealed again to national pride and ensured a widespread popular backing. During the 1950s the League of Communists continued to attract new recruits and by the end of 1960 had over 1 000 000 members. The party would probably have grown even more spectacularly if the Djilas affair had not led to a tightening of party discipline, resulting in a high expulsion rate and stricter admisstion policy in 1953–5, and so caused a temporary drop in the membership figures.[1]

By the beginning of the 1960s the League had become a mass rather than an elite party. The total population of Yugoslavia in 1961 was 18 549 200, and the party membership that year was 1 035 003. In the subsequent 10 years, however, the total membership remained fairly static; and, although there were fluctuations from year to year, in 1971 the total was 1 025 476. This tendency to stagnation was lamented by *Borba* in its assessment of the 1970 membership figures, which indicated a fall in the number of admissions and a large number of people leaving the party.[2] Lack of interest in joining the League reflected in part the political apathy which was becoming evident by the end of the 1960s. The economic problems of this period and the disillusion with self-management, which surveys were also suggesting by 1970, alienated working-class support. The LCY had no success in strengthening working-class representation in the 1960s, since the number of workers who drifted out of the party exceeded the numbers who entered it.

Despite the rapid liberalization after 1966 the membership figures show that the party was failing to attract enough young people into its ranks. There was a special campaign launched to recruit young men and women in 1968, when republican parties enrolled youth *en masse* at big rallies. This youth drive was temporarily successful — reports suggested that the Czechoslovak crisis encouraged many to join the League — and admissions for 1968 shot up.[3] But by 1970 the number of new members had fallen to normal levels and the proportion of young people was falling again.[4]

Two other factors relevant to recruitment to the League are worth noticing. The first is that the gap between the stated aims of the leadership in its admissions policy and the actual results may be due in part to the effective decentralization of this policy to local party organizations, and to their frequent inactivity in recruiting new members. Secondly, the increasing liberalization of the 1960s meant that membership of the party was much less important than it had been earlier, or than it was subsequently to become in the less liberal 1970s, as a stepping stone to a good education, a successful career, economic privileges and social status. The partisan generation had often relied on the party to provide all these personal advantages, but the younger generation in the 1960s had access to education, jobs and status through the schools and universities, and it became evident in the 1960s that professional qualifications were becoming at least as important as party membership in attaining top jobs and effective influence, although the two often overlapped. The logic of the economic reforms required a much greater stress on the importance of professionalism than on party service and loyalty, especially in the economy. Indeed the failure of party membership to secure special job or other advantages was often alleged as one reason for the lesser educated leaving the party.

Party organs and the press expressed concern about the size of the exodus from the League. Many expulsions were due to inactivity and failure to pay membership fees, and therefore reflected the apathy of party members. But the rate of expulsions between 1961 and 1971 was not very high, ranging between 10 000 and 15 000 per year except for 1962, when the political purge initiated by the Executive Committee Letter raised the number of expulsions to almost 23 000. Commentators were usually more worried by the level of resignations,[5] 15 224 in 1970, and by the tendency for substantial numbers to 'lose' themselves from the party records in the process of changing their jobs or their address. During 1967 an unprecedented number of League members, 42 250, dropped out of the official records, and in the course of the period from 1 January 1961 to 31 December 1969 the party lost all trace of 196 174 members.[6]

The League faced serious problems over its membership policy by 1971. An open door policy on admissions, which had included dropping the probationary 'candidate' period in 1952, meant that the criteria for letting people join the party were not strict, and that the League did not enjoy the advantages of a genuinely elitist party which demands high standards of political commitment and discipline. Tito asked angrily in public more than once whether the League could still be called a 'cadre party'. But in the 1960s it failed to realize the potential benefits of being a mass party and tapping the energies and enthusiasm of a large number of people from all social strata.

Social Composition of the Party

There are a number of discernible trends in the social composition of the Yugoslav party. The most striking is the rapid and steady decline in the proportion of peasants in the party after 1952, when according to official estimates they comprised 42.8 per cent of the membership.[7] Collectivization of agriculture was abandoned in March 1953 and many peasants left both the collectives and the party. Nearly 40 000 were expelled in 1953 alone, and others simply walked out of the League. After 1953 peasant recruitment to the party was low not only because of the errors of collectivization, but also because the party ceased to have a positive role to play in the countryside, as party sponsored drives to recruit peasants for industry or to end illiteracy were also abandoned.[8]

The low rates of recruitment of new party members in the villages also reflected the tendency of the young to leave agriculture for higher education or other forms of employment. One study by social scientists suggested that by the late 1960s there were no young people in many villages, especially in Croatia and Slovenia, from whom new members could be recruited.[9] As those who stayed were therefore mostly members of the older generation, either hostile to communism or disillusioned in the early 1950s, it is not surprising they were under-represented in the League. The newly formed Institute for the Survey of Public Opinion found in a

comprehensive suvey in 1964 that only 28 per cent of private peasants
said they wanted to join the party, compared with approximately 43 per cent
of workers and white collar workers.[10]

Nevertheless it is reasonable to look also at the attitudes and procedures
of the party itself in accounting for the low recruitment of peasants.
Official explanations of the decline in peasant membership stressed the
failure of village party organizations to recruit new members: some preferred
to remain a restricted elite in the village, and they all failed to involve
themselves in agricultural problems.[11] Many village organizations were
dominated by their white-collar members, for example shop assistants,
book keepers in agricultural co-operatives, and especially school teachers,
and sometimes party organizations devoted their time to discussing the
school marks of children.[12] A rather different obstacle to recruitment
stemmed from the ideological attitudes of the collectivization period,
when the party only sought to recruit the poor peasants and was hostile
to relatively rich peasants. Party members in the village still tended to view
successful individual peasant proprietors as 'kulaks' — an attitude which
by the mid-sixties party leaders were trying to dispel.[13]

The trends in the proportion of workers who belong to the party have
been less dramatic, but from the standpoint of the party leadership of
greater political importance. By 1952 there were about 204 000 workers
in the League,[14] under 27 per cent of the total membership, and by 1961
the proportion had risen to 37 per cent. This increase in working-class
representation in the party partly reflected the rapid industrialization of
the 1950s, but the proportion of workers in the League was in 1961 higher
than the proportion in the working population as a whole.[15] The trend
after 1961 was less satisfactory and prompted official statements of concern.
Between 1961 and 1971 the number of workers in the party fell absolutely,
and the percentage fell from 37.0 to 28.8 per cent of the total membership.

Party analyses blamed this drop in the number of workers partly on
the strictness of the criteria used by party organizations in enterprises
when admitting workers, pointing to surveys which suggested that many
workers wished to join the party: over 50 per cent of 5000 polled by the
Belgrade University Sociology Department in 1961. Reasons given for
wanting to join included support for the party Programme and 'because
my parents were also workers'. The majority saying 'yes' were young
workers. Those who said 'no' said it was because of youth or old age,
illiteracy or inexperience, conflict in the family, or their religion.[16] The
fact that stricter discipline was invoked against workers than against white-
collar employees in factories, and that workers were expelled for minor
faults like drunkenness, skipping party meetings or failing to pay member-

ship fees also kept down the number of workers in the party. Over half those expelled between 1964 and 1971 were regularly workers.[17] The figures for resignations suggested that workers predominated among those who became disillusioned with the party, either because of the tendency of their party organization to talk jargon rather than act, or because of broader discontent with unequal distribution of wages and salaries and lack of worker power inside enterprises.[18]

Official party comment which deplored the declining number of workers and peasants in the League also tended to condemn the white-collar dominance of the party and their privileged position in implementing admissions and expulsions policy. White-collar workers were more likely to commit serious faults, like accumulating privileges or violating self management rights, but were better placed to escape punishment. In fact white-collar workers have never been in a clear majority in the party, but they have been over-represented in relation to their numbers in the total population.[19] A comparison of the occupational structure of the League with that of the working population in 1968 showed that 77.2 per cent of the managerial stratum was represented in the party, 44.1 per cent of the engineers and technicians, 29.1 per cent of the intelligentsia (within this category education was very strongly represented) but only 15.5 per cent of those in lower level administration.[20] Since the last grouping was the only one in which it could be argued that the League did not require strong representation, these figures suggest that criticism of the proportion of white-collar members in the party was misconceived. It is also obvious that the relatively good educational qualifications of party members, a source of understandable pleasure to League spokesmen in view of the high level of illiteracy and lack of schooling among its members in the early post-war years, were largely a reflection of the qualifications of the white-collar members. It is nevertheless true that given the ideological commitment to a workers' and peasants' party, these sections were under-represented: 14.6 per cent of the working class were in the party, and the skilled were better represented than the unskilled; and only 1.9 per cent of private peasants.[21] The League therefore found itself in the dilemma of all ruling communist parties, that in practice a ruling party is and needs to be a party of the elite; but its legitimacy depends on its claim to be a party of the workers. The fact that during the 1960s in Yugoslavia party membership became less essential to a good career, and professional qualifications more so, did not alter the basic nature of the party.

One noticeable trend which caused the party leaders disquiet was the ageing of the League's membership. Immediately after the war the party had been very young, drawing on former partisans who had very often

joined the partisan army in their teens,[22] and on young people attracted
to the building of a socialist society. The party had naturally aged by 1961,
and enthusiasm among youth for the goals of the party had waned, so by
1961 only 21.6 per cent were under 26, and by 1966 only 11.5 per cent.[23]
An analysis of the reasons for the decline in young people seeking admission
to the party by 1966 suggested that the increasing number who enjoyed
a higher education did not start work until they were 25 and might be
inclined to postpone applying for party membership. The fact that the
Youth Federation (which had itself become increasingly alienated from
young people) had for the previous 20 years been the only channel for the
young to join the party or to assume responsible posts was also suggested
as a reason for slower recruitment. Thirdly, the author observed that
improving the age structure of the League was linked to increasing its
working-class membership, since most Yugoslav workers, especially skilled
workers, were very young.[24]

Women have been continuously under-represented in the party: only
17.3 per cent of the membership in 1948, and this proportion did not
rise until 1968, when it became 19 per cent. The recruitment of women
has been closely related to their social occupation. Peasant women have
been almost non-existent in the party: only 1.9 per cent of all women
communists were peasants in 1964.[25] Despite the important role played by
women as partisan fighters, couriers and political organizers during the
liberation war, it appears that the traditional feeling that politics was not
suitable for women lingered in the villages. Because of these patriarchal
attitudes women tended to be afraid of the disapproval of their neighbours
if they joined the party, according to a survey of the Kraljevo district in
Serbia. Attitudes in the villages there were still influenced by wartime
divisions: while about 80 per cent of former partisans would encourage
their daughters to join the party, only about 60 per cent of the former
Chetniks (whose own motives for associating with the League were liable
to arouse suspicion) said they would do so.[26] Moreover women who stayed
in the villages were usually older and more likely to accept traditional
attitudes. Women workers were also very badly represented in the League:
only 16.8 per cent of the women admitted in the first half of 1964 for
example were workers. The main reason seems to have been the obvious
strain of combining a full time job with looking after a family.[27] There are
very few housewives in the party. The 1964 survey cited earlier found that
housewives were less interested in joining the League than any other social
group – only 15.6 per cent expressed a wish to do so.[28] The majority of
women who are communists are therefore white-collar workers, and
probably mostly to be found in the more highly educated professions.

Yugoslavia does appear to provide very clear evidence in support of the thesis that women's political involvement increases as their educational standards rise. There were in 1961 twice as many women as men who had not been to school, or had spent a maximum of three years at school.[29] It is not therefore surprising that a survey in Croatia found that only half as many women as men claimed to read the daily newspapers and over double the number of women admitted to never reading them, though these findings should perhaps be qualified by noting the very low regular readership for the daily press: 28 per cent of the men in the sample and 13 per cent of the women.[30] It is certainly interesting that Slovenia, which has the lowest illiteracy rate among women, also has a higher proportion of women in the party than any other republic: 28.1 per cent in 1971. By contrast only 12.5 per cent of the Macedonian party were women in 1971 and 18.1 per cent in Bosnia. The fact that over a third of the population is officially Moslem, and the cultural attitudes associated with the Moslem faith, presumably affects the position of women in Bosnia, and Macedonia is one of the most under-developed areas of Yugoslavia. The extent to which women are represented in political life is clearly related to the extent of modernization, for example they would escape from the traditional patriarchalism of village life by moving to the towns, so it is debatable whether education is the primary factor in emancipating Yugoslav women, or whether the fact of their education reflects more egalitarian attitudes in their family and social environment.

The party is committed in principle by its ideology to encourage recruitment of women into the party and to promote their political representation at higher levels. Official commentary on the membership statistics usually included a standard statement of regret that there were too few women in the party, although it is doubtful whether party leaders took it as seriously as the shortage of workers and youth.

None of the tendencies in the social make-up of the party are as contentious as its national composition, though the trend during the 1960s was towards rather better representation of national groups who had felt discriminated against in the party and in other ways.[31] Discrepancies in national representation become most contentious within individual republics: for example, the rather high proportion of Serbs in the Croatian party, 24.7 per cent in 1971 compared with 14.2 per cent in the republican population. Serbs also dominated the Bosnian party, whereas Moslems and more especially Croats were under-represented: in 1971 53.5 per cent of the party were Serbs, who made up only 37.2 per cent of the population. Nationalism caused less difficulty in Macedonia than many other republics, but Macedonians were over-represented in the party, whilst Albanians

and Turks were under-represented. There was in fact evidence of discrimination against Albanians in Macedonia, noted by the republican party
leader Koliševski at the 1959 Macedonian party Congress, and the Albanian
riots in Kosovo in 1968 spread to Tetovo in Macedonia. The political
position of the Albanian majority in Kosovo improved significantly after
the ousting of Ranković in 1966, including their representation in the
League: by 1971 they formed 59.6 per cent of the provincial party and
73.7 per cent of the population. But continuing dissatisfaction was indicated
by the 1968 riots, which led to some further concessions from Belgrade,
for example in education. Hungarians in the Vojvodina had not suffered
from serious persecution like the Albanians, but they also had a number
of grievances about their status as a national minority, and political
representation: even by 1971 Hungarians only formed 9.2 per cent of the
provincial party whilst they comprised 21.7 per cent of the provincial
population.

Quality of Party Members

The most important aspect of party membership is the actual quality of
its members, since the authority of the party rests on a claim to special
political foresight and knowledge, on the political dedication and activism
of its members and on the political and moral example they set. The
power and effectiveness of the party will also depend on the intelligence
and energy of its members, their willingness to put public interest above
personal gain and their party discipline. The weakness of a party staffed
by corrupt careerists and lacking in idealism or ideas has recently been
demonstrated in Poland. When a party tries to loosen its hold on the
cruder instruments of political control and to base its authority on its
ability to persuade people to follow its goals — as the LCY claimed to do
in 1952 and again in the 1960s — then the quality of its membership is even
more significant.

There is some evidence about the degree of knowledge of party ideology
and history among League members, though it is not sufficiently comprehensive to provide a basis for generalization. A small but interesting survey
organized by the party in the Serbian commune of Ilidja in 1964 revealed
an astonishingly low level of knowledge. For example out of 125 members
who had secondary or higher education, 54 did not know one work by
Marx, Engels or Lenin; 'some' did not know the date of the Communist
Manifesto, the former name of the LCY or the date of the Seventh
Congress.[32] The Croatian Ideological Commission revealed in 1963 that an
enquiry in some party organizations showed that 60 per cent of the

members had *not* read the LCY Programme.[33] A survey of 800 communists in Sarajevo, however, found that 55 per cent claimed to have read the Programme and Statute of the LCY and the Bosnian party Statute; 13 per cent the Programme only and 10 per cent the LCY Statute only. Only 11 per cent confessed they had not read any of them.[34]

Newspaper reading appears in general to have been much higher among party members than among non-communists. Mladen Zvonarević's study of newspaper reading habits in Croatia showed that 58 per cent of party members read daily papers regularly and 36 per cent sometimes, whilst only 14 per cent among the rest of the population generally read the dailies, and 29 per cent admitted they never did.[35]

The degree of political activism among party members in the 1960s fell in comparison with earlier periods, a fact which can be attributed to changing social attitudes, for example the campaigning spirit created by constructing a new economic and political order had been lost and replaced in part by greater emphasis on private personal goals and a consumer ethic. There was also a lack of clarity about the role of the party and a consequent disillusionment with party activity both among long-established members and the newly recruited communists.[36] The 1972 Sarajevo survey found that only 43 per cent claimed to participate often in the work of political organizations like the Socialist Alliance, trade unions and Youth Federation, 38 per cent said they did sometimes and 17 per cent declared they never did. Nevertheless party members predictably remained more active in political meetings than non-members,[37] and one study found that former communists among peasants retained the habit of political activism even after they had left the League.[38]

There is plenty of evidence that communists were not particularly conscientious in fulfilling their party duties and attending meetings. For example two commune party conferences in Maglaj and Doboj had to be postponed in 1968 because there was no quorum and some delegates failed to turn up.[39] The Commune Committee of Gadzin Han dissolved two basic organizations in 1969 because for a year only a few members had attended meetings and the majority had not even paid their member-ship fees.[40]

There were also more serious complaints about petty corruption and dishonesty within the League. In 1964 *Komunist* published a general party condemnation of the prevalence of favouritism, receipt of gifts, squandering social property and other dubious practices, and a year later *Politika* drew attention to the habit of treasurers of some basic organiza-tions in Niš pocketing part of the funds they collected.[41] There were also quite a number of cases of high-ranking communists indulging in fraud.

For example an administrative official of the Bosnian Central Committee was tried in October 1963 for embezzling 21 000 000 dinars between 1950 and 1962, and the director of the Skoplje Water Supply was expelled from the party in May 1968 for diverting 7 000 000 dinars to building his personal flat.[42]

Another problem for party leaders was evidence of the lack of unity among party members. Often this appears to have been due to purely personal conflicts and a general tendecy to quarrelsomeness. *Komunist* criticized the 'disorderly internal life' of many basic organizations, noting that in a number of cases communists were bringing libel actions against each other for what had been said in the heat of party meetings.[43] Family and tribal feuds also divided party organizations in some areas. The League committee in the Montenegrin commune of Kolašin had to dissolve the basic organization in the village of Starce, where over half the thirty-seven members were not on speaking terms with one another. *Komunist* explained that the quarrel went back to the 1963 elections when candidates were supported on the basis of their family ties. Fights broke out several times, for example when 'the candidate whose family tribe was the largest and strongest had not been elected'. To make matters worse communists gambled and drank — 'some even used to come drunk to public gatherings and party meetings'.[44]

One reason given by communists who resigned from the League in 1966 was that 'uncomradely and unfriendly relations prevailed'. *Borba* commented that it seemed to be true that 'comradely relations are becoming weaker', and that the level of expulsions from the party seemed to suggest a lack of concern and balanced criticism which might check communists falling into error, before they went too far and got themselves expelled.[45] Some of the divisions in the party at this stage were probably due to more serious causes than personal antagonism and feuds arising out of competition for plum jobs and political posts, since the political divisions between the reformers and the Ranković faction continued to split many commune parties after 1966. Quite often personal and political hostility overlapped. The lack of political and personal unity was most fully demonstrated at the time of the 1967 and 1969 assembly elections.

A picture of party membership which relies primarily on press reports is likely to over-emphasize the negative side, since it is based on reports by control commissions on disciplinary proceedings, comments by party leaders who are always prone to be highly critical of the failings of the rank and file, and on individual scandals.[46] Nevertheless it does emerge clearly from the total evidence available (some of it is in later chapters) that the party during the 1960s had not shed the habits of corruption and narrow localism which had marked the party of the partisan generation. The younger and better educated recruits on the other hand were often influenced by more sophisticated careerism, and more likely to sympathize with a technocratic view of the world, which might be conducive to economic efficiency but was at odds with the radical democratic aspirations of self-management, and lacked the revolutionary vision which attracted the idealism of youth in the early years. The disillusion of workers with the party and the failure to engage many young people in party activities both testified to the failures of the League in these directions. One of the ironies of the 1968 student protests was that the young rebels were making their idealistic demands to their ex-revolutionary fathers, some of whom had manned the university barricades 30 years previously. Finally the League's unity and its ideological clarity was deeply undermined after 1966 by the public revival of nationalist rivalries and passions and symbols, which became more important than the conflict between the reformers and their opponents, and testified to the lack of ideological unity and party discipline at all levels of the party.

Notes

1. See Appendix I for some membership tables and also for a list of the sources for statistics on LCY membership.
2. *Borba*, 18 April, 1971.
3. 152 893 young people under 28 years of age joined in 1968, of whom 75 763 were under 21 years. See *Borba*, 24 January 1970.
4. In 1970 only 31 885 people altogether joined the LCY, although 85.6 per cent of them were under 28 years of age; and whereas at the end of 1968 a total of 24.5 per cent of the membership were under 28 years, at the end of 1970 the percentage had fallen to 20.9 per cent. See Deseti Kongres SKJ: *Statistički Podaci O Savezu Komunista Jugoslavije*, Beograd, 1974.
5. The right of resignation was granted to individual party members in 1964 and underlined in the 1969 Statute.
6. *Borba*, 8 January 1969 and 2 March 1971.
7. This was an artificially inflated figure, the real proportion of peasants was about 31 per cent. See Appendix I.
8. A study of peasants in the Vojvodina cautions against exaggerating the number of peasants who actually drifted away from the party after 1952, because many peasants remained party members and quite often stayed in the village, but changed their jobs. (Borislav Dimković, *Seljaštvo i Komunisti Na Selu*, Centar za Političke Studije i Društveno-Političko Obrazovanje, Novi Sad, 1973, p. 63.)
9. Stipe Šuvar, Jordan Jelić and Ivan Magdalenić, *Društvene Promjene i Djelovanje Komunista u Selu*, Agrarni Institut, Zagreb, 1968, p. 50.
10. *Politika*, 19 December 1964 and *Komunist*, 11 March 1965 both carried summaries of the findings.
11. *Borba*, 20 September 1964.
12. *Borba*, 9 June 1964.

13. See *Borba*, 20 September 1964 and 20 February 1965; *Politika*, 25 April 1966 and *Komunist*, 25 May 1967 article by Stipe Šuvar.
14. The official figure of 249 110 (32.0 per cent) was artificially inflated by about 45 000. See Appendix I.
15. Zoran Vidaković, *Promene u Strukturi Jugoslovenskog Društva i Savez Komunista*, Sedma Sila, Beograd, 1967, p. 23 notes workers comprised 26.5 per cent of the active population.
16. *Borba*, 14 March 1965 reported on the survey.
17. In the period 1965-71 the percentage only fell below 50 per cent once, to 43.6 per cent in 1970. For sources on expulsions see Appendix I.
    VUS, 28 August 1968 gave a breakdown of the reasons for expulsion: 40.9 per cent were expelled for absenteeism from meetings and non-payment of fees. Basic organizations also tended to expel workers for first offences: see *Komunist*, 12 August 1965 and 2 September 1965.
18. For sources on figures on expulsions see Appendix I. For analysis of the reasons for resignation see *Borba*, 17 February 1967 report of Serbian control commission discussions with those who had resigned, and *Borba*, 8 July 1968 discussing resignations in 1967. *NIN*, 4 July 1971 reports on a party survey of those who resigned in 1970, which found the main reason for leaving was a sense of impotence.
19. Vidaković, op. cit. p. 23 notes that white-collar workers comprised 17 per cent of the active population in 1961.
20. Allen H. Barton, Bogdan Denitch and Charles Kadushin, *Opinion Making Elites in Yugoslavia,* Praeger, New York, 1973, p. 113.
21. Ibid.
22. Tito said at the First Congress of Anti-Fascist Youth in 1942 that 75 per cent of the partisan army were under 20 years old. See Stipe Šuvar, 'Omladina i Pomladjivanja S.k.', *Naše Teme*, October 1966.
23. *Yugoslav Survey*, November 1967, pp. 39 and 42 for figures on youth in LCY.
24. Šuvar in Naše Teme op. cit.
25. *Komunist*, 15 July 1965. For sources on proportion of women in LCY see note on general sources in Appendix I.
26. Krsto Kilibarda, *Samoupravljanje i Savez Komunista, Rezultati Socialnog Istraživanja u Srezu Kraljevo*, Sociološki Institut, Beograd, 1966, p. 223.
27. See, for example, *Borba*, 12 November 1964, which refers to an enquiry at the Petar Velebit factory in Belgrade.
28. See *Politika*, 19 December 1964 report on the survey.
29. *Jugoslavija izmedju VIII i IX Kongresa, 1964–1969,* Savezni Zavod za Statistiku, Beograd, 1969, p. 28.
30. Barton, Denitch and Kadushin, op. cit. p. 270.
31. For national representation in LCY and for sources on nationalities in LCY see Appendix I.
32. *Komunist*, 9 July 1964.
33. *Borba*, 13 March 1963.
34. Vladimir Sultanović, Nedjo Miljanović and Ismet Dizdarević, *Struktura i Djelovanje Saveza Komunista u Sarajevu,* Studijski Centar Gradski Konferencije SK B i H, Sarajevo, 1973, p. 156.
35. Barton, Denitch and Kadushin op. cit. p. 270.
36. Sharon Zukin, *Between Marx and Tito,* Cambridge University Press, Cambridge, 1975, discusses the change in political attitudes, pp. 116-52.
37. See Mladen Zvonarević, *Javno Mnijenje Gradjana SR Hrvatske O Samoupravljanu,* Institut Društvena Istraživanja Sveučilista u Zagrebu, Zagreb, 1967.
38. See Dimković, op. cit. p. 113.
39. *Borba*, 11 March 1968.

40. *Borba*, 22 July 1969.
41. *Komunist*, 12 February 1964 and *Politika*, 10 May 1965.
42. *Borba*, 29 October 1963 and *Nova Makedonija*, 24 May 1968.
43. *Komunist*, 14 February 1963.
44. *Komunist*, 21 October 1965.
45. *Borba*, 29 May 1967.
46. A more positive picture is in fact presented by George Zaninovich who did a survey in the 1960s to assess party attitudes in relation to modernization, and concluded that party membership did influence attitudes and values in favour of active political participation and societal commitment and of modernization. He also found they viewed centralized state authority with caution. The survey suggested that attitudes of party members did not vary significantly with age, sex, occupational or political status, or nationality. Zaninovich concludes that 'it can be seen that the League of Communists easily fills the role of an integrating and modernizing elite in Yugoslav society. In fact, Communist Party membership would seem to act as a mitigating force against the excessively fragmenting effects of certain situational variables such as nationality and culture-region'. The survey materials do throw up some interesting divergences between party members and the rest of the population; but the fact that it primarily tests attitudes, and does appear to have elicited the 'correct' responses from party members in the sample on such issues as the virtues of political and economic decentralization, leaves room for doubt about the realism of the conclusions to be drawn from the survey. Some of the evidence of the actual behaviour of party members certainly seems to point in a different direction. For a full account of the survey see: M. George Zaninovich, 'Party and Non-Party Attitudes on Societal Change', in R. Barry Farrell (ed.), *Political Leadership in Eastern Europe and the Soviet Union*, Butterworths, London, 1970, pp. 294-334.

PART II

PROBLEMS OF INNER-PARTY DEMOCRACY

3 Democracy at the Centre

The logic of party reform after Brioni required as a first and minimal step that the Central Committee should put its own house in order. It was at the top of the party that the rules had been flagrantly broken by Ranković. The Central Committee had also signally failed to hold party officials or the Executive Committee to account, and had been willing to act as a rubber stamp for the executive. Any serious attempt to reform the party required that a start should be made by setting an example at the centre, and that democratization should be extended to the operation of the republican committees which had also been affected by Ranković.

The style of Serbian Central Committee meetings under Ranković was described by Dragi Stamenković:

> as soon as we get to the lobbies real discussion begins. We have often heard, or made jokes, about this. If the debates in the lobbies had taken place in the conference hall, every Central Committee meeting would have been lively and what a meeting of the Central Committee is supposed to be.

He added that sessions had been so organized that members were not even asked to express their own opinion, and that many delicate matters were left off the agenda.[1]

The Brioni Plenum itself marked the beginning of a new style of open debate in the party. Miloš Minić commented during the Plenum that: 'The present meeting shows that relations here, in the Central Committee, are being changed. This is very important, the most crucial thing. Democracy is making its entrance to the Central Committee.'[2]

Executive Accountability to the Central Committee.

Final decisions about the best mode of ordering the top bodies of the League could not be made until the next Congress, and although there were calls for an extraordinary Congress at some party meetings the leadership vetoed this idea. The Central Committee therefore agreed to an interim reorganization at its Fifth Plenum in October 1966. The primary aim was the restriction of the power of the Executive Committee, by cutting it down from nineteen to eleven members (although all six republican party secretaries were then co-opted, bringing the total to seventeen), and by creating an authoritative intermediary body between it and the 155-member Central Committee: a Presidium of thirty-five members whose composition was quite separate from that of the Executive Committee. Whilst the latter retained responsibility for the executive functions of the Central Committee, for international links with other parties and for promoting initiatives, the Presidium was to review problems in the work of the Central Committee and it took over responsibility for convening sessions of the Central Committee and for placing items on the agenda. The previously powerful Secretariat was abolished.'[3]

The idea of the Presidium was controversial as Mijalko Todorović admitted in his report to the Fifth Plenum. He mentioned fears that it would hamper the work of the Executive Committee or substitute for it; and that it would become so prominent, especially if the most authoritative members of the Central Committee belonged to it, that it would dominate the Central Committee. He also referred to the quite different objection that the Presidium would not have sufficient functions, an objection which had been made to proposals to create a Presidium before the Fourth Plenum. He admitted that the Presidium might be a temporary body, but stressed that it should reduce to a minimum the dangers of a concentration of power within executive organs. Because it had no executive powers the Presidium could not itself 'seize any monopoly'.[4]

There is very little direct evidence about the role and influence of the new Presidium. Its composition, which included Tito himself, and almost all the members of the former Executive Committee, made it a more prestigious body than the new Executive Committee, but it met much less often. In practice this three-tier system clearly proved too unwieldy and was simplified by arranging joint meetings between the Presidium and the Executive Committee. The Central Committee Report to the Ninth Congress revealed that the Presidium only met twice by itself, but thirteen times together with the Executive Committee. The Executive Committee met sixty-two times between September 1966 and February 1969.[5]

There is some indication that after the Fourth Plenum the Central Committee itself did play a larger role in debating policy than it had previously: it met eight times between July 1966 and the Ninth Congress in March 1969 for sessions averaging 2 days, and the press reports of the meetings of the Committee show a willingness to make specific points, and to propose changes in draft documents submitted to the Committee: for example there was fairly detailed and critical discussion of some drafts of documents for the Ninth Congress submitted to the Eleventh Plenum of the Committee.[6] On the other hand the report on the work of the Central Committee between the Eighth and Ninth Congress was not debated at all, and an article in *Borba* commented unfavourably on the over-generalized nature of the Congress drafts and the failure of the Twelfth Plenum to debate them seriously as a contribution to the necessary public discussion.[7] The reports do moreover suggest that the more prominent and characteristically outspoken members — for example Crvenkovski and Tempo — were more inclined to come out with critical observations.

There were occasions when the Central Committee was clearly relegated to the role of publicly endorsing previously agreed policy; the Ninth Plenum of July 1968 declared uncritical support for the Guidelines on future economic policy which had been adopted in advance by the Presidium and Executive Committee.[8] There was also evidence that the Executive Committee was prepared to pre-empt debate and make somewhat arbitrary decisions. An interesting example occurred in connection with plans to reorganize the top bodies of the League at the Ninth Congress. The new proposals, agreed at the Central Committee Plenum in July 1968, abolished the Central Committee of 155 members and created a Conference of 250–300 members, to meet at least once a year and to represent the rank and file between congresses. The Presidium became the policy making and executive organ of the Conference, but was to be increased from thirty-five to forty-nine members, to allow seven members from each republic and three from each province — a provision in line with the new policy of equal representation of republics in governmental bodies — plus the President of the League.[9] How the members of the new annual Conference should be selected was left open for debate by the July Plenum, which noted there were two schools of thought, one favouring annual election of all delegates by commune party conferences, the other proposing that while a majority of delegates should be elected in this way, there should also be a standing group of permanent members, elected at each Congress, to promote continuity and add weight to the Conference by their experience and prestige. One unstated reason for the standing group, as was clear from later nominations to it, was to provide a niche for veteran figures being shuffled out of the way to make room for the new men and women in the positions of real power. This probably explains why there was apparently strong support for this solution in the Executive Committee. Only a fortnight after the Central Committee Plenum, the Executive Committee issued instructions that there would be a standing group of sixty-eight members of the LCY Conference and required each republican congress to elect ten delegates and the provincial parties four.[10]

The final decision whether to create an inner executive body for the Presidium was also reached arbitrarily. The Conclusions of the July Plenum had been vague about the formation of an Executive Committee, envisaging such a committee without specifying its powers or how its members would be selected. At the Ninth Congress Tito put forward as his personal idea the proposal to create an influential Executive Bureau to be elected directly by the Congress and to be composed of two leading representatives of each republic and one from each province. The Bureau was to be based in Belgrade and was designed officially to be an authoritative forum for resolving disputes between republics and to strengthen the unity of the League, and intended unofficially to curb the independence of republican bosses like Bakarić, who reluctantly was elected to it. The Congress duly greeted Tito's proposal 'with thunderous applause'.[11]

Since the Executive Bureau was composed of the most eminent republican leaders (although the Slovene Prime Minister, Stane Kavčić, reputedly refused to join) it seemed likely that it would become the dominant organ for resolving inter-republican disputes, and would overshadow the Presidium. Fears were expressed that it might exercise dictatorial powers. These fears proved to be groundless, however, because of the increasing independence of the republican parties and the inability of the Bureau to conciliate their interests.

The Bureau did play a predominant organizational role, as indicated by the Presidium Report to the First Conference in July 1970: the Bureau met fifty-three times between the Ninth Congress and the Conference, it considered all proposals made by the Commissions and decided whether to pass them on to the Presidium, and initiated most questions put on the agenda of the Presidium. Although according to its rules of procedures the Presidium should have met once a month, it failed to do so between June and October 1969 and between December 1969 and April 1970, and only held ten sessions.[12] But it is clear that the Presidium was not simply acting as a rubber stamp for the Executive Bureau. It spent 11 hours discussing one item on the agenda — the current political situation — in mid-1969 and important disagreement was expressed on the relative threat posed by 'bureaucratic', 'bourgeois' and 'anarcho-liberal' tendencies, and on how the party should react.[13] The Presidium also rejected parts of the Executive Bureau's draft proposals on tightening up political controls over the press at its Sixth Session in November 1969.[14] This issue had earlier led to unusually lively discussion in the LCY Presidium's Cultural Commission. *VUS* commented that 'what was most interesting and least expected was that the League of Communists should be so recklessly criticised at a session of a LCY Commission'.[15]

After the First Conference in 1970 the Presidium appears to have had a more important political role in resolving inter-republican disputes and greater authority than the Executive Bureau. For example it was at the Seventeenth Presidium meeting at the end of April 1971, which lasted 3 days and was held in secret because of the sensitive issues raised, that republican leaders finally agreed on the form of the Constitutional Amendments and on their immediate implementation. This session also discussed Croatian party leaders' protests about secret police allegations that they were linked to Ustashi emigrés. It was the Twenty-first Presidium at Karadjordjevo which condemned the policy pursued by the Croatian leaders towards Croatian nationalism and initiated the new policy line in the party which led to the defeat of the reformers.

The low status of the Executive Bureau by August 1971 was indicated by the fact that after personnel changes involved in the formation of a new federal government there were still vacancies to be filled on the Executive Bureau. An article in *Politika* commented on fears that if authoritative individuals were not on the Executive Bureau decisions would be taken behind the scenes, and reported that 'some people' were urging that prominent leaders should sit in the Executive Bureau so that it 'would not have to seek agreement from the Presidium for every single move'.[16] The ineffectiveness of the Bureau as a supreme unifying organ of the party was underlined by speakers at the Twenty-third Presidium meeting on 21 December 1971, who discussed reorganization of the Bureau,[17] and by the fact that it was agreed to cut the Bureau down to eight members, a proposal endorsed at the Second Conference in January 1972.

Since the Presidium turned increasingly into a forum where republican representatives bargained for their republican interests, the question of democracy became less relevant, because there was no question of an executive power limiting debate or manipulating decisions. It was also clear that the LCY Conference, which met rather less frequently than once a year in practice, could not exercise any direct control over top organs.

Republican Central Committees

Republican central committees were therefore more likely to exercise their right to debate policy and to amend executive proposals than the LCY Presidium in the period 1969–71. But even during the earlier period 1966–8 there was more evidence of republican committees calling their executives to account than there was in the LCY Central Committee itself. Republican central committees met more often than the LCY Central Committee and some of their sessions resulted in more turbulent debate. All the republican committees had followed the lead of the Central Committee in 1966 in creating their own presidium — even the smaller committees where the value of a third intermediate body was questionable. They then avoided too much duplication of time and effort by arranging joint meetings of the Presidium and Executive Committee. For example twenty-nine out of thirty-two meetings of the Serbian Presidium were held with the Executive Committee, whilst the latter met ninety-seven times between November 1966 and November 1968. The Serbian Central Committee met ten times between its reorganization in November 1966 and the Sixth Serbian Congress 2 years later.[18]

A number of the post-Ranković republican plenums resulted in frank and critical comments about past abuses. In the Serbian committee these comments were in line with the new tone being set by the now dominant reformist leaders; in the Slovenian and Montenegrin committees on the other hand, individual members criticized the Executive Committee report. Jefto Scepanović at the Montenegrin meeting called for a party commission to investigate the role played by Drago Stojović, Secretary to the Central Committee, when he was responsible for Internal Affairs in the republic (see Chapter 1). The Central Committee rejected his proposal, but the majority also rejected a proposal that a specific condemnation of Scepanović's statements should be included in the Conclusions of the Plenum, on the grounds that this would be seen as an attempt to curb freedom of party members to express their views publicly.[19] *Borba* commented on the surprise felt when participants in the Montenegrin Sixth Plenum criticized the official report instead of going up to the rostrum simply to endorse it as in the past.[20]

The reorganization debate later in 1966 sparked off one major controversy at a republican central committee meeting. Press reports stressed that the Sixth Plenum of the Slovenian Central Committee resulted in a 'real polemic' of an unprecedented kind, and that the Committee only voted narrowly, by forty-three to thirty-six, in favour of a proposal that separation of functions between party and state should mean that no top officials in government or 'socio-political' bodies should be on the party Presidium.[21] Several other examples of individuals expressing criticism or dissent at republican meetings were reported in the press in the latter part of 1966. After this period the central committees reverted to more normal business and no instances of violent disagreement at central committee meetings were given prominence in the press during 1967–8, though the Central Committee of the Montenegrin party did split on an organizational question in November 1968.[22] The degree of democracy within a committee cannot be measured only by the amount of dissent and disagreement, but that there were still limits to free and substantive debate in top forums of the League was suggested by the critical observations made by Bosko Siljegović, member of the LCY Central Committee, at the Bosnian republican party Congress, when he called for more dialogue in the League, especially in its top bodies.[23]

After the reorganization of the top bodies in the League the republican parties copied the organizational scheme initiated at the centre, instituting an annual conference between congresses and creating one organ to be responsible for party affairs between conferences. The republics retained the name of 'central committee' for this leading body, but cut down its size. The previous republican committees had ranged from 72 members (Montenegro) to 137 (Serbia), while the new committees ranged from 35 members (Montenegro) to 65 (Croatia). The republican presidiums were therefore abolished but each central committe had an executive committee.

When he was asked in January 1971 to assess the work of the Central Committee elected at the 1968 republican Congress, Franc Popit, President of the Slovenian party, suggested that the committee members participated more actively than in the past.

> It no longer happens that at sessions of the Central Committee its work is exclusively taken up with hearing reports. At every meeting of the Central Committee now fifteen or even twenty members rise to speak. And this means almost always nearly half the total number of members. And it is not always the same members who rise to speak.[24]

He noted that the Slovenian Central Committee had held seventeen meetings in the 2-year period since December 1968.

There were claims that the new Croatian Committee elected at the 1968 republican Congress inaugurated a more democratic tone at its first session: that discussion ranged beyond the text of the programme under consideration to wider questions about the Committee's work, and that demands were made for more precise conclusions.[25] There is in fact some evidence from press reports that both the Slovenian and Croatian Committees did engage in some real debates. The Slovenian Central Committee meeting in May 1969 was the scene of an animated dispute about the levels of pay for party officials. Vinko Hafner, supported by several other members, pressed an amendment that the proposed salaries of top party officials should be increased slightly to denote higher appreciation of political work; he also made proposals about the pay of government officials. Franc Popit, whose own salary as President of the

League was involved, strongly opposed the amendments and after half an hour's debate Hafner reluctantly agreed to withdraw them, commenting that he only did so 'because Popit insists on it'. In the final vote on the salary scales three members voted against and two abstained.[26] The Croatian Central Committee held a marathon 8-hour debate on agrarian policy in October 1970, in the course of which three members pressed strongly, though unsuccessfully, for an increase in the maximum of hectares which individual peasants were allowed to own.[27]

There is, however, also considerable evidence that on key issues of policy Central Committee members were liable to revert to former habits of caution and that the party leaders were still able to manipulate the Committee. The most detailed information available concerns the Croatian Central Committee and in particular its role in 1971 when the nationalist crisis reached its peak. Djuro Kladarin, speaking at the Croatian Central Committee meeting which analysed the failures of the ousted leadership, observed that

> a monopoly of power is always still very much there in the League of Communists, held by the Executive Committee or a group in the Executive Committee. The Central Committee usually serves only as a democratic facade . . . which is manipulated.

He added that when Pero Pirker (then Croatian Party Secretary) misrepresented the meeting held by the Croatian party leaders with Tito in July 1971 many members of the Central Committee knew he was lying 'and we all remained silent'.[28]

On the other hand it is important to note that if Central Committee members were driven towards a timid conformism this was due not only to the machinations of the top leaders (though the Croatian leaders did apparently use cadre policy as a weapon) but also to the increasing intolerance engendered by the nationalist movement and to strong pressures from below. For example the Drniš Commune Committee, a stronghold of the nationalists, tried to revoke the Central Committee membership of Zvonko Jurišić for his speech at the Twentieth Plenum of the Committee, on the grounds that he had contravened the correct Croatian party policy on nationalism; while the party President, Savka Dabčević-Kučar, strongly condemned these moves at a Central Committee meeting.[29]

Nationalist loyalties were being invoked at about the same time in Kosovo, by both the provincial leadership and local party cadres, to suppress individual dissent. Albanian nationalism had become more vociferous in the late sixties and early seventies. This was partly due to the general rise in nationalist consciousness, but it was also rooted in a number of genuine grievances about the status of the Albanians in the province of Kosovo and of Albanian minorities in other areas. Under Ranković the secret police had ruthlessly harassed Albanians, and although after 1966 they were granted cultural rights and greater political recognition, the rapidly growing Albanian population remained the poorest section of Yugoslav society. Albanian aspirations to separate republican status were blocked by Serbian historical claims to the Kosovo area, part of medieval Serbia before the Turkish occupation. The census of 1971 gave rise to nationalist disputes in Kosovo as elsewhere. So when Kadri Reufi, who had recently resigned from the Provincial Committee of the party, opposed the official committee's assessment of the census, and alleged that pressure was brought to bear on Turks to declare themselves Albanians, the Committee anathematized him and the Commune Conference of Kosovska Mitrovica recalled him from the Provincial Conference for his speeches at the Provincial Committee and the Serbian Central Committee. The Secretary of the Provincial Committee said subsequently in a violent attack on Reufi that the League must rid itself of 'reptiles, bureaucrats, pragmatists, nationalists and similar elements'.[30] The Kosovo Provincial President demanded at the Thirteenth Plenum of the Serbian Central Committee that the Committee should dissociate itself from Reufi's statements because they contradicted the assessment of the Provincial Committee and that Reufi's speech should not be published in the press. The Serbian Committee after a discussion refused to endorse these proposals. Commenting on the Reufi and Jurišić incidents an article in *Borba* noted the threat they posed to free speech in central committee meetings, and commented that if dissent met with automatic calls for dissociation, and expulsion of the offender, it would be a step back to former undemocratic practices.[31]

The Control Commission

The role adopted by the party Control Commission, the body responsible for party discipline but also in principle responsible for ensuring proper observance of the party statutes, is clearly important in any programme for party democracy. The Eighth Congress measures of organizational reform required that for the first time the Control Commission should be formally elected instead of being appointed. Koliševski claimed in his speech to the Congress that by becoming independent of the Central Committee and responsible to Congress, the Commission could safeguard the application of the statutes with greater authority. He went on to qualify possible radical implications, however, by stressing how closely the Commission would work with the Central Committee.[32]

During the period of reassessment of the party in 1966, Control Commission members criticized their own work, which had been limited to considering complaints and admitted that they had been subordinate to party leaderships. This passive attitude by control commissions was blamed on the compromise nature of the 1964 Statute, and it was suggested that they should be authorized to see whether decisions passed by leaderships were in accord with the Statute and Congress decisions.[33] A specific example of the subordination of the Control Commission to Ranković was provided by the case of Predrag Ajtić, who was dismissed from his post as Ambassador to Sofia and expelled from the League at the end of 1962 (see Chap. 1). Ajtić appealed to the Central Committee against his expulsion and received no reply. He then appealed to the Control Commission, who dissuaded him from complaining to the Eighth Congress, and recommended him to write to Ranković. His letter was annotated by Ranković to the effect that his readmission could be considered, but any re-examination of his case was 'out of the question'. The Commission duly informed Ajtić there was no objection to his renewing membership of the League. When Ajtić tried again to have his case reviewed, by writing to the Serbian Committee, he was stalled.[34]

The Control Commission noted a complete lack of interest in its future during the 1967 discussions on reorganization and therefore undertook to debate the question itself.[35] It rejected views that control commissions had become superfluous, urged that their independence should be maintained by direct election at central and republican congresses, and agreed a division of powers between the central Commission and the republican commissions. The latter became the final courts of appeal on disciplinary matters while the LCY Commission acquired a broader jurisdiction to ensure democratic procedures were observed in the party, to consider possible amendments to the Statute and to be responsible for the co-ordination of the republican party Statutes.[36] To mark its new role it was called the Commission for Statutory Questions. It was active during 1969 in overseeing co-ordination of republican statutes with the statutes of the LCY (see Chapter 3), but apparently took a rather narrow view of its commitments to oversee observance of statutory norms, as a member of the Commission was moved to remark in April 1971 that the time had come to stop worrying about basic organizations and to direct attention to the Presidium and the republican committees.[37]

Central Committee Commissions

Dissatisfaction with the work of the Central Committee before Brioni extended to its commissions, which were criticized by the Commission on Reorganization for their lack of independence and their total subordination to the Executive Committee.[38] The 1966 plan for reorganization set up new policy commissions, which were intended to reinvigorate the Central Committee by involving all its members in activity and connecting the Committee to lower bodies. Todorović said that in addition to those specifically appointed all other Central Committee members would have the right to take part in the work of commissions. So that the commissions could act as a direct link with other party activists the Central Committee would only nominate an 'initiating group', which could then co-opt qualified people inside the party, or even outside it. The Fifth Plenum specified that the commissions should be independent and should report direct to the Central Committee, to reduce the danger of their being subordinate to the Executive Committee. This provision could also be seen as an aid to efficiency: a discussion in the Bosnian Central Committee had noted that because the Executive Committee was overburdened it had in the past formed a bottleneck for commission reports.[39] None of the five new commissions was concerned with internal party matters; they all dealt with broad policy issues, including one devoted to inter-republican relations.

The Ninth Congress brought about further changes in the commissions. Those set up in 1966 had apparently proved unsatisfactory because in May 1969 the new Presidium replaced them by fourteen permanent commissions to deal with political, economic and social policies as well as ideology, propaganda and the internal development of the party, plus two temporary commissions for agricultural policy and for youth.[40] The principle of separating the commissions from the executive was obviously abandoned after the Ninth Congress. The Presidium's report to the First Conference of the League in 1970 noted that commission proposals were all considered first by the Executive Bureau, and after that if necessary there was co-ordination between the Bureau and the commission to prepare a draft for the Presidium. The Bureau also held occasional (but rare) consultative meetings with the chairmen of commissions or individual chairmen. The commissions do appear to have had some importance in studying problems facing the Presidium; the Report claimed they had made a significant contribution, especially in relation to certain social problems. They involved a fairly large number of communists from various economic, professional, academic and political spheres — about 270.[41] How far they exhibited much intellectual or political independence is less clear. The controversial discussion in the Cultural Commission during 1969 (cited earlier) was clearly exceptional.

Conclusion

There is a disappointing lack of assessment by the League itself of the results of the reorganization undertaken at the top after Brioni. When the new proposals for a further organizational change were made in July 1968 there was no attempt to analyse shortcomings in the work of the Central Committee in the two previous years, or to examine the new role of the Executive Committee and the part played by the Presidium. There was no attempt either to explain the rationale behind the new structure. One reason for this silence may have been that organizational questions had become fairly insignificant beside more pressing problems: the July Plenum which agreed the proposed reorganization was concerned with the important economic Guidelines, the aftermath of the student protests and the crisis over Czechoslovakia. There also appears to have been a public mood of impatience with purely organizational issues. When NIN questioned Mirko Čanadonović, as a member of the Commission for reorganization, about preparations for the Ninth Congress, their reporter began by asking why the focus was still on 'technical organisational matters instead of dealing with the essence of relations as well'.[42] After the Ninth Congress the deepening nationalist divisions pushed organizational issues even further to one side except where they impinged directly on the powers of republics and national representation on central bodies.

The available evidence suggests that some aspects of organizational reform at the top of the League — in particular the constant revamping of the commission structure — failed to achieve very significant results. Even the creation of the intermediate tier of the Presidium between the Executive Committee and the Central Committee in 1966 appears to have been a form of organizational tinkering without obvious substantive results. Where the reforms did have genuine if very partial success, in livening up central committee meetings and creating some willingness to criticize and amend executive proposals, it seems likely that organization was secondary to the new spirit of independence engendered in party members at many levels. While factors like the size of committees and the frequency of meetings clearly do have importance, the willingness of executives to be accountable and the willingness of central committee members to engage in real debate and criticism are essential to make any formal system of party democracy work in practice.

Notes

1. *Politika*, 15 September 1966.
2. *Borba*, 3 July 1966.
3. *Borba*, 17 September 1966.
4. *Yugoslav Survey*, February 1967, pp. 46-7.
5. *Deveti Kongres SKJ, Stenografske Beleške, Knjiga 1*, Kommunist, 1970, p. 158.
6. *Borba*, 3 December 1968.
7. *Borba*, 7 February 1969.
8. *Borba*, 17 July 1968.
9. *Komunist*, 1 August 1968. The Eleventh Plenum in November decided to add three representatives from the army and accepted the names of three candidates (*Borba*, 3 December 1968).
10. *Komunist*, 1 August 1968.
11. *Borba*, 13 March 1969.
12. *Borba*, 26 July 1970.
13. *Ekonomska Politika*, 2 June 1969.
14. *RFE Research Report*, 4 December 1969.
15. *VUS*, 12 November 1969.
16. *Politika*, 4 August 1971.
17. *Borba*, 21 December 1971.
18. *Isvestaji VI Kongresu Saveza Komunista Srbije,* Beograd, 1968, pp. 12-13.
19. *Politika*, 23 September 1966.
20. *Borba*, 25 September 1966.
21. *Borba*, 18 October 1966.
22. *Borba*, 13 November 1968.
23. *Ekspres Nedelnja Revija,* January 1969.
24. *Komunist*, 21 January 1971.
25. *Vjesnik*, 3 January 1969.
26. *Borba*, 13 May 1969.
27. *Borba*, 21 October 1970.
28. Dennison Rusinow, *Crisis in Croatia*, Part I, American University Field Service Reports, 1972, p. 4.
29. *Borba*, 10 July 1971.
30. *Borba*, 31 July 1971.
31. *Borba*, 22 July 1971.
32. *Osmi Kongres SKJ, StenografskeBeleške, Knjiga 1*, Kultura, Beograd, 1965, pp. 571-2.
33. *Borba*, 12 November 1966.
34. *VUS*, 9 November 1966. Report based on shorthand minutes of LCY Control Commission meetings of 17 September 1966, which rehabilitated Ajtić.
35. *Borba*, 13 January 1968.
36. *Borba*, 3 December 1968.
37. *Borba*, 22 April 1971.
38. *Borba*, 17 September 1966.
39. *Politika*, 23 August 1966.
40. *Borba*, 13 May 1969.
41. Report on the Work of Presidium of the LCY on Implementing Decisions of the Ninth Congress, printed in *Borba Reflektor*, 26 July 1970.
42. *NIN*, 8 August 1968.

4 Devolution of Power and Local Reorganization

Introduction

The development of the reform movement in the Yugoslav League during the 1960s was closely linked to attempts to reorganize the party at all levels, both because the spirit of reform required certain changes in the method of work and internal processes of decision making of the party, and because organizational changes tended to reflect the redistribution of effective power within the party and political life as a whole. The organizational reforms took place in a number of stages, starting with the Eighth Congress in December 1964, when the new Statute incorporated a number of clauses designed to enhance the power of republican and lower bodies. The statutory changes were primarily a matter of verbal emphasis — the only procedural innovation of importance was the requirement that in the future republican congresses should meet before the congress of the LCY — and their practical significance in the context of the political climate in 1964 was doubtful.

There is general agreement that no major changes occurred in the party's habitual procedures until after the fall of Ranković. The extensive and frank criticisms of Ranković's 'factional activity', and of the way in which party bodies had allowed themselves to be manipulated, promoted a more critical and independent attitude among party members. The demotion of Ranković was also a signal for comprehensive reorganization of the party. It gave impetus to the demands of the republican parties for greater independence, and increasing republican power was reflected in the revised Statutes published in 1968, the manner in which the Ninth Congress was organized in March 1969, and in the selection of personnel to the top organs of the party at this Congress. There was also some decentralization of power to the commune parties. It was reorganization at this level that the League debated throughout 1967, in an attempt to improve the efficiency of local party activity and to make the League a more suitable instrument for fulfilling its guiding role in a self-managing society. The reform leaders wanted to curb centres of arbitrary power in commune parties in order to promote rank and file democracy inside the party, and because the role of local party bosses clashed with attempts to promote genuine self-management in commune administration and in enterprises.

Devolution of Powers to Republican Parties

The most significant development during the period 1964 to 1971 was the steady increase in the independence and power of republican parties. This trend was initiated at the Eighth Congress, greatly accelerated after the demotion of Ranković and fully recognized by the time of the Ninth Congress.

Greater formal recognition was accorded to republican parties under the revised Statute drafted for the Eighth Congress. This Statute gave back to the republics a limited right to decide policy, which had been accorded in 1952 but withdrawn in the 1958 Statute.[1] The 1964 Statute also stipulated that for the first time the republican congresses should be held before the Congress of the LCY, instead of after it. While this provision did not automatically ensure the republican parties much greater independence than before — it was after all bringing the Yugoslav party into line with the practice of the Soviet party in this respect — it clearly created much greater opportunity for republics to formulate their own policies and to choose their own nominees for central organs.[2]

The realization of genuine autonomy for republican and provincial leaderships was, like the realization of broader democratic reforms, to a large extent blocked by the personal and organizational power wielded by Ranković. There was, however, no immediate move to federalize the party after his fall. The weakening of the power of the Executive through the creation of a buffer in the Presidium could be seen as indirectly increasing the latitude allowed to republican committees: Bakarić is quoted as saying that they would have a 'free hand' as a result of the reorganization at the top.[3] On the other hand the republican committees all felt obliged to adopt the organizational pattern initiated by the Central Committee, only showing slight divergence when deciding how many commissions to create. The republican parties were still represented on the Executive Committee and Presidium roughly in proportion to their population (though weighted in favour of the smaller republics), not in equal numbers on a strictly federal basis. It is not clear how the members of the new Presidium and Executive Committee were chosen in the autumn of 1966. The Slovenian Committee publicly named candidates for these bodies to be 'proposed' to the Central Committee.[4] But since the Slovenian Committee met only a few days before the LCY Central Committee Plenum which ratified the members of the new bodies, presumably the candidates had already been cleared centrally. The Slovenian Committee was perhaps asserting a right of nomination which was to be granted to the republican parties in 1968.

Moves to consolidate republican powers proceeded much faster in the governmental sphere, with the passing of the 1967 and 1968 Constitutional Amendments, than within the party. During 1967 attention was focused on reorganizing the League at commune level, and although the republican central committees had final jurisdiction over the precise forms of re-organization, they followed the guidelines established by the LCY Central Committee, set out in the Theses published in April 1967 and endorsed at the Seventh Plenum on 1 July.

Preparations for the republican congresses and the re-drafting of the Statute in 1968 did, however, result in formal alteration of the status of the republican parties. Because republican congresses were held in advance of the Ninth Congress the newly elected republican leaders could go with enhanced authority to the Congress. Republican committees were also able to nominate candidates for the central party organs and have these nominees publicly endorsed by elections at the republican congresses, so that the composition of the LCY Presidium and of the standing part of the Conference was decided in advance of the Ninth Congress, which simply confirmed the republican candidates. This apparent republican freedom to decide the composition of the central party bodies was limited by a stipulation in the Executive Committee Instructions on the selection of candidates that the Executive Committee and Presidium must consider republican nominations in advance of the republican congresses.[5] Nevertheless, the procedure adopted tended to turn the central party organs into federal bodies composed of republican delegates rather than the central bodies of a unified party, and this federalism was underlined by giving each republic equal representation.

Federalism was also implied by the new draft Statute, which for the first time recognized the republican Leagues as separate organizations within the LCY, and by the right given to the republics to draw up their own republican statutes as a symbol of their new authority. As a result republican parties were free to adopt slightly different organizational forms. Although there were no major deviations from the established pattern, the Slovenian party used its autonomy to give rather wider powers to the republican conference, and — as a result of an amendment passed at the Slovenian Congress — elected members of the conference for a 2 year instead of a 1 year period.[6] The degree of independence which republican parties could enjoy in drafting their statutes was restricted by the problems of ensuring co-ordination with the Statute of the LCY, although the latter was of course influenced by proposals from the republics — for example the Macedonian party proposed amendments to the draft LCY Statute.[7] The Ninth Congress inserted a clause in the Statute requiring republican statutes to be brought into line with the LCY Statute within 1 year in order to tidy up the anomalies that existed.

The role played by the Statutory Commission during 1969 in overseeing the amendment of republican statutes, and giving rulings on points of uncertainty, suggested that at the formal organizational level there was still a tendency towards centralism in the party. The Commission met in June 1969 to discuss the extent of co-ordination required to bring republican statutes into line on all essentials, which meant incorporating clauses included in the LCY Statute after the republican congresses — for example the clause in Article 25 creating 'comradely courts' as part of the disciplinary process. The Commission issued a statement requiring republican parties to comply.[8] Meeting again in November the Commission noted that the republican statutes had been duly amended. It also gave rulings on some matters of detail: that the republican conference could dissolve a commune conference (although the LCY Statute left this decision to the republics); and on whether republican conferences should endorse co-options on to central committees by secret or public ballot.[9]

The party leaders were anxious at the time of the Ninth Congress to dispel any impression that the League had become a federal party, not only in deference to Leninist insistence on party unity transcending state federalism, but because of the immediate political importance of retaining party unity as a unifying factor. Mitja Ribičić, the Executive Committee member responsible for drafting the new Statute, stated in an interview that it was wrong to believe that 'the centre of the Party now represents some sort of a federation in the League of Communists, and that it sums up republican views, which are then co-ordinated'.[10] The specific organizational and statutory innovations at the Ninth Congress were in fact sufficiently hedged by central controls not to pose in themselves a threat to the unity of the League. A minor illustration of the organizational relations between the centre and the republics in 1969 was the decision reached on the new scale of membership fees. The LCY Presidium took the decision setting maximum and minimum limits for both poor and rich members, but the republics had discretion within these limits to lower or to increase the fees.[11]

The creation of the Executive Bureau, however, could be seen as a recognition of the actual independence being exercised by republican parties in policy spheres. Stane Dolanc indicated in a talk to *Komunist* in December 1971 the extent of republican independence between 1969 and 1971, when he observed that the Presidium meeting at Karadjorjevo was the first time a central organ of the LCY had commented authoritatively on the situation within a particular republic since the Executive Bureau reached conclusions on the demonstrations in Slovenia over allocation of World Bank money for roads in 1969, because assessing the responsibility of republican party leaderships had been viewed as the exclusive right of republican organs. He confirmed that the Presidium had recently been a place where republican bodies stated their views and LCY policy was usually based on compromise between republics, or else decisions were deferred.[12]

It was not until 1971 that there was public comment on the extent to which the League was becoming a confederal body. Crvenkovski for example spoke in May 1971 on the advantages and disadvantages of republican bodies taking up firm stands in advance of LCY Presidium meetings, noting that this practice allowed for the inclusion of broader circles in policy making, but tended to result in rigidity and mutual polemics, instead of the necessary dialogue on social problems.[13] Tito took up the issue in June and rejected as totally unacceptable recent views 'about some sort of a league of republican leagues of communists' and insisted 'we must have one League of Communists of Yugoslavia';[14] and an article in *Borba* in August commented on the need to avert a situation in which there could be six or eight separate political movements connected only by the same name.[15] Nevertheless even in 1971 certain habits of formal deference to central party decisions could be invoked: all republican committees felt bound to meet to endorse formally the conclusions of the Seventeenth Presidium session which agreed the Constitutional Amendments and to justify subsequent policies by citing the authority of the decisions reached at this session.

Devolution of Power to the Communes?

Whereas organizational changes in the League led to an increasing devolution of power to the republican parties, the tendency to give greater autonomy to commune parties was much less marked. Because the reformers were committed to the idea of decentralization in opposition to the centralized hierarchy, which they alleged existed until 1966 in the party, they were bound by ideological consistency to promote some degree of organizational autonomy at commune level. On the other hand there were several reasons why the reformers should not lay primary stress on the devolution of further powers to the commune parties. First, even if the commune committees were subject to strict control by higher levels of the party in certain spheres like cadre policy, they also enjoyed considerable administrative and economic powers within the commune as a result of governmental decentralization of powers during the 1950s — whereas the republics only gained substantial governmental and economic autonomy after 1966. There was also evidence during the 1950s and early 1960s that the commune party bosses were able to abuse their powers to secure privileges, and to usurp the rights of self-governing bodies in the commune and in enterprises without being checked by higher party organs unless a full-scale scandal erupted. Secondly, since these middle-level officials were frequently opponents of the reformers' policies, it would have been counter-productive to have given much greater organizational power to the commune committees. Thirdly, the reformers' commitment to ensure broader democratic control over small executive committees meant that they could quite consistently lay primary stress on strengthening democratic forms of organization at commune level in order to check arbitrary domination by local party bosses. Finally, the party leadership was concerned not only with internal democratization but also with reorganization to promote greater party efficiency in fulfilling its role at a local level.

There was, however, some slight emphasis on the desirability of enhancing the role of the commune at the time of the Eighth Congress. Crvenkovski advocated their greater autonomy at the Central Committee of the Macedonian party when he spoke of essential changes in the position of the commune committees and noted that they were no longer solely transmission belts for the higher bodies 'but were increasingly shaping the policy of the communes independently'.[16] Koliševski suggested that the 1964 Statute was meant to give greater independence to the commune in deciding the pattern of work and detailed the rights of communes to found basic organizations and to decide on other forms of organizing communists.[17]

A real key to the basis of power inside communist parties is who controls cadre appointments. During the debate before the Eighth Congress an article in *Komunist* raised the question of centralized control of cadre policy, and urged commune and district committees to abandon their practice of electing secretaries under direction from above. A contributor to *Komunist* noted that consent of senior leaderships to the election of lower leaderships was not written into the Statute, but that 'certain jurisdictions which it seems to me are today unnecessary are still being maintained'.[18] The President of the Serbian League admitted on television in February 1967 that in the past the republican central committee had made cadre decisions, but by then he could say that the republican committee 'does not even decide any longer who will be the secretary of a district committee, and least of all a commune committee . . . Personnel policy has been decentralized'.[19] This issue was refered to in more detail by a commune committee secretary from Serbia writing in *Komunist* in July 1966.[20] The author claimed that his commune had for the first time decided on its own commune committee political secretary, an appointment previously made by the district committee, which had meant that the secretary remained subservient to those who had appointed him. This account suggested that cadre policy rested as much on the personal patronage exercised by former commune officials who had moved up a rung in the hierarchy as on a formal organizational chain of decision making — it noted for example the tendency of a parliamentary deputy (probably a former commune assembly president) to keep 'all the commune strings in his hands for many years' after leaving the commune. But it did characterize the district committee as the chief focus for arbitrary exercise of authority. This view is supported by evidence which emerged in connection with the decentralization of cadre policy in both party and government at the time of the contentious 1967 assembly elections. *Borba* observed in an analysis of a factional struggle that surfaced in 1967 in the Macedonian town of Delčevo that, although personal feuds had existed for a long time, they had come into the open because in the past the key to all cadre moves, up or down, was in the district committee cadre commissions which held the strings. When the district was abolished, 'the commune was left to take care of its own cadre problems'.[21]

It seems, therefore, that one of the most important steps towards increasing communal independence was not a result of the party reforms designed to eliminate the deformations of the Ranković era, but a result of an earlier administrative decision to abolish the district as a governmental unit, which led to the dissolution of the district committees of the League in 1966–7. The dislike felt by communal officials for the supervisory role of the district was suggested during the discussion of local reorganization in 1967, when it was proposed to set up inter-communal conferences within the League to ensure the co-ordination previously achieved by the district committees. When the Serbian draft proposals provided that these inter-communal bodies should have their own executive organs a critical article in *Komunist* suggested that the Serbian draft had revived the ghost of the district committees under a new name, especially as the inter-communal committees would presumably draw on the former district personnel. The article noted that in the past the district committees had 'often played the role of tutor to commune committees' and that communists in the communes were opposed to a system which might lead to the intercommunal committees being 'above' the communes.[22] Despite this communal opposition the Croatian Central Committee — after leaving the question open in its original draft proposals on reorganization — also included a clause specifying the election of inter-communal executives.[23] In practice, however, communal fears that they would be dominated by these bodies do not appear to have been realized.

There are problems in finding adequate evidence to chart the nature of the relations between the republican committees and the commune committees after 1967. There were certainly signs of increasing defiance. The Kraljevo commune committee for example clashed with the Serbian party control commission in October 1968 over their decision to expel a member of the commune conference. The republican commission ruled that the committee had contravened the statute by taking the decision in the man's absence, noted that the proper body for such a decision was the basic organization, and suggested that if in this instance another body were to take the decision, it should be the commune conference. The commune committee replied by stating its unanimous opposition to the republican commission's decision and asking that it should be reconsidered. *Borba* observed that 'this is an act without precedent', and pointed out that the proper courses open to the commune committee were either to comply with the republican commission's proposal or to appeal to the control commission of the LCY.[24] During the 1969 assembly elections some candidates openly defied orders from the republican party committee to stand down.

Nevertheless some commune parties may have retained a habit of checking with higher authority before reaching decisions. Latinka Perović suggested that this happened during an interview in 1970, when she observed that 'Some commune committees come to the Serbian Central Committee and ask "Do we enjoy your support?" We tell them: "You were elected by the members, it is they to whom you must account for your activity . . . You have not been nominated by us." '[25]

Reorganization of the Commune Parties

In pursuit of the goal of reforming the League at local levels, to enable it to perform its guiding role more effectively and to enhance rank and file participation and independence, the party leaders launched a prolonged debate on how to organize the party within the commune.

The debate about reorganization focused on to two main issues: whether the party should retain its primary base in enterprises and other places of work or whether all communists should be linked directly to the commune:[26] and on means of making the commune committee more responsive to the rank and file members in the commune. Mijalko Todorović, Secretary of the Executive Committee of the League, explained on Belgrade television that party organizations in the enterprises confined their members' attention to relatively narrow interests and issues, and that he believed that since the commune was the main unit for realizing the common interests of the 'working people' it should be the focus for party organization. As the commune was too large to act as a basic organization where all members could assemble it would be necessary to devise ways of dividing them up, either by organizing sections to deal with specific areas of the economy, education or culture, or by setting up *aktivs* in places of work and residence.[27]

VUS ran an article in February 1967 in which it asked secretaries of commune and factory committees from various republics to give their views on the best organizational base for the party. The respondents opted for organizing communists in enterprises, arguing that the main task was to promote self-management in the economy, and that in practice territorial bodies did not achieve the ideal of engaging themselves with the social interests of the commune as a whole. One Zagreb factory-party secretary recalled the experience of territorial *aktivs* which had been tried 2 years previously with the aim of introducing self-management attitudes from the enterprises into the settlement of problems of the commune. He noted:

> But in the end it turned out that the Socialist Alliance was using us to collect membership fees . . . There were lamentations over lack of quorums at election meetings, over people not attending and debates not being prepared.[28]

The Croatian party leaders made it clear from the outset of the debate that they were committed to maintain party organizations in enterprises, thus opposing the preference of LCY officials for the territorial solution, indicated by Todorović's speech. Miko Tripalo said in an introductory report to the Croatian Central Committee in February 1967 that the Executive Committee stood by the view that it was impossible to remove the party from process of production, although he conceded that basic organizations in the workplace were often too fragmented.[29] In a later speech Tripalo explained this commitment to keep the party in the factories not only in ideological terms — that the League remained primarily the party of the working class, a term he extended to cover the technicians and scientists in industry and 'working people in other spheres' who identified with the interests of the workers – but also in political terms. He said that, while Croatian Communists welcomed an end to the insulation of communists in work organizations, they feared that 'if the LC were to be dragged out of the work organisations, it might be a bureaucratic measure', because of the problems of communists drawn from different spheres discussing authoritatively a wide range of social problems. Tripalo observed that: 'This situation might really provide a favourable opportunity for the chief bureaucrats in the commune to impose their own view on all problems.'[30]

The Theses published by the Central Committee Commission on Reorganization in April 1967 represented a compromise. A speaker in a debate on the Theses at Sarajevo University observed that they bore the typical stamp of the professional politicians in the party.[31] The Theses rehearsed what were clearly familiar arguments, that the activity of communists had been confined too narrowly either to the factory or institution in which they worked, or to the immediate area in which they lived. Party organizations in streets or housing blocks, which were mainly composed of pensioners and housewives, were particularly inclined to be inactive and limited in their horizons. The Theses proposed retaining both types of basic organization, but in order to widen the interests of communists in both, and to promote efficiency, it stated that communists attached to party organizations at their work place would in future be required to join also in the activities of the territorial body in the area in which they lived. The Theses expressed grave doubts about forming party organizations in administrative agencies, arguing that this separated communists into a white-collar stratum and promoted a 'civil service mentality' among them, which encouraged them to meddle in the running of these agencies to the detriment of their efficiency. Communists in government administration were to join their local territorial organization. In addition the Theses recommended that both the scope and efficiency of basic organizations could be increased by a process of amalgamating small organizations, so enlarging their number of members and the area for which they were responsible.[32]

The other problem discussed in the Theses was the best means of overcoming the isolation of basic organizations and their subordination to the instructions of an overpowerful commune committee. A number of suggestions had been thrown up in the preliminary discussion. Tripalo referred to the idea of setting up broad *aktivs* of for example those engaged in education, health and culture and attaching them to the commune committee. He also said that support should be given to proposals from

Slavonski Brod for commune conferences to be set up as permanent bodies meeting three or four times a year in order to debate major policy issues of the commune.[33] An alternative proposal canvassed was for the holding of a series of specialist communal conferences drawing on different personnel, instead of one permanent conference. The Theses opted for a permanent commune conference which would represent the basic organizations and give them a voice in policy making (previously relations between the commune committee and the basic organizations had been officially confined to organizational questions) and would − it was hoped − enable them to prevent the commune committee 'from taking over prerogatives which do not belong to it'.[34]

The reorganization debate indicated that within enterprises there was a good deal of grass roots feeling in favour of abolishing the party factory committees, though not of course party organization in the workplace. The *VUS* interviews with party officials cited earlier indicated that even a number of factory-committee secretaries favoured this move. A Titograd construction-enterprise secretary observed that if anything should be abolished, it was the factory committees, which were responsible for bureaucratic interference. A secretary from a cotton industry in Djakovica said that the factory committee was a bad mediator between communal committees and the basic organizations in the factory. A third from Pula reported that 900 communists in his shipbuilding enterprise had discussed more flexible forms of organization and agreed not to elect a factory committee. *Politika* noted in December 1966 that the Zemun commune committee had accepted demands from three enterprises that factory committees should be abolished.[35] The reorganization of the Zagreb party in August 1967 entailed abandoning factory committees in almost all enterprises and setting up conferences where this seemed necessary.[36]

One important organizational issue which was not examined in the Theses concerned the enterprises which as a result of mergers had factories in a number of different communes. The Executive Committee of the LCY noted this problem at its meeting of 20 July 1967, which was devoted to issuing directives on various unclarified questions arising from reorganization, condemned an occasional tendency to insist upon 'vertical linkage' which would deviate from the principle of basing party organization on the commune, and advocated further consultation by those concerned.[37] The Serbian Executive Committee proposed that in these 'integrated enterprises' there should be party conferences composed of delegates from all sections, but that the party organization should be related to the commune and should not parallel the structure of the enterprise.[38]

In view of the time and effort spent by the League in the mid-sixties
in discussing forms of reorganization, and the importance assigned to it in
ideological terms, the end results of the process were disappointing. This
was particularly true at commune level. After prolonged debate and
disagreement, commune-party organization did not change in essentials.
The principle of having party branches in the workplace and at ward level
was retained, the only difference being that working communists were
obliged to belong to both.[39] The most systematic change carried out in
all republics was a reduction in the number of basic organizations through
a process of amalgamation.[40]

Rights of Basic Organizations

The effectiveness of the local reorganization in achieving its goals of
revitalizing the basic organizations and in promoting democratic participation within the commune depended in part on the degree of involvement of the membership as a whole in the process of reform. Tempo
in a characteristically frank and critical article in *NIN* commented on
the fact that rank and file members were being given no really detailed
and concrete advice about how to overcome old methods of work and
avoid insularity within their basic organizations, and noted that the
findings of various enquiries 'show that a considerable section of the
League of Communists either ignore what changes have been taking place
in the current reorganization, or have a completely wrong picture of
the nature of these changes'.[41]

There is some evidence of a greater willingness by basic organizations to
assert their independence in relation to higher party organs, although this
was probably a product of the new atmosphere in the party rather than of
the reorganization, and in some instances pre-dated it. For example the
republican control commission for Macedonia noted in a report in August
1967 that there had recently been increasingly frequent instances of basic
organizations appealing against commune commissions which had annulled
or mitigated punishments. The republican commission judged that some
of the complaints by basic organizations were justified and upheld them
against the commune, but also noted that some basic organizations indicated
an obstinate determination to stick to their original punishment regardless
of the views of both the commune and republican commissions, and had
refused to readmit members whose expulsion had been annulled. The report
attributed this attitude in part to factions within the basic organizations,
and quoted a number of examples.[42] An interesting declaration of independence by basic organizations on a policy issue occurred in Zagreb in

December 1968 when organizations refused to discuss the new Croatian draft statute until they could compare it with the draft statute of the LCY, then still unpublished.[43]

On the other hand, there is also evidence that commune committees tended to exercise arbitrary powers in relation to basic organizations, quite frequently usurping the statutory rights of the basic organizations to decide on punishment of individual members. Commune committee intervention in expulsions policy was a well-established practice. In 1963 the LCY Control Commission criticized the tendency of factory and commune committees to mete out punishments direct.[44] Press reports indicated that commune committees quite often continued to take the initiative in deciding on expulsions. The Serbian party Control Commission report covering 1966, for example, commented unfavourably on the arbitrary action by commune committees.[45] A *Borba* reporter asked the President of the Serbian Statutory Commission in May 1969 whether it was possible to deduce from the complaints received what kind of opposition there was to democratization, and was told that 'the old practice' of commune committees pronouncing punishments, instead of leaving this to basic organizations, was continuing.[46]

There were certainly cases where commune committees and secretaries exceeded their powers and imposed their will on basic organizations on wider issues. *Komunist* publicized in February 1968 the 'Hafiza Demirović' scandal, which concerned the unconstitutional intervention of the Novi Pazar commune committee in job assignment in a Social Insurance Institute, and its attempt to quash resistance by the basic organization in the Institute by expelling Hafiza Demirović and pronouncing disciplinary measures against the other members of the organization. When Demirović demanded that her case be discussed by her own basic organization the commune Secretary referred the matter to the commune control commission.[47]

It is difficult to generalize about relations between commune committees and basic organizations, or about the effectiveness or otherwise of the new commune conferences on the basis of individual 'cases'. There is also the problem that party attitudes and practices at the local level might vary between regions and republics. Nevertheless the general impression which emerges from examining the role of the party in the commune and from the electoral conflicts which took place in 1967 and especially in 1969 was that power at commune level was normally wielded by a group of party bosses, sometimes co-operating to run the affairs of the commune and sometimes engaged in bitter personal power struggles, and that the attempt to curb their activities through the broad democratic forum of the commune conference failed as an institutional device. Tripalo commented in the wake of the 1969 elections 'that these elections have shown that the commune bureaucracy is being considerably strengthened'.[48] This comment referred to commune government as well as party officials — the two being closely linked — but indicated the failure of commune parties to achieve internal democracy or to encourage real self-management.

Notes

1. The 1952 clause allowed republican parties to 'determine within the framework of the political line of the LCY the political line of the League of Communists of the people's republic', whereas the 1958 version simply accorded them the right to decide 'the tasks of the League of Communists in the people's republic'. The 1964 Statute amplified republican rights in Article 28 to read:

   > The Congress of the League of Communists of the socialist republic . . . establishes the policy, positions and tasks of the League of Communists of the socialist republic in accordance with the policy of the LCY and conditions in the republic; and initiates consideration of specific individual questions by the Congress and Central Committee of the LCY (*Osmi Kongres SKJ*, Stenografske Beleške, Kultura, Beograd, p. 2029).

2. A move to enhance republican rights also entailed re-examination of the status of the two provincial party bodies. The 1964 draft reverted to the format of the 1952 Statute and devoted a separate section to the provincial organizations, which had in 1958 been grouped with the commune and district levels of the party. Under the new rules the provincial conferences were — like the republican congresses — to be held every 4 years, which implicitly gave them comparable status and distinguished them from the district and commune conferences to be held every 2 years. The Statute did not specify whether the provincial conferences should be held before or after the Serbian party Congress: they had previously been held afterwards, a practice maintained in 1965. This question does not seem to have been accorded much political significance, since in 1968 the Kosovo conference met just before the Serbian Congress and the Vojvodina conference just after it. The provincial organizations gained the right in 1964 to propose policies to higher bodies, a right described as an important innovation in a *Borba* article discussing final changes in the text of the draft Statute (*Borba*, 28 November 1964).
3. *Vjesnik*, 17 September 1966, cited by Paul Shoup, *Communism and the Yugoslav National Question*, Columbia University Press, New York, 1968, p. 214.
4. *Borba*, 2 October 1966.
5. *Komunist*, 1 August 1968.
6. *Komunist*, 30 January 1969.
7. Ibid.
8. *Politika*, 26 June 1969. Comradely courts (renamed comradely councils in the final draft of the Statute) would be appointed *ad hoc* by a party organization to investigate charges against an individual communist and make recommendations about appropriate disciplinary action.
9. *Borba*, 13 November 1969.
10. *Komunist*, 30 January 1969.
11. *Borba*, 16 December 1969.
12. *Socialist Thought and Practice*, October–December 1971.
13. *Borba*, 15 May 1971.
14. *Politika*, 20 June 1971.

15. *Borba*, 4 August 1971.
16. *Komunist*, 24 March 1964.
17. *Osmi Kongres SKJ*, p. 2026.
18. *Komunist*, 16 July 1964.
19. *Borba*, 17 February 1967.
20. *Komunist*, 28 July 1966.
21. *Borba*, 26 February 1967.
22. *Komunist*, 5 October 1967.
23. *Komunist*, 5 October and 17 October 1967.
24. *Borba*, 31 October 1968.
25. *Politika*, 26 July, 1970.
26. The reformers had discussed the principles on which the League should be organized in discussing the Statute for the Eighth Congress according to Krsto Bulajić, speaking at the Commission for Reorganization in July 1967 (*Borba*, 16 July 1967).
27. *Borba*, 16 December 1966.
28. *VUS*, 8 February 1967.
29. *Vjesnik*, 8 February 1967. See also *RFE Research Report*, 18 October 1967 on Croatian Committee independent stand on reorganization.
30. *Borba*, 24 September 1967.
31. *Pregled*, 1967, no. 2, p. 77.
32. The Theses were published in *Yugoslav Survey*, August 1967, pp. 45-74.
33. *Vjesnik*, 8 February 1967.
34. Budislav Šoškić on the reorganization proposals in *Komunist*, 23 May 1967.
35. *Politika*, 28 December 1966.
36. *Borba*, 9 August 1967.
37. *Komunist*, 20 July 1967.
38. *Borba*, 12 September 1967.
39. There was some divergence from the prescribed pattern by certain Slovenian commune parties. Some decided to abolish party bodies in factories, except in the biggest enterprises, and to found single local territorial organizations in their place. Others set up 'associated organizations' in education, the health service, government administration, militia and customs, despite criticisms that they were acting against the Slovenian Central Committee Resolution on reorganization (*Komunist*, 3 August 1967).
40. The Croatian Central Committee for example reported to their republican congress at the end of 1968 that territorial organizations in the countryside had been cut from 2318 to 1134 and in the town from 769 to 321, while the number in enterprises had been reduced from 3854 to 1778 and in other institutions from 1271 to 603 (*Sesti Kongres*, SKH, Knjiga I, 5-7 December 1968, Stenografske Bilješke, *Komunist*, 1969, p. 90).
41. *NIN*, 10 September 1967.
42. *Komunist*, 3 August 1967.
43. *Borba*, 3 December 1968.
44. *Komunist*, 7 November 1963.
45. *Borba*, 6 May 1967.
46. *Borba*, 1 May 1969.
47. *Komunist*, 28 February 1968.
48. *Borba*, 24 May 1969.

5 Rank and File Democracy

When the reformers took up the struggle to promote democracy in the League, and campaigned for statutory recognition of greater democratic rights in the 1964 Statute, they had a number of specific aims: to encourage debate and criticism, to safeguard the right of individual dissent, to promote much greater participation in policy making, and to give rank and file members more influence in the selection of party leaderships through the electoral process. In addition the reformers stressed the importance of making the work of the party committees and local organizations open to the press and also to the public, a facet of democratization in relation to the broader population. This chapter examines how far each of these goals was embodied in the Statutes and in the actual practice of the League at various levels.

Freedom of Criticism and Debate

The Eighth Congress Statute set out to strengthen the rights of the individual to criticize the work of party officials and committees and their right to defend their views in party publications and to make proposals to higher bodies or ask questions. Koliševski underlined in his introduction to the new Statute that members had the right to query adopted policies, on the grounds that party decisions may have to be revised in the light of practical developments.[1] The need to guarantee the right of criticism had been indicated by a report of the LCY Control Commission in November 1963 which noted that party members including leading officials tended to resent justified criticisms; that individuals had been punished for criticism and for complaining to higher bodies; and that individuals had also been penalized when their criticism was wrong in minor details even when its substance was correct.[2] During the debate on the drafting of the Statute a party member wrote to *Borba* proposing that individual rights should be strengthened in view of the fact that 'there are not a few basic organizations where proposals made by leading officials are formally approved in their presence in order not to offend them', and that there had been press reports about people being dismissed from their jobs for addressing higher bodies or criticizing leading officials.[3] A district conference in Valjevo suggested that communists in villages were prepared to be outspokenly critical of government and party bodies — as revealed at a consultative conference for 300 village members — but that communists in factories, who were much more numerous than communists in villages, tended to keep quiet for fear of losing their jobs.[4]

It appears that the Eighth Congress did not mark any striking increase in the freedom felt by ordinary members to indulge in outspokenness. A report in *Borba* noted the prevalence of 'phrase mongering' in party meetings because there was no risk in repeating the correct phrases and they masked the speaker's real opinion.[5] In the aftermath of the Fourth Plenum *Borba* quoted workers in a Belgrade factory who complained about lack of democracy in the party and commented on 'this silence of communists at meetings which has lasted for a fairly long time, this fear to advance one's opinion'.[6] Apart from fear of criticizing those above — a Control Commission report in May 1966 found that people were often punished for opposing certain officials[7] — there were still pressures against dissent even on minor matters. A discussion among political officials in Skoplje indicated that basic organizations often insisted on members taking unanimous stands on practical questions, like recommending an individual for a post, where disagreement would be perfectly reasonable.[8]

After Brioni there was in general greater freedom of criticism and greater willingness to express disagreement about policy or even to state reservations about the correctness of decisions reached by top party organs. High-ranking members of the party were prepared to air publicly their individual differences, though not all communists approved of this tendency. A perturbed reader from Priština wrote to *Borba* in June 1967 to complain that he had always assumed that statements by party and state officials represented League policy, and said that where there were disagreements party forums should decide what was right and what was not. His letter was a response to comments by Crvenkovski saying that party members must understand that disagreement at the top was not bad and that speeches by high officials were not to be considered the party line until a policy had been officially adopted.[9]

There were also instances of representatives of commune organizations voicing open criticism of republican policies. A delegate from Zadar at the Croatian party Congress in 1968 stated in the debate on the Statute that the majority of communists in his commune were against adopting a republican statute, which might lead to disunity.[10] Members of the

Ljubljana City Committee protested vigorously at a meeting in June 1971 because the Slovenian Central Committee had taken a decision about the reorganization of the City party, reinstating the five commune organizations abolished 3 years previously, without prior consultation with the City Conference or wider discussions in the party. Tone Preloznik, member of the City Committee, said in an introductory speech that the City Committee still believed, in contrast with the views of the Central Committee, that weaknesses in the City party were not caused by the existing organizational structure. Since the republican Central Committee had decided to form commune organizations, however, he observed, 'we, in keeping with the principles of democratic centralism, must implement the decision, regardless of whether we agree with it or not'.[11] Ljubljana representatives pressed their grievance at the Third Conference of the Slovene party in November 1971, when during discussion on Central Committee reports a spokesman demanded more consistent respect for the Statute and called for the text of the resolutions to incorporate the fact that the Central Committee had disregarded the Statute in omitting to consult the City Conference about reorganization.[12]

There is, however, room for doubt how far freedom of criticism was fully enjoyed by rank and file party members at local level. Two speakers at the Montenegrin Congress in 1968 said that criticism was still considered risky in the League and even sincere critics were denounced as 'petty critics'.[13]

Special difficulties in ensuring freedom of criticism arose inside party organizations in the armed services. *Komunist* reported a discussion at an electoral conference in an army unit. Soldiers at this party meeting did criticize their commander for not concerning himself enough with their activities outside basic training, but they also noted the difficulty of promoting real criticism in any military unit, because subordinates cannot know properly what their superior officers are doing.[14] The article also suggested that communists refrained from criticizing errors by commanding officers for fear of damaging the officer's reputation, even when the whole unit knew about the mistake. A more frequent explanation given for hesitancy among party members in the army to voice criticism was that ordinary soldiers were afraid to criticize their military superiors, though spokesmen for the party organization in the army tended to insist that there was a tradition of criticizing superiors.[15] Similar statements about the obstacles to criticism by communists in the army were being made after Brioni.

Right of Dissent

One means of expressing major disagreement with party policy is resignation, and as an extension of the individual right of dissent the 1964 Statute granted individuals the right to resign from the party. The phrase inserted in the Statute provided that membership would lapse 'on voluntary withdrawal from the League or on expulsion'. Kolišhevski gave a gloss on this formulation explaining that the idea was to emphasize that members who wanted to leave the League would not be formally expelled as a result, and that the clause would enable anyone who could not accept the party Programme or its obligations to withdraw.

The right of resignation was gradually adopted after 1964, with the number prepared to take advantage of this option growing in 1966 and 1967. Nevertheless *Komunist* noted in August 1967 that there were still considerable obstacles to resignation, partly because there was no clarity about procedures and some basic organizations made the process more rigorous than others, partly because some party organizations still disapproved and formally expelled those who asked to resign, and partly because in some places leaving the League was interpreted as a repudiation of socialism and viewed as more serious than expulsion.[16]

The Croatian Central Committee extended the right of resignation to members of the Committee at its Plenum in October 1966. Resignation was granted to members who could not perform their duties adequately, or those who disagreed with the actions and policy of the Committee. Resignations could be both individual and collective.[17] The Dubrovnik Commune Committee invoked this right of collective resignation in the aftermath of one of the crises that enlivened the 1967 elections to the communal, republican and federal assemblies. *Komunist* noted that it was 'the first case in the history of the LCY of the collective resignation of a party committee' and Crvenkovski singled the incident out for special mention.[18]

This right of resignation by committees was subsequently incorporated into the revised party Statute of 1969, which specified that: 'Every elected organ and executive unit of the League may submit collective resignations and their members may submit individual resignations.' The initial draft suggested that resignation was not only a right but a duty where members could not conscientiously implement agreed tasks or accept the collective views of their organization, or if they acted to block policy and undermined party unity. The final draft passed at the Congress, however, omitted the clauses implying obligation to resign in such circumstances.[19] The Statute also spelt out much more clearly the right of individual resignation: Article 28 of the adopted Statute specified that a member could voluntarily leave the League. The numbers availing themselves of this right tended to rise steadily, despite a slight fall in 1969 compared with 1968, reaching 15 000 in 1970.

One crucial issue concerning the limits of dissent and the nature of party discipline was raised during the debate about the Statute in 1964 and in 1966–7; whether to allow organized factions in the party. A number of party spokesmen felt obliged to condemn advocacy of factions during 1964. Milentije Popović said in an interview with *Socijalizam* that factions would lead to a multi-party system.[20] Marijan Cvetković, Organizational Secretary of the Croatian party, castigated 'liberalistic pseudo-democratic trends' and trends 'towards allowing the minority to defend its opinion, even after the decision has been made, in the press, meetings, etc.'. He added that there was an attempt to introduce 'alien theoretical conceptions into the revolutionary monolithic organization of the League of Communists'.[21]

It is not however clear if there was any pressure at higher levels of the party for a relaxation on the traditional ban on factions, or if these attacks were directed solely against the academic reformers who had been involved in the conference on Marxism and Contemporary Reality in June 1964, some of whom had overstepped the line. Besim Ibrahimpašić had attacked the Leninist concept of the party for laying the foundations of Stalinist bureaucracy and called for changes in the League's Statute to allow the expression of various tendencies in the party press. He also specifically urged that communists who remained in a minority in their beliefs had the right to defend them, although they were obliged to accept majority opinion on the plane of action.[22] Svetozar Stojanović, later to become a prominent radical as an editor of *Praxis* and member of the Philosophy Department at Belgrade University, had also come out clearly for the rights of minorities.[23]

Questions about the principle of democratic centralism, or of the correct interpretation of the principle, arose naturally in the debate about the future of the party after the Brioni Plenum. But proposals to legislate in favour of minorities in the party were being canvassed sufficiently often before the July Plenum for Bakarić to deal with the issue in a speech during May 1966. He characterized discussions on how the League should be organized as part of an anti-Stalinist campaign:

On the whole the purpose of this anti-Stalinist criticism has been to assert that the League of Communists, as well as all other communist parties, has retained the oldest principles of organization; that it is dogmatic; that it adheres to democratic centralism — and consequently, is not democratic at all; that the principles of self-management initiated by the League of Communists are in contradiction with democratic centralism. The conclusion is then drawn that one should organize, as a minimum, the rights of the minority within the League of Communists, or adopt some other 'democratic' forms.[24]

Later in his talk Bakarić reverted to the thesis that 'the "minority" has always been the standard bearer of what is progressive' and it was therefore necessary to assure minority rights. Bakarić attacked this argument with the rather indirect claim that while minorities were the champions of progress, any real attempt to institutionalize the minority's role was to miss the point, which was the necessity of minority progressive ideas being propagated among the majority, who left to themselves would lag behind social developments and act conservatively.

Explicit support for legalizing factions did not find expression in the official party press, *Komunist* and *Socijalizam*, but there were more generalized statements stressing the creative role of minorities and criticizing 'formalistic' interpretations of democratic centralism: for example an article by Muzafer Tufai writing in *Komunist*.[25] The theoretical journal of the party, *Socijalizam*, printed two articles in 1967 highly critical of automatic adherence to democratic centralism. Tomislav Čokrevski underlined the fact that Lenin's conception had been formulated to meet the problems of an underground party in Tsarist Russia, stressed the need for party organization to reflect changing social conditions, indicated that the organizational principles devised for a conspiratorial party of professional revolutionaries could not be applied unchanged to mass proletarian parties, and quoted Gramsci in support of a more flexible interpretation of democratic centralism.[26] Vojislav Stanovčić in a more specific article in the same issue argued that belief in democratic centralism had previously favoured the conservative and bureaucratic forces in the Yugoslav League, and suggested unity was necessary on some but not all issues.[27]

These views which threatened the principle of democratic centralism were rebutted by some party officials, including some of the leading reformers. Bakarić came out in July 1966 with a much more sharply worded attack on the idea of an organized minority in the party and also condemned the *Praxis* group (though without specifically naming them) for calling the League Stalinist.[28] Tripalo in a discussion about reorganization in September 1967 asserted the need to maintain the principle of democratic centralism: 'Of course, I am not referring to democratic centralism of the Stalinist type.'[29] While an official of the Belgrade

University Committee wrote in *Komunist* that 'the recently propagated thesis' that minorities were always the bearers of progressive ideas overlooked the reactionary and divisive theories more often promoted by minorities.[30]

In assessing the strength of those seeking an end to the ban on factions it is important to clarify the position held by the Macedonian reformers. Milosavlevski made a case for legalizing factions in his book *Revolucija i Anti-Revolucija*, published in September 1971; but he did so as part of a general theoretical discussion about maximizing democracy in socialist regimes and not as a concrete recommendation for the League.[31] The section of his book directly on Yugoslavia is understandably less radical than the more abstract analysis, and he wrote after the main debate on the party statute. It is of greater importance to examine the line taken by Crvenkovski, who was a central figure in the debates of the 1960s, and who is credited by some Western and Yugoslav sources with supporting for a time the 'rights of minorities'. The evidence for this interpretation of his position appears to rest primarily upon an interview with *Politika* in October 1966, but scrutiny of this article does not suggest that Crvenkovski committed himself to supporting organized factions. Asked about the implication of democratic centralism that the minority should be subordinated to the majority, Crvenkovski replied that:

> this principle should not be formulated in a military fashion as in the past . . . we must proclaim that the minority which advocates a different attitude is not expected to fight unconditionally for the standpoints of the majority, but that it is necessary that the minority should be loyal to the decision, that it should not, for example, oppose them. This is necessary if we do not want to break individuals, their thoughts and ideas, to turn a revolutionary into an obedient bureaucrat . . .

He went on to note that while progressive ideas were always initiated by minorities, these ideas can only be successful if endorsed by the majority. 'Therefore we must give enough room for minorities and individuals to express their ideological and political creativity, and we must also strive to ensure that what is endorsed will be democratically endorsed by the majority. . . . '[32] This latter formulation is not far from Bakarić. Speaking almost a year later Crvenkovski suggested that democratic centralism was modified by the right of resignation, which signified abandonment of the conception of the party as a sectarian organization and of the pretence of monolithic unity.[33] A link between the right of resignation and the acceptance of democratic centralism was also made by Milutin Baltić addressing the Croatian Central Committee in October 1967, when he argued that the republican Decisions on Reorganization were binding and that individuals unable to implement them had the freedom to resign; only in this way could the principle of democratic centralism be correctly observed.[34]

The substance of Crvenkovski's wish not to impose a false monolithic unity, and to allow individuals to maintain their personal beliefs, was incorporated in the draft of the 1969 Statute, in a clause which specified that the individual had a right to retain his own opinion when a decision was being made in the party, though he was obliged to accept the agreed conclusions. This provision was the source of considerable confusion and disagreement, both during the discussions of the draft and after the Statute had been adopted. An article in *Borba* complained, with justice, that it was ambiguous.[35] The author of this article interpreted the clause as legalizing abstention during discussion and voting on an issue, an interpretation accepted by some other commentators. But the official explanation given by Budislav Šoškić introducing the new Statute at the Ninth Congress stressed the right of the individual to retain his own opinion even *after* a decision had been agreed, a provision which was, he said, designed to safeguard the integrity of the individual and to avoid the hypocrisy of verbal obeisance to the majority view. But this provision did not in any way mitigate the obligation of party members to accept majority decisions: discipline in action was necessary although discipline in thought could not be imposed.[36] The final text of the Statute had reduced the emphasis on party discipline in this clause, omitting the injunction: 'he is not allowed to oppose the implementation of the accepted decision nor may he in any way render difficult the implementation of an adopted decision'.[37] Party members remained uncertain what this clause meant in practice: the Commission for Statutory Questions noted in April 1970 that there had been 'a great deal of dispute over the provisions of Article 17'.[38]

The party statutes did allow a loophole for those dissatisfied with adopted policies to press for their reconsideration in light of difficulties revealed by experience. Koliševski drew attention to the clause in the 1964 Statute, which kept open the possibility of policy review, but he presented it less as an individual right than as a safeguard to ensure party policy kept pace with social developments; and the wording of the clause indicated that pleas for reconsideration of adopted decisions were to be made to party committees rather than to be discussed among the rank and file.[39] The 1969 Statute retained this right to query agreed policies in the light of experience and to seek further discussion – the relevant organ had to decide whether there were sufficient reasons for renewing the discussion.

This right was granted in the same article of the Statute which allowed individuals to retain their personal opinions. In order to clarify the limits of these two concessions, which suggested a degree of scepticism about adopted decisions was allowable, Article 17 specifically forbade 'grouping and fractionalism' in the League.

One of the effects of the reformers' emphasis on giving content to the 'democratic' aspect of democratic centralism was to alter the statutory formulations of this principle. The 1958 Statute of the League had taken over almost exactly the definition adopted in the Soviet Statute: (a) all leading organs of the League, from the lowest to the highest, are elected; (b) all organs of the League are bound to account for their work to the organizations which elected them; (c) the minority is bound to accept and carry out the decisions of the majority; (d) organizations and lower organs are obliged to carry out the decisions of higher organs. The 1964 Statute modified and elaborated its interpretation of the essentials of democratic centralism. It specified that all organizations must 'work independently',[40] that leading organs should work collectively, and that higher organs must consider proposals and criticisms from lower bodies; but it retained the requirement that lower bodies must implement the decisions of higher organs. The demand that the minority obey the majority was also retained, but incorporated in a clause elaborating on the democratic manner in which decisions ought to be reached: through comprehensive debate and majority vote.

Crvenkovski suggested in 1966 that participation in policy making was essential to a reinterpretation of democratic centralism:

> In the future, this democratic centralism will have to be changed in the sense of making the base become the body which will assume an increasingly important and probably decisive role in the adoption of decisions. This means that already now we can speak of the possibilities for individual basic, commune or republican organizations to come forward with draft resolutions before the Central Committee or the Congress and for these proposals to be taken into consideration . . .[41]

The effect of the more liberal views which predominated after 1966 and of the acceptance of the need for broader consultations within the party was a further erosion of the centralist element in democratic centralism.

Indeed, it is arguable that the statutory formulation adopted in 1969 went far towards abandoning it altogether. The Ninth Congress Statute omitted the requirement that lower bodies obey higher organs, replacing it by a clause obliging smaller organs to observe the decisions of broader bodies and binding all organizations to observe the Programme, Statute, policies and decisions of the LCY. It did however maintain the requirement that majority decisions should be binding on all members. The main emphasis of the new ten-point definition of democratic centralism was on the need for maximum participation by all members in policy making at every level of the League and in the selection of party organs.

Participation at Party Congresses

Party congresses provide occasions when it is possible to make some assessment of the genuineness of claims to have promoted participation in policy making in the League. Because the proceedings cover a brief period and are well reported it is possible to assess them in terms of specific criteria: the degree to which members of the Central Committee dominate the proceedings; the numbers of delegates who participate in discussion; whether or not this discussion is substantive and critical; whether many amendments are proposed and accepted; and whether or not voting is unanimous. Since congresses of ruling communist parties are normally well orchestrated occasions designed to demonstrate party unity to the world at large, and to herald policy changes or provide a forum for ideological innovation, any change in the nature of a party congress signifies a new tone in party practices and relationships. The Fifth, Sixth and Seventh Congresses of the Yugoslav League all fulfilled the traditional function of acclaiming the policies initiated by the party leadership, and although there was some increase in the extent of rank and file participation at the Eighth Congress, this Congress too observed the conventions of lengthy official speeches and absolute unanimity in plenary sessions. The Ninth Congress did therefore constitute a significant break with this pattern, cutting official speeches down to a minimum so that four and a half out of five days were spent in discussions in commissions.

Central Committee domination of the proceedings on the floor of the Congress was minimized at the Ninth Congress by the elimination of long official reports. Over 400 delegates took part in discussions in the six commissions at the Ninth Congress — more than a third of the delegates, compared with 230 who made speeches at the four Eighth Congress commissions. In the most popular commission at the Eighth Congress, on Socio-Economic Development, only 76 delegates spoke out of the 600 attending; 20 out of the 99 delegates attending the least popular commission on International Problems were able to speak, but 10 of them were Central Committee members. About 200 amendments were submitted to congress documents at the Ninth Congress and a number of them were accepted. The Eighth Congress report notes two amendments proposed to the Statute, one of which was accepted by the Statute Commission: it concerned reformulation of the role of the executive committees of republican central committees.

The liveliest debate at the Ninth Congress occurred in the commission for the Development of Socio-Economic Relations, which was debating the Congress Resolution on this topic. Groups and individuals had submitted fifty-eight amendments to the text, twelve of which were adopted. Two votes had to be called on an amendment from Zagreb calling for inclusion of a provision to abolish the rate of interest on the business fund. The spokesman for the working group of the commission noted that the Federal Assembly had already reached a decision to abolish the interest rate and urged that it was therefore unnecessary for the League to reiterate this policy. The first vote disclosed 148 delegates for the amendment and 147 against. A second vote taken later in the day passed the amendment by 248 votes against 229. (The reporter commented that the increase in the number of delegates was presumably due to the fact that the commission started work at 8 a.m.) A second issue which evoked strong disagreement was the question of whether or not republics should be compensated for negative economic effects resulting from federal customs, foreign trade or taxation policies. The Congress Resolution included such a provision, but some delegates pressed for its deletion. Several speakers suggested that since the question had not yet been studied 'we do not know what we are deciding about'. After a long debate the move to delete this provision in the Resolution was defeated. The delegates adopted amendments specifying that 'the general growth of personal earnings outside the economy cannot increase faster than the growth of earnings in production' and calling for the intensive development of the shipping industry — though it was argued that the latter would prejudge the 5 year plan to be discussed by the Assembly. Discussion about the Fund for the Undeveloped led to the adoption of an amendment to delete references in the text to the lesser economic efficiency of undeveloped areas.[42]

Dissension at the Ninth Congress did not, however, disrupt the harmony of the plenary session, and there had been more striking examples of active involvement by the congress delegates in all stages of the debate at some of the republican congresses held before the LCY Ninth Congress. At the Slovenian Congress speakers seriously criticized the Resolution on Future Tasks and pressed amendments at the final plenary session. The Congress voted in favour of including three amendments proposed during the discussion: that communists must strive for a more rapid application of legality in social life, especially in state organs; that communists must resolve the problems of young people more successfully and ensure that all youth had equal opportunities irrespective of social origins, and that pension differences due to the time of retirement and anomalies in the tax base would be eliminated in 1969. The Commission for the Resolution, in light of the criticisms that the text was too generalized, accepted a proposal that the Resolution should be taken together with the reports of discussion in commission when viewed as a guide to further action. The Congress eventually adopted the amended Resolution; three delegates abstained on the final vote.[43] There were also a number of amendments tabled to the Slovenian Statute at the plenary session. A spokesman for the commission on Organization and Development of the League suggested that the delegates elected by commune conferences to the annual republican conference should be elected for a two-year period, not one as envisaged in the draft agreed by the commission on the Statute. The Congress voted in favour. Another delegate raised again a proposition which had caused disagreement in the commission for the Statute: that the Statute should specify that there should be a post of President of the Conference with statutory rights to ensure the independence of the Conference from the Central Committee, but only forty-five delegates voted for the motion. This debate on the Statute involved a procedural dispute with the Chairman about the correct procedures for voting on the Statute, and the Congress agreed to vote on the amendments prior to voting on the draft Statute as a whole as presented by the commission for the Statute.[44]

A few individual voices of dissent were raised at the plenary session of the Sixth Croatian Congress. A delegate from Zadar, as noted earlier, protested against the concept of a republican statute, but his amendment that the Statute should not be introduced was defeated with only one vote in favour.[45]

The most radical challenge to the leadership occurred at the Congress of the Montenegrin party, where there was a rebellion from the floor on the question of creating a standing section of the annual conference. The draft statute originally submitted to the Central Committee had proposed that all delegates should be re-elected annually, and the grounds given for this decision were that it reflected the opinion of most commune organizations. The Central Committee decided by a majority vote to provide for a standing section nevertheless, giving as a reason the need to ensure continuity.[46] At the Congress in December the Congress Commission on the Statute endorsed the Central Committee decision by fourteen votes to six, but the plenary session challenged it. A delegate from Cetinje claimed that fourteen out of twenty commune organizations were against a standing conference because they believed it might degenerate into an organ which would either control the Central Committee or become a counter-weight to it — especially as the two bodies would both be composed of thirty-five members. The Congress then voted by 130 votes to 103 not to elect a standing section.[47] The Montenegrin party therefore became the only republican party without a standing section and diverged from the model for the LCY laid down by the Executive Committee in August 1968.

Protests were made at several republican congresses about the lists of candidates for the top bodies of the republican party and the LCY. At the Montenegrin Congress there were a number of proposals from the floor to alter or add to the list of candidates proposed by the Nominations Committee, but these alterations were not accepted by the Congress.[48] Delegates to the Croatian Congress complained that three prominent officials had been omitted from the list of candidates, and two were proposed as additional candidates for the LCY Presidium.[49] In the event they received only two and eight votes respectively.[50] Tripalo explained to a journalist after the Congress that the third person nominated from the floor, Mika Špiljak, who was at the time Prime Minister, had written asking not to be nominated for any party forum because of the policy of separating party and government posts.[51] The Macedonian Congress transferred one candidate from the list for the Revision Commission to the list for the Central Committee and added a candidate for the Revision Commission, but this was effected without heated criticisms.[52]

There was considerable protest from the floor of the Serbian Congress because there was no choice of candidates. (Most republican congresses in 1968 allowed some choice.) Argument about the list started early in the Congress, when Mijalko Turtić, member of the Serbian Central Committee, proposed that the Nominations Committee should be asked to ensure that Congress was presented with more candidates than there were places to be filled. A number of delegates supported him on the grounds that it would be more democratic, and one speaker argued that the list was of a compromise nature and there should be more candidates from direct production. The spokesman for the Nominations Committee defended the list, claiming that it was based on extensive consultation and represented a balance of social categories, which additions to the list would upset. The Congress rejected Turtić's proposals by a majority, though they accepted a second amendment that the Committee should suggest more candidates from industry without extending the list.[53] Two further challenges were made to the proposed candidates for the Serbian Central Committee during the final discussion of the proposals of the Nomination Committee. A delegate from the Savski Venac commune, complained that there were too many professional politicians, and proposed that seven of the candidates (whom he named) should be deleted from the list and replaced by others more representative of society as a whole. He did not have any alternative names to offer. A delegate from Belgrade University suggested that one candidate, Mirko Stamenković, editor of the internal policy column of *Večernje Novosti*, should be omitted and replaced by a student in psychology. The Chairman of the Nominations Committee pointed out that the nomination of Stamenković had been approved by all Belgrade communes and that to drop him would be an affront to the whole Belgrade organization, but thirty-seven delegates voted in favour of replacing him by the student. The more drastic resolution from Savski Venac was rejected overwhelmingly by Congress, though nineteen delegates did vote for it.[54]

The Vojvodina Conference in December 1968 resulted in further dissent over the candidates for higher bodies. The proposed candidates for the Provincial bodies of the League were adopted with only one objection, which came from a Zrenjanin delegate who said there were not enough direct producers on the list. But three members of the University organization spoke against the list of candidates for the standing section of the Conference of the LCY, objecting that the list had more outsiders than Vojvodina candidates and that there was no choice of candidates for the LCY body. The President, Mirko Čanadanović, replied that the comrades in question were now representing provincial organs in Belgrade and would return to the Vojvodina, and that the list of candidates had been considered by all commune organizations, so there was no need for an excess of candidates over places. A university spokesman declared he was not satisfied with these answers and that there was an implied contempt for candidates for provincial organizations, where there was a choice. Mirko Čanadanović then replied in detail, explaining there had been proposals to extend the list of candidates for the LCY Conference but the names suggested had been ruled out because they were already performing other state or party functions.[55]

Elections in the League

One standard test of democracy is the conduct of elections, and the reformers in the League did make consistent efforts from 1964 to make the procedures for electing party committees more democratic. *Komunist* noted in an article about the election of commune and factory committees in 1964 that the old practice had been for the committee (or its secretariat) to draw up the list of candidates, which the conference then accepted as announced without amending or adding to it.[56] Two main innovations were intended to enhance the influence of party members in elections: widespread consultation at the stage of drawing up nominations — the 1964 Statute gave basic organizations the right not only to elect delegates to commune conferences but to discuss nominees for membership of the commune committee; and a choice of candidates in the final election. Practice during elections in 1964 suggested there were moves towards implementing both principles, though there was still considerable opposition to them. The Macedonian Central Committee when assessing electoral conferences in the Republic concluded that whilst elections to the secretariats of basic organizations and factory committees did involve wide participation in nominating candidates, and allowed for disagreements to be voiced, there was more resistance to consultation when it came to commune committees, though in some communes there were large numbers of nominations by basic organizations.[57] There was press comment on a number of 'upsets' in elections at district and city conference level when members stated to be members of the secretariat, or even secretary of the committee, failed to be elected.[58] But Tripalo condemned elections in this period in which there had been a choice of only twenty-seven candidates for twenty-five seats.[59]

When elections to commune committees were being held 2 years later, in 1966, there were indications that the principle of consultation was often being applied so as to make it largely or wholly meaningless. An article in *Komunist* commented that it was not enough for basic organizations simply to propose nominees from their own ranks. It also pointed out that lists could be compiled either by members taking the initiative in nominating candidates, or by the committee sending out its own provisional list for comments and amendments, or by a more complex process involving greater consultation between the committee and members at both the initial nominating stage and in drawing up a final list. *Komunist* complained that whichever method was chosen, 'many purely formal approaches, obsolete methods and violations of members' rights' could be noted. Moreover most election conferences did not discuss at all the proposed lists of nominees.[60] *Borba* described in May a specific case in which the commune committee made the requirements of consultation about candidates and about the criteria for choosing them completely farcical.

> The present committee (or rather a few members of the committee) entrusted this job first of all to the personnel commission. But, at the same time, it sent the commission a list of the names of the 27

candidates who had already been envisaged, representing in fact the complete composition of the future committee.

The commission then had to invent a set of election criteria based on the list to be submitted to the public for discussion. *Borba* suggested that 'such drastic forms of slighting democracy are rare', but that they alerted people to the much more frequent and less striking violations.[61]

Nevertheless the practice of consulting members about nominees for party committees was well established before the Brioni Plenum. Republican committees undertook an elaborate process of consulting district, commune and factory committees about candidates for the new central committees and control and revision commissions to be elected at the 1965 republican congresses. First the central committee proposed criteria for the candidates, then the lower level committees suggested individual candidates, and on the basis of these suggestions the central committee drew up a provisional list, which included more names than there were places on the committee. District and commune committees were able to comment on this provisional list before it was finally scanned by the central committee and turned over to the nominating committee of the congress. During this process 200 candidates were nominated for 103 Central Committee seats in Bosnia-Hercegovina, 444 in Montenegro for 72 Central Committee seats, 350 in Slovenia for 99 Central Committee seats and 327 in Macedonia for 87 Central Committee seats.[62] (These nominations also covered control commissions of approximately fifteen members and revision commissions of about ten members in each case.)

When, in the course of 1966, republican central committees reorganized themselves they also engaged in consultation about the membership of the new presidium and executive committee. The Bosnian Central Committee for example consulted party leaderships in twenty communes and as a result sixty members were proposed for the Presidium and twenty for the Executive Committee.[63] The Serbian Committee asked provincial and district committees to nominate any members of the existing Committee, and then had to whittle down in further consultations the unwieldy number of nominees (sixty-seven for the Executive Committee for example and eleven for the Secretary of the Committee.)[64]

A process of consultation was automatically adopted prior to the republican congresses at the end of 1968: for example *Borba* reported that commune party organizations had elected 182 candidates for leading bodies in the Slovenian League (30 more candidates than places) and there had initially been 1550 nominations.[65] The Central Committee had final discretion in slightly reducing and amending the list. The representative

of the Candidates' Committee at the Slovene Congress explained that the
Executive Committee had supplemented the original list of candidates in
response to demands from many commune parties, by adding the names
of six veteran party leaders; but as this move 'had not been well received
by the public', and the six concerned had asked to withdraw, their names
had been omitted from the final list before Congress.[66] The process of
consultation for republican candidates was somewhat broader at commune
level than in 1965 because commune conferences as well as committees
had an opportunity to make proposals: 525 nominees in Croatia were put
up by commune conferences, before the committees sent in their lists;
apparently in Serbia the Personnel Commission chose directly from 1808
candidates proposed by commune conference.[67] *Komunist* complained
about the diverse ideological views reflected in the choice of nominees
at commune level.[68]

Consultation, even as a two-stage process, necessarily leaves final power
in the hands of those with ultimate discretions to draw up a list of names.
Choice between candidates at the electoral congress or conference can
therefore be seen as a necessary complement to any policy intended to
maximize democratic participation and choice in selection of candidates.
The Macedonian League laid particular importance on the principle of
choice. It was the only republican party to present a choice of candidates
for republican organs during the republican congresses of 1965, when the
Nominations Committee proposed ninety-four candidates for eighty-seven
seats on the Central Committee, nineteen candidates for fifteen seats on
the Control Commissions and twenty candidates for thirteen places on
the Revision Commission.[69] The Serbian Central Committee adopted the
principle of allowing a choice of candidates for its top bodies in 1966,
when five extra candidates were nominated for the Presidium, and three
extra for the Executive Committee. The Belgrade press, apparently out of
a sense of discretion, did not however print the names of the defeated
candidates.[70] The Montenegrin Central Committee, which also allowed
a choice of candidates for its Presidium and Executive Committee, banished
the press for the ballot,[71] but the Vojvodina Provincial Committee allowed
the names of defeated candidates for its Presidium and Executive
Committee to be published.[72]

Most, but not all, republican congresses had a choice of candidates
before them in 1968-9. Two exceptions were Serbia and Bosnia-Hercegovina
— although as noted earlier the lack of choice led to bitter complaints
from the floor in the Serbian Congress. The Croatian Congress was offered
a choice in elections to both republican and LCY bodies: ten candidates
were put up for five places on the LCY Presidium; fifteen candidates for

ten places on the LCY Conference standing section: seventy-eight candidates for sixty-five seats on the republican Central Committee and eighty-two candidates for seventy places on the standing section of the republican Conference.[73] The Slovene and Montenegrin Congresses and the Vojvodina Conference had a choice of candidates for republican (or provincial) bodies only and not for LCY bodies.[74] The Macedonian Central Committee selected candidates for LCY bodies in advance[75] but allowed the republican Congress some choice in elections for republican organs, and the Congress added one name to the list of Central Committee candidates.[76]

One possible objection to the hypothesis that choice of candidates leads to more democratic control in elections is that delegates may have no real basis for choice where long lists are involved and where some candidates may be unknown to most delegates. A press article alleged that in an election in the Socialist Alliance delegates had simply tended to tick the required number of names at the top of the list, so all candidates whose names came below the letter S failed to get in. This interpretation was denied by the President of the Bosnian Socialist Alliance, who said that only 10 per cent of the delegates had mechanically ticked those at the top of the alphabet, so that many candidates who failed to get elected only had five or ten votes less than those who were successful.[77] It is, however, doubtful if elections in the League in 1968–9 were directly comparable with Socialist Alliance elections: the lists for the party organs were all much shorter – in the Socialist Alliance election cited there were 199 candidates for 171 seats; and with the possible exception of the standing section of the republican conference it is probable that delegates at party congresses were more interested in the composition of their leading bodies. There is not in fact any real evidence that at the republican party congresses delegates ticked names on a purely alphabetical basis: in all cases some candidates whose names came high on the list failed to get enough votes and well-known names near the bottom were decisively elected, although there was a slight tendency in the case of republican central committees and standing sections of conference for fewer to be elected towards the bottom of the list. Todorović summed up on the republican congress elections in a speech to directors of press, radio and television. He admitted there had been shortcomings, 'elements of political confrontation between generations, and the like' instead of choice purely on individual qualifications. He continued:

All this, however, can be explained by the fact that our democratic election system is still new in many respects. Earlier, as you know, we have had very narrow and exclusive cadre commissions which so-to-speak appointed people to the LC bodies, after consultations with a close circle of people and forums, all of which corresponded with the conditions and relations prevailing at the time. Today we have a democratic procedure instead. Practice will certainly lead to further progress in future elections.[78]

There was no change in the voting procedures adopted at republican congresses in 1968-9. Voting at congresses had by statutory requirement been by secret ballot (true of 1948, 1952, 1958 and 1964 Statutes). The election data published for the Eighth Congress of the League in 1964 show that not all candidates received a full quota of votes and that a substantial minority of delegates 'wrote in' the names of individuals whom they thought should have been included on the list of candidates: Latinka Perović collected four such write-in votes. This was not new — nine people got write-in votes in 1958, and at that time only Tito and Kardelj were endorsed by all 1791 delegates; the lowest number of votes, 1766, was polled by a relatively unknown candidate.[79] There was, however, apparently greater emphasis on voting by secret ballot in committees after Brioni. The Serbian Central Committee insisted when electing their new executive organs in November 1966 that the President and Secretary should also be elected by secret ballot, even though there was only one candidate for each post, in order to avoid creating a precedent for voting by a show of hands.[80]

Openness of Party to Public

One of the measures pressed by the reformers was a return to the principle enunciated at the Sixth Congress: that the work of party organs should be open to the public — in general this meant that the press and mass media should be present to report meetings, though at the local level of the basic organization it also included the right of individual members of the public to attend party meetings. Both the 1958 and the 1964 Statutes included a statement in the Introduction that the work of the League was public; the latter explained the importance of openness in terms of promoting the active participation of members and other 'working people' and strengthening the social responsibility of party members and organs. The 1969 Statute laid more stress on the importance of making the work of the party public by incorporating this requirement not only into the Introduction, but also making it one of the elements of 'democratic centralism' in the new extended ten-point interpretation.

The standard method of publicizing the work of party organs is to publish full or edited versions of the proceedings of congresses and central committee plenums. All the LCY Congresses since 1948 have been well publicized and reports are available for republican congresses. Edited proceedings of Central Committee plenums were published regularly after 1964, but were also issued in the 1950s and early 1960s. The Presidium of the League normally published reports of its meetings after the Ninth Congress. In addition the party weekly *Komunist* carried LCY and republican central committee reports and of course extensive congress materials.

Making the work of the party accessible to the general public must mean, however, reports in the daily press – though in practice the low proportion of the Yugoslav public who read a serious newspaper, and the high boredom factor in reading reports of official party meetings, must limit the extent to which most members of the public are exposed to this information. The press, in particular *Borba*, does give full coverage to party congresses and the meetings of central and republican organs. There is a significant difference, however, between allowing the press to publish official communiques, or the prepared speeches and conclusions of central committee meetings, and allowing journalists to be present, to decide what is newsworthy, and to make their own critical comments on the proceedings. It is difficult to compare press coverage of central committee meetings before and after Brioni because the style of the central committee meetings themselves changed, but it is clear that the press had been in the habit of exercising great discretion in reporting party affairs. The fact that the public was given no explicit information about the struggle at the top of the League until the Third Central Committee Plenum of February–March 1966, when the press was apparently encouraged to print fairly fully all the speeches made, indicates the tacit conspiracy of silence between party leaders and journalists. So it is reasonable to date real openness in the work of the top party organs from Brioni, and a number of incidents after July 1966 indicated the difficulties of both press and party leaders in adjusting to the new role of reporters. The suppression of the names of candidates who failed to be elected to the Presidium or Executive Committee of the LCY (mentioned earlier) is an indication of the caution still felt about fully publicizing party affairs. Journalist Milan Bajec came under fire from Stevan Doronjski in December 1966 for having written a critical commentary on one particular report made to the Serbian Central Committee, and for expressing his views 'in an unqualified manner'. Bajec replied that real debate required taking up specific views of a specific individual, and commented that even 'very prominent forums' tended to 'content themselves with presenting views without confrontations, with maintaining an atmosphere of general coexistence of views by some sort of diplomatic language'.[81]

In the period 1967–71 the press became accustomed to printing fairly detailed reports of sometimes contentious meetings of central committees (and of the LCY Presidium after March 1969), and more ready to criticize the central committee or its documents.[82] Only one session of the Presidium was closed to the press: the crucial Seventeenth Session in May 1971 which dealt with the most difficult issues of disagreement and mutual suspicion between republics, where the political advantages of confidentiality clearly clashed with the general commitment to open policy making, and the Presidium felt obliged to justify this secrecy in public. Meetings of Central Committee Commissions were sometimes reported in detail. Executive Committee meetings prior to the Ninth Congress and Executive Bureau meetings after it were reported through brief official communiques only.

Before Brioni the work of the LCY Central Committee and of the republican committees were better publicized than the work of lower-level committees in the League. Krsto Bulajić speaking at the Commission on Reorganization of the League in July 1966 noted that the discussions and conclusions of district and commune committees were very rarely reported at all.[83] Local meetings were quite often closed to journalists when contentious issues arose. *Politika Ekspres* reported in February 1964 that a basic organization in Sabac had on the suggestion of the Secretary of the Commune Assembly decided to ban journalists from the meeting. *Politika Ekspres* was particularly interested in the meeting because one of its journalists was being disciplined for writing critical articles about the local health centre.[84] *Komunist* commented critically on the fact that in August 1966 the Commune Committee in Vojnić (in the Karlovac district) held a 13-hour session behind closed doors at which it decided to reprimand five of the commune's top leaders for their power seeking methods and for bypassing self-management.[85] The Commune Committee meeting with secretaries of basic organizations in Kragujevac refused to allow members of the public to attend the session, which dealt with the decisions reached at the Brioni Plenum, and *Borba* reported on the same day that their correspondent had been refused admission to attend a meeting of the basic party organization in the Secretariat for Internal Affairs in Bor. The request was turned down by the Secretary of the District Committee.[86]

It seems that until Brioni meetings of basic organizations were often closed to the public, who had a statutory right to attend. (At this level the principle of 'openness' meant accessibility to both press and individual members of the general public, though at higher levels only the press could attend.) Exclusion of the public was raised periodically in the correspondence columns of *Komunist*. A letter from a commune party official in March 1966 said that some basic organizations ignored the Statute and shut out the public and suggested, in explanation, that one reason was lack of advance preparation. The writer thought the public was willing to be involved in local party meetings, and cited the example of one village where the communists were outnumbered two to one by the villagers, who joined vigorously in the discussion.[87] A week later two employees at an Institute wrote to complain they had tried to attend a meeting of the basic party organization but had been turned away after the secretary asked for a vote on whether to open the meeting and the vote decided it was closed. Editorial comment confirmed that all meetings of basic organizations should be open.[88]

The Secretary of the Kosovo Provincial Committee noted that in his province there had been greater insistence on publicizing the work of the League since Brioni.[89] There was apparently in general greater willingness to honour the principle of open meetings after July 1966, since party bodies felt themselves obliged to justify certain exceptions to this principle. *Borba* discussed a recent occasion when it had been decided to close the meeting because elections to leading bodies were to be discussed. The organizers explained that the audience was being excluded to make possible freer discussion about proposed candidates, while the members of the public and journalists attending criticized the decision. The argument in defence of excluding the public noted the unfairness of discussing individuals in open session.[90] A similar point was raised by the Control Commission of the LCY which expressed reservations about discussions in control commissions of individual faults if these were to be publicly announced, especially in delicate cases where the facts were in dispute.[91] Apart from these reasonable reservations about fully publicizing the work of the League, there was still a tendency to resort to secrecy to avoid political embarrassment. For example *Politika* protested about a breach of the principle of open party meetings when the press was excluded from a basic organization meeting in Belgrade during a crisis over an unwanted candidate in the 1969 assembly elections.[92] A delegate to the Slovene party Congress in 1968 complained that various party organs in the republic often supplied information to the public through communiques instead of opening up their meetings, but it is not clear to which level of the party he was referring.[93]

One interesting issue on which the League maintained total secrecy until 1969 was that of the salaries and expenses paid to party officials.

A journalist writing in *VUS* welcomed the fact that the Croatian Central Committee had released to the press details of the remuneration of its full-time officials, noting that in the past 'we have not had even the most basic data' on the salaries of top party officials. A Croatian party executive committee member commented on the undesirable results of such secrecy which had encouraged speculation and sometimes malicious gossip.[94]

Mijalko Todorović discussed limits to publicizing the work of the League in a meeting with editors and radio and television directors shortly before the Ninth Congress. He noted that there had been suggestions that the party could have gone further in publicising election of members to party forums, and commented:

> Maybe we could, but one should bear in mind that the transformation of the League of Communists is still under way, and that differentiation in its ranks is only now assuming greater dimensions. Fears are justified that in an organization like this, which is still insufficiently differentiated, and when the public knows too little about the qualities of each individual personality . . . public discussion and consideration of each individual could lead to the setting up of groups and factions, to gathering around personalities, and not around ideas and ideological and political platforms.[95]

Conclusion

The record in the crucial area of internal democratization of the party is therefore patchy, but it is possible to discern a trend towards greater willingness to criticize party leaders, towards freedom of individual dissent, and towards more genuine choice in elections. There is also clear evidence of a move towards a more independent role for party congresses and the possibility of amending policy from the floor. It is therefore possible to postulate that if the process of reform had not been interrupted in 1972 the habits of independence from below and tolerance from above which were being tentatively established might have been consolidated and have led to a genuinely democratic spirit at various levels of the party.

One of the main obstacles to this progress — as suggested in the previous chapter — was probably the attitudes of middle-level party officials in the commune and city committees. While they demonstrated increased willingness to criticize and even openly defy their republican committees, this spirit of independence towards higher authority often did not involve a reciprocal tolerance to opposition from below. The attitudes of many commune committees raises the interesting question whether a degree of bloody-mindedness promotes democracy by refusal to conform timidly,

or whether it obstructs democracy by elevating self interest above respect
for agreed procedures. The answer may depend in part on the level at which
intransigence is being displayed. It is ironical that one of the more interesting
innovations in the party rules, granting the right to committees to resign
collectively on issues of principle, should have been used by the Dubrovnik
Committee to show their pique at their failure to force 'their man' on the
Commune Assembly, and hence in defiance of the declared new role of
the party.

The most sensitive question involved in attempts to promote democracy
in any communist party is whether or not the principle of democratic
centralism is being maintained. The Yugoslav League went some way in
modifying the emphasis on central control and hierarchical discipline, but
the reform leaders drew back from the decisive step of abandoning the
principle, and also refused to countenance organized opposition to official
policy by maintaining the ban on factions. This tendency to fall back on
the orthodoxy of democratic centralism when under pressure illustrated
the limits of the reformers' willingness to take risks in promoting democracy
inside the party and also set important limits to their readiness to relax
party control over political and economic life.

Notes

1. *VIIIth Congress of the League of Communists of Yugoslavia: Practice and Theory of Socialist Development in Yugoslavia*, Medjunarodna Politika, Beograd, 1965, p. 221.
2. *Komunist*, 7 November 1963.
3. *Borba*, 7 October 1964.
4. *Borba*, 13 November 1964.
5. *Borba*, 30 May 1965.
6. *Borba*, 10 July 1966.
7. *Komunist*, 26 May 1966.
8. *Borba*, 13 August 1966.
9. *Borba*, 15 June 1967.
10. *Borba*, 7 December 1968.
11. *Borba*, 1 June 1971.
12. *Politika*, 18 November 1971.
13. *Politika*, 14 December 1968.
14. *Komunist*, 9 December 1965.
15. *Narodna Armija*, 5 December 1964. See also *Kommunist*, 1 September 1966, which quotes a captain at the Banjaluka garrison who said that it was 'rather inconvenient for the young to criticise seniors at party meetings'.
16. *Komunist*, 17 August 1967.
17. *Borba*, 27 October 1966.
18. *Komunist*, 8 June 1967 and *Politka*, 7 June 1967. The Dubrovnik case raised interesting questions about the proper role of the party in elections and is discussed further in Chapter 8.
19. RFE Research Report, 26 March 1969.

20. *Komunist*, 20 August 1964, reprinted a summary of the interview.
21. *Vjesnik*, 14 October 1964.
22. *Marks i Savremenost*, Prvi Deo, Institut za Izučavanje Radničkog Prokreta, Institut Društveni Nauka, Beograd, 1964, p. 101.
23. See also Svetozar Stojanović, *Between Ideals and Reality*, Oxford University Press, New York, 1973, Chapter Four and note on p. 82.
24. Vladimir Bakarić, 'The League of Communists today', *Socialist Thought and Practice*, July–September, 1966, p. 24.
25. *Komunist*, 5 January 1967.
26. Tomislav Čokrevski, 'Oblik organizacija u zavisnost od istorjske i društvene funkcija', *Socijalizam*, No. 10. 1967, pp. 1240-7.
27. Vojislav Stanovčić, 'Nužnost prilagodjavanja SKJ procesmia demokratizacije društva', *Socijalizam*, No. 10. 1967, pp. 1291-7.
28. *Borba*, 24 July 1966.
29. *Borba*, 24 September 1967.
30. *Komunist*, 16 January 1967.
31. Slavko Milosavlevski, *Revolucija i Anti Revolucija,* Revija, Beograd, 1971.
32. *Politika*, 23 October 1966.
33. *Politika*, 7 June 1967.
34. *Borba*, 17 October 1967.
35. *Borba*, 30 January 1969.
36. *Borba*, 13 March 1969.
37. RFE Research Report, 26 March 1969.
38. *Borba*, 16 April 1970.
39. *VIII Congress of the League of Communists of Yugoslavia*, op. cit., p. 221.
40. This formulation is an adaptation of Article 10 in the 1958 Statute, which appeared immediately after the definition of democratic centralism, and specified that all organizations and leaderships of the League are independent in making decisions in the sphere of their own work, and in accordance with the Programme, Statute and policy of the League.
41. *Politika*, 23 October 1966.
42. *Borba*, 15 March 1969.
43. *Borba*, 16 December 1968.
44. *Borba*, 11 December 1968.
45. *Borba*, 7 December 1968.
46. *Borba*, 13 November 1968.
47. *Politika*, 15 December 1968.
48. Ibid.
49. *Borba*, 27 November 1968.
50. *Šesti Kongres SKH, Stenografske Bilješke,* Komunist, 1969, Knjiga III, p. 379. Cvetković two votes and Čalić eight votes.
51. *Politika*, 12 December 1968.
52. *Borba*, 21 November 1968.
53. *Borba*, 22 November 1968.
54. *Politika*, 24 November 1968.
55. *Politika*, 22 December 1968.
56. *Komunist*, 16 July 1964.
57. *Komunist*, 20 August 1964.
58. *Politika*, 15 November 1964.
59. *VUS*, 14 October 1964.
60. *Komunist*, 14 April 1966.
61. *Borba*, 22 May 1966.
62. *Komunist*, 22 April 1965.
63. *Borba*, 15 November 1966.

64. *Borba*, 10 November 1966.
65. *Borba*, 6 November 1968.
66. *Borba*, 11 December 1968.
67. *Borba*, 13 and 27 November 1968.
68. *Komunist*, 13 October 1968.
69. *Borba*, 1 April 1965.
70. *Borba*, 10 November 1966.
71. *Borba*, 15 November 1966.
72. *Politika*, 22 December 1977.
73. *Šesti Kongress SKH*, Knjiga III, pp. 379–82.
74. *Borba*, 16 December 1968 covers the Slovene Congress, which had a choice between fifty-one candidates for forty-five members of the Central Committee and between seventy candidates for five places on the standing section of conference. *Borba*, 13 November 1968 reports on the Montenegrin Central Committee decision on candidates to be put before their republican congress. *Politika*, 22 December 1968 covers the Vojvodina Conference debate on candidates.
75. *Politika*, 3 November 1968.
76. *Borba*, 21 November 1968.
77. *Borba*, 29 January and 13 February 1966.
78. *Komunist*, 23 January 1969.
79. VII Kongres SKJ, Stenografske Beleške, Kultura, 1958, p. 1145.
80. *Borba*, 10 November 1966.
81. *Borba*, 24 December 1966.
82. See for example *Borba*, 7 February 1969 which was critical of the Twelfth Plenum of the LCY Central Committee, and *Ekonomska Politika*, 13 January 1969 commenting on draft document on 'Tasks of the LCY in the further construction of self-managing socio-economic relations' for the Ninth Congress.
83. *Borba*, 16 July 1966.
84. *Politika Ekspres*, 15 February 1964.
85. *Komunist*, 11 August 1966.
86. *Borba*, 26 July 1966.
87. *Komunist*, 24 March 1966.
88. *Komunist*, 31 March 1966.
89. *Politika*, 19 August 1966.
90. *Borba*, 30 October 1966.
91. *Politika*, 23 February 1967.
92. Dennison Rusinow, *Yugoslav Elections 1969,* Part II, American University Field Staff Report, July 1969. Another example of the party shutting its doors to the press occurred in Mostar in October 1970 in connection with the Alilović case (discussed in Chapter 10), when the conduct of defence lawyers in a trial involving charges of hostile nationalist propaganda was being debated. *Borba* complained that the commune party was beginning to add elements of mystery to the case (*Borba*, 11 October 1970).
93. *Borba*, 11 December 1968.
94. *VUS*, 16 April 1969, cited in RFE Research Report, 17 April 1969.
95. *Komunist*, 23 January 1969.

PART III

SEPARATING THE PARTY FROM POWER

6 The Party's Guiding Role and the Socialist Alliance

Problems of Interpreting the Guiding Role of the League

One of the central themes of the reform was the necessity of fulfilling the Sixth Congress declaration that the party would cease to dominate political life and would instead play an ideological guiding role. The reformers had succeeded in putting this question on the Eighth Congress agenda, but progress on this, as on other issues, remained minimal until the Brioni Plenum of 1966. Crvenkovski commented in a *Politika* interview in October 1966:

> I think that nothing essential has happened since the Sixth Congress . . . when it was proclaimed that the League of Communists should no longer be a factor of power but rather a political, ideological guiding force, to justify any fundamental change in this general concept. The problem lies in struggling to realise it, since relatively little has been done in this respect.[1]

One of the difficulties of the concept of 'a guiding role' was that liberal leaders who espoused this approach seldom spelt out clearly to their own rank and file precisely what this meant. But there was some open debate about the ambiguities of interpreting the role of the party, especially during 1966, a period of unusual frankness and self-questioning about fundamental political issues.

Bakarić had pronounced on the correct interpretation of the role of the party in a speech he made during the crucial period between the Third and Fourth Central Committee plenums in 1966. He noted that in general terms its role in the current phase of social development was to direct self-management and help to build self-managing bodies at all levels up to the federal government. He went on to explain briefly 'why it is sometimes demanded that various forums of the League of Communists play a greater or direct role in government and sometimes that they should not play such a role'. The reason was that: 'one has to appraise where something should be done because of the incomplete character of the system and where this does not happen to be the case'.[2]

Slavko Milosavlevski tackled the problem of the role of the party in mid-1966 and drew similar conclusions. Ideally the task of communists in self-managing bodies was to work with non-communists to accomplish the programme devised for a given period by the League (which would encompass the nature of self-management and general economic policy — Milosavlevski cites the 1958 Programme and the Eighth Congress resolutions); but they should not be implementing detailed party resolutions, which should in any case become unnecessary. Party committees should, however, take responsibility for deciding concrete issues where they were the source of acute conflict or where other groups showed themselves incapable of action. The necessity of this kind of direct intervention was a sign of the undeveloped nature of self-management.

The pitfalls to be avoided by the party in interpreting its role were set out frankly in Milosavlevski's article. He argued that the belief that the League should operate through its members in executive organs and 'realize' party policy undermined the initiative and purpose of representative bodies, meant that those who were members both of executives of self-managing bodies and of party committees were primarily responsible to these committees and not to their electors, and that party leaders continued in their old habits of acting more or less directly through the executives of self-managing institutions. He also pointed out that communists who worked formally through the structure of self-management, but were organized in informal groups, had 'a decisive influence on the outcome of policy because other members of self governing organs were not so organised and were not able to agree in advance on their policies and views on every given problem'.[3]

Milosavlevski also tackled the theory of the role of the party in relation to the mass political organizations like the Socialist Alliance in an article for Gledišta, and examined ways in which the latter might maintain relative independence from the League. First, he suggested, they could adopt policy resolutions in areas not covered by specific party resolutions. This proposal, like Hobbes's thesis that 'liberty lies in the silence of the law', could leave open an area of genuine independence, but its scope would depend entirely on the degree of latitude left by the party. Milosavlevski supplemented this proposal with two more substantial suggestions:

that the mass organizations should be free to adopt their own resolutions on issues that the party had already pronounced upon, and should be able to differ from the party; and that they should be free to elect their own leaderships, so that any communists who were elected enjoyed their position by virtue of their activity inside the organization.[4]

Two critical questions continued to arise after 1966 in discussions about the role of the League with other political bodies: the degree to which these bodies could be allowed to diverge from the stated policy of the League; and the obligations of individual communists in their capacity as members of self-governing bodies or mass organizations to abide by party decisions. The first question was one on which party leaders differed, but some prominent reformers were prepared to say publicly that the possibility of such divergence was the logical conclusion to be drawn from the new definition of the role of the party. Miko Tripalo took a relaxed view of possible discrepancies between the policy of the League and that of other bodies when interviewed by *Politika* in December 1969:

Q. Would you consider it a social disturbance or danger if in a centre of decision-making such as the Assembly, the Trade Unions, a work organization or cultural institution a decision or measure was taken in spite of a reserved attitude towards it by the Central Committee?

A. I think that cases like this have occurred and that in all probability there are going to be similar occurrences in the future. If we take the stand that no decision of the League of Communists is formally and automatically obligatory for various centres of decision-making, such cases must be expected . . . no dramatic conclusions should be reached on these grounds, but decision on action should be taken . . .

Q. Since the League of Communists is a ruling party, what should members of such a party do if and when they find themselves in a minority?

A. Everything depends on the question under review. If it were some crucial matter, I would not rank among those who consider that democracy is an end to which everything should be sacrificed. If the fate of socialism in Yugoslavia were at stake, of course we would use every possible measure to avert that. Yet, there are many more problems which are not of this nature. That is why one should remain within the framework of a normal ideological and political discussion.[5]

When delivering his report to the LCY Presidium, in his capacity as a member of the Executive Bureau, Tripalo presented a more restrictive view:

> The League of Communists opposes instances of an ideological or political emancipation of centres of decision making that may lead to the emergence of parallel organizations and of 'leaderships' which enable individual officials under the guise of 'popular support' to drift away from the LC and oppose it . . .[6]

He noted that there had been examples of this tendency in commune assemblies, government organs and Socialist Alliance committees, and recommended that the guiding role of the League could be strengthened by electing presidents of commune assemblies and leaders of 'socio-political organizations' to the higher organs of the Conferences of the League. Commenting on the relationship of the party to the state, he observed that there was a 'mistaken conception' of the dissociation of the party from political power and that communists were responsible for the work of the authorities.

Tripalo's position on the obligation of communists to adhere to party policy was firm in the *Politika* interview as well as in his report to the LCY Presidium. In the latter he observed that 'certain misunderstandings have been used by individual members of the League to secure their own autonomy from the party on the grounds of the League's alleged lack of interest in wielding power'. There was a need to stress the duty of all communists to put party decisions into effect. Srecko Bijelić, speaking at the same Presidium meeting, stated:

> We cannot permit communists in workers councils, in the republican or Federal Assembly, to bring up questions in the course of discussion which are evidently not in accord with the line the League of Communists has adopted.[7]

General pronouncements on the role of the party usually covered the whole spectrum of political activity in central and republican government, in the mass organizations and in local self-government and the enterprises. But the need of the party to maintain close control over various areas of political and economic life is greater at the top than at the local level, and it is easier to concede a degree of autonomy to bodies representing various social interest groups, like trade unions and student unions, than to an organization with a specifically political function like the Socialist Alliance. This generalization is over-simplified, because an economic policy which minimizes the part played by central government may in practice require greater party intervention at enterprise level, and in a communist context worker demands for real trade union autonomy may be politically explosive, as the Polish strikes of 1970 and 1980 have demonstrated. Nevertheless it is analytically useful to distinguish the problems of separating the party from political power at the federal and republican level, from the problems of allowing some degree of political and social pluralism outside the centres of power, or of granting some autonomy to local self-management bodies. The experience of the Yugoslav party in the period 1966–71 also suggests that in practice it was harder to separate the party from political power than to concede a degree of pluralism and dissent, at least until nationalist aspirations converted claims to interest group autonomy and free speech into a direct political threat to the party's control; and that the party was not necessarily the main obstacle to real self-management in enterprises.

The goal of 'separating the party from power' required the League to stand back from direct participation and control in three central areas: the actual operations of federal and republican government; the activity of the parliamentary assemblies; and the election of parliamentary deputies, which also of course affected the choice of government ministers. It also required the League to stop exercising direct control over the Socialist Alliance, the mass organization representing the great majority of citizens (in 1965 8 000 000 citizens belonged to the Alliance, 69 per cent of all voters) which was formally responsible for political direction of the parliamentary elections, and for the work of the deputies in the assemblies. Before assessing the degree of independence exercised by government, the assemblies and various electoral bodies it is necessary to know in general terms whether or not the Socialist Alliance acquired its own degree of autonomy or remained simply an extension of the party itself.

The Significance of the Socialist Alliance

Yugoslav commentators on the meaning of the new role of the party in the early 1950s had laid considerable stress at that stage on the need to grant autonomy to the Socialist Alliance and other mass organizations, and denounced the Soviet practice of treating trade unions, youth and student bodies as 'transmission belts' of the party. Particular attention was paid to the new role to be assigned to the Socialist Alliance, the new name given to the People's Front at its Congress in February 1953, which heralded the transformation of the Front into a suitable vehicle for socialist democracy. Djilas announced that the new Socialist Alliance was designed to promote livelier mass participation in the political life of the country.

The Alliance would make its own decisions on the basis of free discussion and communists would not have a privileged position inside it.[8] The *Christian Science Monitor* reported that the party was to cease making decisions in advance of Front meetings and all party activity was to be conducted inside the Front. The reporter commented that Tito was deliberately adopting the methods he had been accused of by the Soviet letter of 1948, which said that the party was hiding its activities behind the screen of the People's Front.[9] Djilas observed in this connection that he expected other East European countries would attack the LCY for being 'diluted' in the Front, since they espoused the idea of the party being separated from the people as a privileged caste, as in the USSR. When addressing the 1953 Congress Kardelj explained that the party had no monopoly in building socialism, and that the Socialist Alliance was not a party but a political alliance of the working class who should determine policy. He added that the Alliance should be a 'broad parliament' of the people which all well-intentioned citizens could join.[10]

The possibilities of democratic participation and decision-making promised early in 1953 failed to materialize. Probably the average citizen was at a loss how to use these opportunities and local party bosses unwilling to let him, although some party members were being carried along throughout 1953 on a wave of enthusiasm for political reform. There was also undoubtedly opposition at the top to so radical a relaxation of the hold the party had on political life. According to the *Christian Science Monitor* report some party members had resisted these changes as being premature because they feared 'hostile elements may grab power'. Given the typical style of Yugoslav rhetoric about democratic reform, which always seemed to promise more than the reformers meant to give, it is doubtful how much real change was intended. Nevertheless the element of genuine commitment, pride in the Yugoslav experiment and utopian aspiration among party leaders should not be underrated – particularly in the early 1950s. The man who epitomized these qualities, and whose extremism in the search for truth undermined his own goals, was Djilas himself, who no doubt did mean what he said about the Alliance. His proposals, first voiced tentatively in his *Borba* articles, that the party should disband itself altogether and individual members work through the Alliance, took the reforms announced in February 1953 to their logical conclusion. It also convinced his colleagues that the reform movement was getting out of hand, and in practice brought attempts to democratize the party or to limit its role to a halt in 1954. Djilas's heretical ideas no doubt also made it harder in later years to propose major changes touching the Alliance.

The Alliance did, however, continue to have some importance in official Yugoslav theory during the 1950s. Speeches and articles expounding the Yugoslav version of democracy stressed the role of the Alliance in giving a forum to all the citizens and underlined its autonomy. The existence of the Alliance served to meet Western criticisms of the exclusiveness of a one-party state. The Alliance fulfilled in addition a foreign policy function as a socialist body which could ally itself with other socialist parties in the West and in the non-aligned states of Africa and Asia, and could front for foreign policy initiatives which the government or party did not wish to make directly.

Official party spokesmen maintained their formal commitment to avoid using the Alliance as a transmission belt, but up to 1966 this seems to have meant that the party would avoid direct and overt interference, but that the Alliance would operate within the limits set by the League and would in practice be led by high-ranking party members. This interpretation ruled that party organizations must not usurp the rights of Alliance members or issue direct orders. For example, *Komunist* formally condemned a village organization of the party in the Titovo Užice district which decided to expel the president of the local Socialist Alliance organization and selected a former secretary of the League for this post. The same party meeting had also decided on the plan of work for the Socialist Alliance.[11]

When reform was in the air during the mid-sixties it was inevitable that the question of the future of the Alliance should be placed on the agenda. In principle the Alliance was the means of enabling the majority of citizens who were not party members, but did accept the general socialist goals set down by the League, to take part in general policy discussions and in political activity which transcended purely local and work issues or sectional interests. A democratic reform programme logically concerns itself with the problem of granting genuine political rights to non-party members, and the role of a popular front (which for historical reasons exists in East European socialist states as a means of incorporating and then transcending the previous non-communist political parties) presents obvious opportunities for popular involvement without granting the much more dangerous and contentious right to form opposition (even socialist opposition) parties. It is, therefore, not surprising that Imre Nagy attempted to enhance the powers of the People's Front during his reform premiership of Hungary in 1953-4, and that the Prague Spring threw up a number of ideas for revitalizing the National Front and its electoral role. The same logic applied to the Yugoslav reformers, although the origins of the People's Front, which was a continuation of the wartime People's Liberation Front and had always been primarily a communist-dominated organization rather than a coalition of political parties, made it a rather different body from the Hungarian or Czechoslovak Fronts. There was less danger that former political parties might use democratization of the Alliance to revive themselves as independent political parties, but perhaps more difficulty in breathing life into a body habitually subordinate to the party.

The Alliance Role in Theory

The problems of finding a real role for the Socialist Alliance were expressed cogently at an interesting debate on the Alliance held in January 1966 under the auspices of the Belgrade High School for Political Science. An article in *Gledišta* summarizing the conference commented:

> A number of analyses carried out recently show that citizens are less active in the Socialist Alliance than in other organizations and organs. This is usually explained by the fact that citizens will devote more energy where they can satisfy and realise their own concrete and immediate interests and goals. . . . Participation in the work of the bodies of self-management is of greater interest to the citizens than work in the Socialist Alliance.[12]

One reason suggested for this indifference to the Alliance was that it often spent time organizing big drives and general demonstrations which were intended to help the work of other political organs, rather than concentrating on 'settling certain common problems of all citizens of an established area, in which citizens would certainly find greater interest'.

The Socialist Alliance differed from the Trade Unions and Youth or Student Federations in failing to represent any clear sectional interest group which could make limited but specific demands. The ability to transcend sectional interests could be represented as one of the strengths and purposes of the Alliance. This was the stand taken by the Federal Chairman of the Socialist Alliance in an interview with *Borba* in November 1969. After noting the diversity of interests stemming from social and regional differences he continued:

> There are various bodies, representative bodies, self-management organs, and other socio-political organizations which are also on the scene, which interpret certain class interests of various strata of the population or interested communities. The interpreters of these interests want to influence decision-making in representative bodies, self-management

organs, or other centres of decision-making. The Socialist Alliance
cannot avoid paying attention to it all. It has been trying to resolve
differences through a democratic confrontation, by giving a chance
for everybody's interests to be expressed, but in the end trying to find
out the common interests of both the working people and the
citizens.[13]

Dr Jovan Djordjević, one of the leading theoretical exponents of the
Yugoslav brand of socialism, made a similar point at a consultation in
Serbia in 1970, when he argued that the Alliance was designed to meet
'the needs of a stratified society where a whole series of interest groups
and individuals outside the League of Communists are politically
articulated'.[14] It was not, however, at all clear that the Socialist Alliance
could in practice pursue this aim of discovering and declaring a general
interest; and if it were to suggest policies designed to harmonize the claims
of differing interest groups, it would be in danger of usurping the role of
the League as the body primarily responsible for integrating divisive forces
and pointing the way to socialist solutions.

A series of public statements by political scientists and leading political
figures suggested that it was widely held throughout the period 1966–71
that the Alliance remained a transmission belt for the party. Critical
contributors to the 1966 symposium on the Alliance elaborated on this
view. *Borba* observed that a 'wrong understanding of the nature of the
Socialist Alliance and its new role was frequently manifested':

> It was even stated that the Socialist Alliance is still a replica of the
> LCY . . . the fact that the views of the SA and the LCY have been
> continuously and absolutely identical in making various important
> political decisions was quoted as evidence of the Alliance's lack of
> emancipation.[15]

The critics suggested that an autonomous Alliance would need its own
programme as this was one factor determining the independence of an
organization. They noted as other signs of the Alliance's dependence on
the party that the League controlled its cadre policy and the predominance
of communists in leading Alliance bodies.

The official response to the critics at the symposium was to claim that
they misunderstood the role of the Alliance and the nature of its links to
the League. *Komunist* reprinted the speech made by Najdan Pašić arguing
that the Socialist Alliance adopted the League's Programme in the sense
of accepting a general orientation towards socialism and that the Alliance
was the broadest form of political association and activity. Pašić referred

in passing to typical Western misunderstandings of the Alliance, and how certain formulations adopted at the Fifth Congress of the Alliance in 1960 had given rise to reports in the West that Yugoslavia had declared in favour of a 'two party system'.[16]

Nevertheless official spokesmen for the Alliance and the party were quite often prepared to admit that the Alliance had appeared to act as a transmission belt. *Komunist* printed an interview with the President of the Slovenian section of the Alliance, Vida Tomšić, in April 1966. During the interview she observed that:

> sometimes it seems as if the Socialist Alliance is being used as a propaganda service which is to campaign for the measures of the authorities or of the party leadership. If such things were adequate in a certain period, they are certainly an anachronism today and are impeding the development of the system of self-management.[17]

Marko Nikezić aired frankly the problems facing the Alliance at the 1970 Conference of the Serbian section:

> Recently and at the meeting here today we have spoken about two dangers: that the Socialist Alliance may be understood to be a transmission belt of the League of Communists, and secondly that it may become a parallel and in some way a rival organization.

Nikezić said that both dangers could be averted if communists acted within the framework of the Alliance, but went on to admit:

> However, the very fact that communists have a special organization — which it is necessary to retain even now — may inevitably mean a possible rebirth of sectarian tendencies. To begin with, a tendency to hold discussions behind closed doors about questions of importance to society as a whole . . . tendencies to seek the shortest and easiest way to implement the policy of the League of Communists. That is, to keep the executive mechanism of social-political organizations directly in the hands of leading bodies and organizations of the League of Communists. A relationship of this kind between the executive organs of the League and the executive organs of other bodies . . . is of course comfortable.[18]

The Federal President of the Alliance, Veljko Milatović, told *Borba* in November 1969 that the transmission role of the Alliance: 'has not yet disappeared everywhere. Or, to express it better, it has not disappeared in the minds of all individuals, either those working in the Socialist Alliance or those working in other political structures.'[19] When *Borba* interviewed

Milatović again early in 1971 the reporter pressed him on whether the Alliance would remain an 'interpreter' of decisions already adopted elsewhere. Milatović replied that it depended on the League's tolerance of public discussion of certain issues. 'The present degree of intolerance probably stems also from fear of some in the League of Communists of losing their monopoly.' Despite his candour about the defects in the way in which the Alliance operated, however, Milatović also made a strong statement about its importance in the Yugoslav system reminiscent of the theoretical claims for the role of the Alliance in the 1950s, but with a 1970s slant:

> True, a socialist society can exist without a Socialist Alliance. . . . Only, to bring the existence of the SAWP into question would, in my opinion, be conducive to a return to a one-party system. This in practice means centralism, less national equity and autonomy and less freedom.[20]

The Party and Alliance in Practice

Very little evidence emerged to suggest there were moves towards independence in the Alliance itself. One obvious occasion for demonstrating such tendencies was the Sixth Congress in June 1966, and some Western press and academic commentators have suggested that the Sixth Congress marked a significant change of course by the Alliance. The *New York Times*, for example, reporting on the Alliance's new statute, predicted the evolution of a 'one and a half' party system, and noted that although not granted full autonomy, its relations with the party were to be based on independence and co-operation.[21] This interpretation is not, however, supported by the available evidence.

The Alliance could have moved towards greater autonomy at its Sixth Congress if the League had ended the practice of staffing the top Alliance bodies with prominent party officials and ceded independent control over some political activities to the Alliance. The party was, however, only prepared to make gestures towards a separation of cadres. Before the June 1966 Congress twenty-eight out of thirty-five members of the Alliance Executive Committee were also on the LCY Central Committee, among them twelve members of the League's Executive Committee; and nine out of eleven members of the Alliance Secretariat were LCY Central Committee members. After the June Congress there were still seventeen LCY Central Committee members on the forty-three member Alliance Presidium, though only three members of the League Executive; while one third of the new Alliance Executive Committee of eighteen were LCY Central

Committee members.[22] Perhaps more significant is the fact that Lazar Koliševski, a member of the LCY Executive Committee and a moderate conservative in the battle over the reforms, continued to be President of the Alliance after the Congress. The Secretary General, Milentije Popović, also remained. As for ceding more autonomy to the Alliance, the 1966 draft Statute in fact spelt out the relations between the party and Alliance, which had previously been taken as read; the official reason given was that 'certain misunderstandings' had arisen. Indeed the discussion in the Congress Statutory Commission included demands for greater emphasis on the interdependence between the party and the Alliance.[23]

If there had been rank and file demands at the Congress either for greater democracy within the Alliance itself, or for more independence in its political activities, these might have presaged a change of direction. But the detailed reports of the Congress in the Yugoslav press suggest it was phenomenally dull. In the elections to the federal conference 185 candidates were proposed by the nominating commission for 185 seats to be chosen by public ballot, on the grounds that the federal body was composed of delegates already selected by the republican Alliance committees. The Congress duly elected the candidates by acclamation. The only issue seriously debated in the Statutory Commission, which went to a vote on the floor of Congress, was on the question of what the central Alliance body should be called. *Borba* allowed itself in an otherwise respectful account of the whole proceedings to call this discussion tedious. The only really lively debate took place in a commission where young delegates complained about the lack of self-management rights for students in schools and universities.[24]

The timing of the Alliance Congress was in fact unpropitious for making significant changes. If it had taken place some months earlier it is at least possible that the party reformers would have expended some effort to swing it in their own direction, but by June 1966 they were engaged behind the scenes in a final settlement of accounts with Ranković. On the other hand if the Congress had taken place a few months later it would probably have reflected the post-Brioni willingness to criticize and debate, and there might have been more pressure from below. As it was the Alliance was largely ignored in the post-Brioni ferment, though in the course of the various cadre changes at the top Rato Dugonjić, a former President of the Bosnian Socialist Alliance who was promoted to the new League Presidium in the autumn of 1966, took over the Alliance presidency from Koliševski. Dugonjić was replaced in 1969 by Veljko Milatović, who held no position in the central bodies of the LCY, though he had earlier worked in the Central Committee Secretariat.

One incident demonstrated clearly that the party was, at least in some republics, still prepared to assert its primary authority over the Alliance quite unequivocally. The Montenegrin party Central Committee met in October 1969 to discuss cadre problems in the republican Alliance. The party accused the executive committee of the Alliance of suppressing its presidium, so violating internal democracy; and of failing to co-operate with other 'social factors', that is of acting too independently of the party. Alliance spokesmen for their part complained that the party had intervened in cadre policy, so violating 'the independence of the Socialist Alliance'. The actions of the Central Committee seemed to vindicate the accusations of dictatorial behaviour. It met the day before the Alliance Conference and decided to recommend dismissal of the Alliance Secretary and to make the position of the party clear at the Conference session. It also affirmed that the party Secretariat had acted rightly in intervening in the personnel policy of the Alliance.

The Central Committee statement underlined the ultimate right of intervention of the League:

> The Central Committee considers that every political and self-managing factor should carry out its role independently, and that every one of them should contribute to the unity of social activity and bear responsibility before the public for the role it is playing. But the League of Communists bears full responsibility for making sure that the democratic course of development will not be used in such a way as to lead to a disintegration of social activity, or, under specific conditions, to antagonisms of political structures and the setting up of closed and independent political centres.[25]

At the Montenegrin Alliance Conference the next day the Federal President of the Alliance commented on the need for the work of the Alliance to be more public and for freedom to express divergent views and interests, criticized undemocratic methods of work and said they could lead to the Alliance becoming 'an expression of the narrow minded and personal interests of individuals'. He went on to warn that outside initiatives and criticisms of the work of the Alliance should not be received defensively, even if there were demands for individuals to resign. The Conference then duly endorsed the view of the Montenegrin party Central Committee that the Alliance Secretary should resign, and also accepted the resignation of the President, who was replaced by Dobroslav Čulafić, the Secretary of the Central Committee of the Montenegrin League and a member of the LCY Presidium. This apparent disregard for the principle of the separation of functions suggests that the Montenegrin party was anxious to ensure full party control over the Alliance, although it was apparently not prepared to publicize the real political reasons for its dispute with the Alliance Secretary, since they are notably absent from the *Borba* reports of this affair.[26]

Conclusion

There seem to have been two main reasons why the Alliance always tended to remain subordinate to the party. One was its lack of any clear-cut function in its day-to-day activity — the only important task allotted to it was to mobilize citizens at elections, and even here it operated parallel to the formal machinery of voters' meetings and electoral commissions. There was therefore no incentive for independently minded activists to involve themselves in the Alliance. Even more important, however, was the fact that the general policy-making and co-ordinating roles assigned to the Alliance duplicated the functions which the party claimed as its own prerogatives. If allowed genuine autonomy the Socialist Alliance would inevitably become an embryonic, if not an actual, opposition party. Its electoral and parliamentary roles made this potential opposition immediately dangerous to the party.

It is not, therefore, surprising that the League, despite official disclaimers, tended to use the Alliance as a transmission belt for its own decisions. This conclusion must be tempered by awareness of the way in which political conflicts inside the party might result in the leadership of a republican section of the Alliance disagreeing with a new liberal party leadership. A crisis like the student demonstrations of June 1968 could elicit (particularly in the early days) varying responses, and in fact the Serbian Socialist Alliance, headed by former Serbian Prime Minister, Dragi Stamenković, who was considered a conservative, initially adopted a more critical line than the Presidium of the Serbian Party. Factional and personality clashes could also divide party and Alliance officials at commune level, as happened at times in the parliamentary elections. Nevertheless the standard tendency was for the Alliance to act on behalf of the League, and the evidence in the two succeeding chapters confirms the view that it was primarily an instrument to achieve the aims of the party.

Notes

1. *Politika*, 23 October 1966.
2. Vladimir Bakaric, 'The League of Communists today', *Socialist Thought and Practice*, July–September 1966, pp. 34–5.

3. Slavko Milosavlevski, 'Demokratski Odnosi u Političkoj Akciji', *Socijalizam*, July–August, 1966, p. 894.
4. Slavko Milosavlevski, 'Društveno-Političke Organizacije U Nas', *Gledišta*, October–November 1966, pp. 1232-3.
5. *Politika*, 28 December 1969.
6. *Komunist*, 11 December 1969.
7. *Borba*, 16 December 1969.
8. *Tanjug Bulletin*, 28 November 1952.
9. *Christian Science Monitor*, 18 February 1953.
10. *Tanjug Bulletin*, 23 February 1953.
11. *Komunist*, 7 October 1965.
12. V. Vasović and V. Stojković, 'Socijalistički Savez i Radnik', *Gledišta*, February 1966, p. 238.
13. *Borba*, 15 November 1969.
14. *Politika*, 30 May 1970.
15. *Borba*, 12 January 1966.
16. *Komunist*, 20 January 1966.
17. *Komunist*, 7 April 1966.
18. *Borba*, 16 June 1970.
19. *Borba*, 15 November 1969.
20. *Borba*, 7 February 1971.
21. *New York Times*, 24 May 1966.
22. Sources for Socialist Alliance bodies: Roster of Federal and Republican Officials and of LCY, SAWPY and Federation of Trade Unions, Joint Translation Service Supplement, 12 February 1964; and *Borba*, 11 June 1966. There was considerable, but not total, overlap between the two top bodies of the Alliance, so that the total of LCY Central Committee members on both was before June 1966 thirty-one, and after the Congress eighteen. Apart from the LCY Central Committee members on the Alliance executive bodies there were also high ranking republican party members represented both before and after the Sixth Alliance Congress.
23. *Borba*, 9 June 1966.
24. *Borba*, 9 June, 10 June and 11 June 1966.
25. *Borba*, 10 October 1969.
26. *Borba*, 11 October 1969. The report notes that the Montenegrin party President gave the Conference the reasons for the party wishing the Alliance Secretary to resign, but gave no further information. Dobroslav Ćulafić was replaced as Montenegrin party Secretary in November 1969. (*Borba*, 26 November 1969.)

7 The Party and the Government

One of the most important but ambiguous aims entailed in the League's new guiding role was, as often proclaimed, to 'separate the party from power'. It was obvious that this aim could not be taken too literally. Even if the party leaders were willing to abandon their hard-won power, which was almost inconceivable — especially for the generation which had fought in the partisan war, it was a course at odds with the League's own principles and basic rationale. A party committed to a specific programme for a socialist society could not abandon its control of governmental power and allow the adoption of measures which were in conflict with its own policies.

After the Brioni Plenum in 1966 intellectuals and officials in the League took up the problem in public. Veljko Cvjetičanin noted in a critical article that despite the decisions taken at the Sixth Congress on the new role of the League, the party had not put this into practice. He continued:

> Despite the thesis that we have transcended a one-party system and the possibility of a multi-party system, our state organization still has very strong elements of a one-party system. Party leaderships make the chief decisions at their own levels of social power. The League of Communists still has a monopoly in our society, especially in the sphere of ideology and the distribution of cadres. The organization of the League of Communists is parallel to the state organization and is functionally intertwined with it.[1]

A very frank debate about the possibility of separating the party from power was published by *NIN* in October 1966. Dr Najdan Pašić, then Chief Editor of *Socijalizam*, the League's theoretical journal, observed that 'our present discussions do not give evidence of an effort to define in more precise and definite terms what "putting the party at a distance from power" means'. He went on to suggest that those using this slogan did not always grasp how far social change must be inaugurated by political means, and asked whether the League could be the guiding force in a political society 'and at the same time renounce its influence, its direct influence on authority, on the substance of policy which is carried into effect through the channels of government authority?' Miroslav Pečujlić, a member of the LCY Central Committee, replied that 'The programmatic thesis about separation from power, does not in any way imply a renunciation of influence on the state'.[2]

Zoran Vidojević writing 2 years later in *Gledišta* was forthright about the need for the League to exercise political power. 'It is a fact that today, in our society, those belonging to the vanguard, that is, the communists, hold all the most important positions in government and in society at large.'[3] Asking how this fact squared with the declared goal that the League should act upon social consciousness rather than wield power, he admitted that this was a 'programmatic orientation' rather than a statement of the existing reality. So long as there were conflicts between different interests and social groups, the League must keep a hold on power 'to assure the predominance of the most progressive interests'. The need for a vanguard which holds power can only be dispensed with when self-management is sufficiently highly developed.

Miko Tripalo, despite his relatively relaxed view of the degree of party control necessary in many spheres, insisted on the need for the party to retain its hold on political power.

> There are certain disagreements about relations between the League of Communists and the state. It is said that the League is not concerned with the state any more, but with self-management . . . It would however be very mistaken if we were to draw the conclusion that there are not elements of authority (vlast) in the League of Communists and that these elements could or even should be immediately eliminated. Because the League . . . represents also the instrument for realising the historic interests of the working class . . . When we say that the League of Communists distances itself from the state, we do not mean to say that it abandons control of the destiny of the socialist state. That would have dangerous consequences.[4]

Practical implementation of the goal of (partially) separating the party from power raised three main questions: cadre policy in staffing top party and government posts; the functions of party committees and secretariats in relation to the corresponding government organs and in relation to formulation of policy; and the degree of control to be exercised by the party leaderships over members of parliamentary and government bodies both collectively and individually. The other important question of the role of the party in the electoral process is examined in the next chapter.

Cadre Policy

After Brioni it was generally agreed that people with key posts in the League should not simultaneously hold government office, with the automatic exception of Tito himself. Pečujlić commented during the *NIN* discussion that there was a discrepancy between frequent repetition of the refrain that the party should be distanced from power and practical steps, and it was therefore a prime necessity to end the practice of the same individual combining party and state offices, especially in the case of members of party executive committees. Obviously such a separation of personnel need not imply relinquishing power to forces outside the party, since government and party posts could simply be divided between prominent party members. Indeed a reallocation of party and government jobs could be carried out to ensure that the dominant grouping within the party acquired a monopoly of all key political posts. The reshuffling of top leaderships in the period 1966-9 at both federal and republic level was carried out on both these principles. Initial moves to separate party and state functions took place in the autumn of 1966 by general agreement in all republics; for example, *Komunist* commented on the new executive organs of the Bosnian Central Committee that they contained nobody with executive or other top posts in the republic, or in socio-political organizations, so that the party was observing the principle of separating functions.[5] In November 1966 two members of the new Executive Committee of the Serbian party resigned their posts on the Serbian Executive Council, the republican government.[6] The press reported a quarrel in the Slovenian Central Committee on the question how rapidly this policy should be implemented. Liberals on the Committee insisted that the principle 'those performing functions in state organs and those performing other social functions connected with government affairs may not, as a rule, be members of the Presidium of the Central Committee' be adopted immediately.[7]

There was a government reshuffle in May 1967, following the parliamentary elections, which did result in an unprecedented rotation of cadres — only four top officials (excepting Tito) kept their previous federal jobs — and did also result in a substantial separation of top party and government personnel, Tito again excepted. Only two members of the League's Presidium were also on the Federal Executive Committee: President of the FEC (i.e. Prime Minister) Mika Špiljak and one of the Vice-Presidents, Rudi Kolak; though six other FEC members were on the LCY Central Committee, including the other Vice-President, Kiro Gligorov, seven were not. The Secretaries of State for Defence and

Foreign Affairs (not formally members of FEC) were in addition both LCY Central Committee members.[8]

There was a corresponding changeover in republican cadres in May 1967, as a result of which there was a substantial, but not total, separation of party and government posts. There was no overlap in Serbia and Bosnia between membership of the Republican Executive Council and the republican party Presidium and Executive Committee. Only one member of the Executive Council in Croatia, Milka Kufrin, was also a member of the Croatian party Presidium, possibly because of a shortage of women at the top. The Presidents of the Executive Councils in Montenegro and Slovenia were both members of their republican party Presidiums, and there was some additional overlap of government and party posts in both republics. A number of top republican figures were at the same time members of the LCY Central Committee or Presidium, but only the Slovene Stane Kavčić combined his job as head of the republican government with membership of leading bodies in *both* the republican party and the LCY.[9]

The republican congresses of the party at the end of 1968 and the subsequent Ninth Congress of the League created the opportunity for a more thorough separation of posts in the party and the government, especially as the central committees were to be reduced in size in the republics, and at the federal level a fifty-two-member presidium was to become the main central party organ (see Chapter 3 for details). A critical article in *Komunist* queried whether the party intended in practice to implement the cadre principle endorsed at the Ninth Plenum of the Central Committee: 'the separation of executive functions in the League of Communists and in other socio-political organizations, assembly bodies, and the state administration'. The article said that similar statements had been made in connection with discussion of the future structure of party leaderships, 'but the principle of separating functions only provides explicitly for members of future executive organs of the LCY Presidium'. No decisive position had been adopted on whether or not chairmen or vice-chairmen of assemblies, executive councils, or conferences of the Socialist Alliance and trade unions, should simultaneously be members of the leading organs of the party at federal, republican or communal level. The author complained that 'to this day' individual officials in state administration or the political organizations were simultaneously members of 'the highest party forums' and had 'insisted on concrete decisions on numerous vital problems'. Greater clarity about the degree of 'personal union' permissible would be a real step towards achieving the goal of a separation of the party from power.[10] There was some ambiguity also as to the importance of preventing an overlap between governmental and other executive political posts and membership of the LCY Central Committee. In practice in the period 1966-9 the emphasis was on freeing party executive members from other posts; after March 1969 the fact that the Presidium was much smaller than the old Central Committee partly solved the problem.

The re-allocation of posts at the top of both the party and the government in 1969 did in fact result in a considerable, though not complete, division of functions at this level. When a new FEC was selected in May 1969 none of its twenty-two members were on the LCY Executive Bureau and only the Prime Minister and Secretaries of Defence and Foreign Affairs were on the Presidium, though four other members belonged to the seventy-strong standing section of the LCY Conference.[11] The President of the Federal Assembly, a post which Milentije Popović (who had replaced Kardelj in 1967) continued to hold until his death in May 1971, was also on the new LCY Presidium elected at the Ninth Congress. It is interesting, however, that by the time of the governmental reorganization of July 1971 the principle of dividing party and state posts seems to have had lower priority. It is true that the new FEC (half of whose members had been newly appointed) only overlapped with the LCY Presidium in the persons of the Defence and Foreign Secretaries, as the new Prime Minister, Džemal Bijedić, had been brought in from a republican post in Bosnia. But an Executive Bureau member, Mijalko Todorović, was brought in to replace Popović as Assembly President, while the newly created Collective Presidency, designed to solve the succession problem at governmental level and to help deal with the immediate republican conflicts, which looked like outranking the FEC, included three members of the party Executive Bureau and seven other LCY Presidium members among its total of twenty-two.[12] The pressing problems of nationalism were supplanting concern with reform in cadre policy as in other areas.

It is worth noting in connection with the separation of personnel, that the impact of this measure may in any case have been reduced by the device of including relevant officials in party consultations affecting their areas of policy. Reports of presidium and executive committee meetings quite often noted the presence of other officials. For example the League Executive Committee met on 22 June 1968 with the Chairman of SAWPY the Vice-Chairman of the Youth Federation and the Secretary of the Student Federation.[13] The presence of the youth and student officials was no doubt due to the crisis caused by the Belgrade student unrest that month. But outside officials were not only summoned to deal with crises. The Presidium meeting on 3 July 1970 to discuss economic affairs for example was attended by the Chairman of the Alliance, the Chairman of the Trade Unions, a Vice-Chairman of the Federal Executive Council and the Director General of the Federal Institute for Economic Planning.[14]

Separation of Functions

If there is to be a real purpose in separation of personnel — beyond a probable increase in efficiency and a broadening of the number of top posts available — it must imply a separation of functions between the party and the state. Milosavlevski suggested in the *NIN* discussion that a differentiation of functions would enable the League to realize its role 'in the sense proclaimed by the Sixth Congress, but still not realized in practice'. Pečujlić indicated that one reason why a division of functions was desirable was the need for objective criticism. He noted the basic contradiction that:

> the League of Communists is the social force which expresses and formulates the main objectives and the general political line . . . and at the same time the League should be its own opposition and its own critic; it should not identify itself with every direct measure of state authority and simply explain it, but should view it critically . . . [15]

The second reason Pečujlić adduced for the need to separate party and state functions was the importance of individuals taking direct responsibility for particular measures and being held accountable for them, if necessary to the point of resigning for mistakes made. He hoped that enforcing public responsibility on officials would help to prevent the practice of declaring publicly for a policy but taking action to obstruct its implementation.

Both the principle that the party should be in a position to exercise a critical oversight of state operations, and the principle that individual officials should be held personally responsible for their decisions and action, require that there should be a fundamental division of roles between the party and the government. The division of functions that was generally recommended in principle was the same as that proposed for the party in its relations with self-managing bodies in enterprises: the party should be responsible for the overall formulation of long-term policy on the basis of its interpretation of socialist ideology, while the government should concentrate on immediate political and economic decision making. The need for the top bodies of the party to observe this distinction of functions was stated with some impatience in the report submitted by the Secretary for Ideological Affairs, Veljko Vlahović, to the Brioni Plenum of 1966. The report noted that it had already been agreed several times that:

> the leading bodies in the League of Communists should not concern themselves with those issues which fall within the jurisdiction of elected, responsible bodies, but should rather concern themselves with questions of relations among people, and should channel the work of members towards essential problems of self-government in practice and the role of the working man in society.[16]

The division of functions was, however, easier to interpret in principle than in practice. Responsibility for general policy on the development of self-management, the economy and relations between nationalities could not easily be divorced from concern with the details of immediate constitutional changes, economic problems and outbursts of nationalism. It also left unclear how far party organs could or should initiate proposals to resolve immediate issues and disputes, how far governmental organs were obliged to consult with federal or republican party committees before taking any significant action, and how far federal or republican governments were at liberty to adopt measures which party committees had criticized. These uncertainties also left open how far in practice party executives would be seen as publicly responsible for resolving urgent political and economic problems.

These uncertainties were reflected in public discussion in the press and in the actions and statements of various party spokesmen. When *Politika* interviewed Tripalo in December 1969 the following exchange took place:

Q. The Executive Bureau and the Presidium of the LCY discuss all walks of public and economic life. What criteria are now being used to avoid exceeding their competences?

A. At present we work under somewhat changed circumstances as compared with the situation in the past. Other centres of decision-making have evolved in the interim, and no one can abolish them even if anybody wanted to do so. Consequently, the current action of the Executive Bureau and the Presidium has a different meaning and quality from that in the recent past when those centres were not as developed as they now are. Moreover, the Executive Bureau and the Presidium put on the agenda problems concerned with the future development of the political and economic system, along with problems on which there is such a broad division of opinion among communists that this could paralyse decision-making even in the centres of decision-making mentioned above.[17]

An example of Executive Bureau involvement was given by Pečujlić in an interview with *NIN*, in which he disclosed that his main concern in his work for the Executive Bureau at that time was the shortage of railway wagons, which gave rise to inter-republican friction despite the apparently trivial nature of the problem.[18]

Occasion for clarification of the role of the League in formulation of government policy arose in connection with the uncertainties about the division of governmental powers between the federation and the republics. Mijalko Todorović suggested in an interview in *Komunist* that the party had an active role to play in assisting in policy making.

> Nobody thinks that current problems, either economic or other problems, can wait for all questions of the political system to be solved . . .

> At the present moment the Federal Executive Council is in a way blocked, as a result of the general atmosphere, tension and divergent viewpoints, etc. But the Executive Council is a responsible organ, and we as the League of Communists should try and help it to come forward with a programme of measures for a consolidation of the market and economic trends.[19]

When the retiring President of the FEC, Mitja Ribičić, was interviewed about his difficulties during his 2-year spell in office as head of the federal government, at a time of increasing republican independence and discord, he suggested that the government worked closely with top party organs and relied on them for support. One question put to Ribičić inquired about the kind of help his government received from the League of Communists, Socialist Alliance and Trade Unions. He answered:

> The Federal Executive Council would be unable to survive in office even for a month in such a difficult economic and political situation without relying in its work not only on the Federal Assembly, to which it is responsible for its work and by which its programme is approved, but also on other federal institutions. As is known, we constantly kept the LCY Presidium and its Executive Bureau informed about our work, about all economic and other current problems.[20]

One issue which had required close co-operation between the Executive Bureau and the Federal Executive Council was the Slovenian roads crisis which erupted in the summer of 1969. When the FEC distributed a World Bank loan for building roads to various republics there were vigorous protests in Slovenia because they had not been allocated funds for a Slovenian motorway. Official protests by the Slovenian republican government and spontaneous protests by the public who took part in mass demonstrations alarmed other republics and exposed the fragility of the federal government. The LCY Executive Bureau met with the FEC and with presidents of the Republican Executive Councils to support Ribičić and to condemn 'undemocratic forms of pressure' used in Slovenia. The Federal Assembly, which was in recess, was not recalled to consider the crisis. The Slovenian Party was mobilized to support the Executive Bureau pronouncements and condemn both the methods of protest and the 'chauvinism' expressed through these protests. The League undoubtedly figured as the more authoritative body in this crisis,[21] but the Executive Bureau was careful to stress that: 'the controversial issues concerning the financing of the further construction of roads will be settled and solved successfully in competent federal organs, on the basis of agreements with the republics'.[22]

A picture of relations between the party and federal government, which projected the party as the senior partner with overall responsibility, but stressed that the FEC was responsible for detailed implementation of policy, appeared in *NIN* in August 1971. The author noted that the LCY Presidium had ditched its proposed discussion on the League itself at the forthcoming annual Conference of the party and put as the first item on the agenda the economic situation. The article, 'Between the Party and the State', commented that it was in the economic area that the party must show its ideological creativity and political ability to unify society, and that the public looked to the party to have a clear role on economic issues. But specific political responsibilities rested on the federal government:

> Work in the LCY is of course valuable and important, but it would be too bad if organs which are, under the Constitution, responsible for the economic situation, and for finding solutions in the economic sphere, could look for and find an alibi in the guise of their party work. The League of Communists does not adopt solutions, it does not make laws, and does not count the money. This will have to be done quietly, both before and after the Conference, in the federal state organs.[23]

The definition of principles of federal cadre policy was another sphere in which the League had taken overall responsibility, in view of the increasing sensitivity of republics to their federal representation, but had delegated the detailed implementation. The Eleventh Session of the LCY

Presidium in September 1970 considered draft resolutions on cadre policy, drawn up after several months' discussion involving consultation with the Federal Assembly, the FEC and the Socialist Alliance, as well as two debates in the Executive Bureau and, of course, consideration by the Presidium Commission responsible for the draft. Tripalo said when presenting the draft resolutions that agreement in principle had been reached. He continued:

> The draft resolutions of the LCY Presidium cover only some essential problems from this area in which the League of Communists has been especially interested, whereas a more elaborate version will be produced in the documents to be issued by the Federal Assembly and other organs of the Federation.[24]

Crvenkovski made a speech in October 1970 which threw some light on the relations between the League and government. He commented that the Executive Bureau had been under the impression that it was excessively engaged in discussions of economic policy, but that it had really been little engaged. He then made the very interesting disclosure that the Executive Bureau had made objections to a number of measures proposed by the FEC – he did not specify what these were, but in the context of his speech they appear to have been economic measures – but that the government had nevertheless passed them. Crvenkovski allowed that this divergence from the views of the party was reasonable, since the FEC had agreed the measures with the Assembly. But he then went on to stress the prime responsibility of the League 'for the lag in the development of the concept of the socio-political system' and continued that the League 'has taken and must take into its hands the working out of these methods'.[25] Nevertheless Crvenkovski was prepared to maintain the independent role of the federal government. A later report in *Politika* quoted him as saying that: 'The FEC has its responsibilities and its rights, for which it renders account to the Federal Assembly'. The reporter noted that this apparently admirable statement of the autonomy and accountability of the government was – in the context of economic conflict in which the federal government appeared disunited and ineffective and caught in a stalemate – interpreted as an attempt by the party to avoid responsibility. Discussion of the responsibility of the FEC 'was met with the cynical remark: "After all, the Yugoslav government is going to be blamed for everything".'[26]

Any attempt to reach a clear conclusion about the respective roles of the party and state bodies in the period 1969–71 is complicated by the intensity of republican conflicts which tended to paralyse the federal government and made agreement in central party organs extremely difficult.

Judgements about the responsibility of the FEC and the degree of its responsiveness to the Federal Assembly must be hedged by awareness of the increasing importance of another state institution – the Collective Presidency created in 1971, which was generally believed to be a second government, and of inter-republican governmental consultations in newly created policy committees which during 1971 increasingly pre-empted the role of both the FEC and the Assembly.[27] Nevertheless there seems little doubt that the party organs retained the power to influence specific governmental decisions and the exclusive right to initiate major policy changes. Budimir Košutić, in a very critical contribution to a debate printed in Gledišta, adduced as evidence that the party had never in practice separated itself from political power the fact that the League launched the most important proposals, citing in particular the 1965 economic reforms and the 1971 Constitutional Amendments, which were finally agreed by the party Presidium. He concluded that basic political decisions were initiated by the federal or republican organs of the League, not through the constitutionally designated institutions, and that the methods of the League of Communists differed less from other ruling parties in practice than it was claimed in theory.[28]

It is arguable that the party leadership was forced into assuming direct responsibility for the Constitutional Amendments because of the increasing political heat being engendered by this debate and the inability of republican leaders to reach agreement. Kardelj told the LCY Presidium in December 1970 that the planning of how to change the political system would be the responsibility of the Federal Assembly Commission on the Constitution rather than the party Presidium, though he also announced the creation of three Presidium working groups to cover aspects of the constitutional changes.[29] But there is also evidence of the LCY Presidium adopting specific economic decisions: for example the Eighth Session meeting in April 1970 discussed the problem of assistance to Kosovo and passed a resolution which stated more funds should be secured by donations from the Federal Budget,[30] and the Ninth Session endorsed proposals for financing the Fund to aid Under-developed Republics, although the level of compulsory contributions was left to the republics and Federal Assembly to decide.[31]

In view of the complexities of federal politics it seems reasonable to look for a clearer picture of relations between the party and government organs in the republics. The most interesting evidence of governmental independence from the party comes from Slovenia. The Slovenian government headed by Janko Smole startled everyone by resigning in December 1966 after a government bill to reduce the level of social insurance

contributions made by enterprises and increase workers' contributions had
been defeated in the Health and Welfare Chamber of the Slovenian
Assembly, by forty-four votes to eleven. The resignation of the government
is most often noted as the first occasion on which a communist government made itself fully accountable to parliament. (In fact the Chamber
later reversed its vote and the government withdrew its resignation, but
this does not reduce the significance of the original government action.)
But what chiefly agitated the Slovenian party was that the republican
government had acted without first consulting the party Executive
Committee. The initial response of the Executive Committee was to
complain about the lack of consultation. On second thoughts the
Committee formulated its position more carefully. *Politika* reported that
it was explained at a second meeting of the Executive Committee that the
criticism voiced at the previous meeting about the failure to consult the
republican party leadership did not refer to 'behind the scenes consultation but to open dialogue, after which the independent decision of the
Executive Council would have been strengthened'.[32] The Executive
Committee of the Slovenian Socialist Alliance also met and approved the
resignation, but discussed too the question whether the 'socio-political
organizations' should have been consulted first.

The meeting agreed that it should not demand obligatory consultation,
which would imply arbitrary interference in the constitutional relations
between the Executive Council and the Assembly. 'However, this responsibility is not contrary to the principle of consultation of socio-political
organizations'.[33] The apparent message of these official statements was
that the government could not now be formally required to consult the
party but that in practice it was expected to do so.

After the Slovenian roads crisis in the autumn of 1969 the Slovenian
party leaders stressed the necessity of party control and blamed the crisis
on the republican governmental representatives. Franc Popit, Slovenian
party President, stressed in a report to the Executive Bureau in September
1969 that the republican party secretariat had underlined the need for the
League to adopt its own policy stands on vital issues 'and to oppose the
tendency towards limiting the activity of the League of Communists to
the issuing of general guidelines which can be interpreted in a different
way in each place'. He went on to suggest the dangers of governmental
independence:

It was established that instead of the previous monopoly, against which
we have fought in the League of Communists, several other monopolies
have appeared simultaneously in other political centres of decision-

making. It was stated that certain vital problems . . . are not dealt with in the League. It was stated that this leads to autocracy, to the rule of individuals under the cover of the slogan 'We and the Nation', and this would necessarily lead to the ruin of self-managing democracy . . . We agreed during the discussion that the Republican Executive Council, the Assembly, and other political decision-making centres are autonomous, but that none of them can be a vehicle for monopolies.[34]

Popit also revealed that the Slovene party EC adopted Kardelj's analysis of the situation in Slovenia and reached certain 'practical conclusions', for example the need to convene the Republican Executive Council and the Assembly, and 'the necessity for the Executive Council to explain the roads situation from the political viewpoint'.

One obvious question to be considered when assessing the role of the party in government is whether the central committee secretariat has any responsibility for supervising the activities of government departments or for vetting appointments to various levels of the administration. The Central Committee Secretariat of the Soviet Party is pivotal to the whole system and any real move to repudiate Soviet-style party control would certainly imply limiting the power of the central secretariat. This is not an issue which was openly debated by the League, although the emphasis in the early fifties and the renewed stress in the reform movement of the sixties on cutting down the size of the professional staff at all levels in the party could be taken to include reduction in the powers as well as the personnel of central and republican secretariats.

The composition and activities of the central secretariat were not as widely publicized as some other aspects of the League's internal affairs, but in line with its general policy of openness the party did allow some information about the organization and activities of the secretariat to be published during the sixties. *Komunist* reported in 1965 on an Executive Committee decision on the organization of Central Committee bodies, and listed by name the permanent secretaries attached to each Central Committee commission. At that stage there were four commissions dealing with issues of organization and political activity within the League (under the general auspices of Ranković) and four commissions covering aspects of ideological education inside the party, the role of the party in the social sciences and culture and national attitudes inside Yugoslavia (under Vlahović). There were also five commissions in the sphere of social, economic and political relations (under Kardelj), three of which probably had general responsibility for policy in the spheres of the economy and administration. The secretariat also staffed the League's two specialized commissions on international links with other parties and on the history of the LCY. Four other Central Committee sections listed were for editorial work and filing of documents, for petitions and complaints, for finances, and for general affairs.[35] It is not possible to deduce the scope of the activities of the secretariat from this organizational breakdown, but the relatively small number of high-ranking party *apparatchiks* then employed in the Central Committee Secretariat — reported as forty-seven 'political workers'[36] — suggest that their main energies were directed to servicing the central party organs, in particular the commissions.

When the Executive Bureau was set up after the Ninth Congress, a long article in *Politika* discussed the responsibilities of individual Bureau members, who shared out a range of jobs between them, and also asked what the specialized services responsible to the Bureau were supposed to concentrate upon. Miroslav Pečujlić suggested in reply that their main task was to present concise analyses of issues for the agenda of the Executive Bureau meetings and to help in preparing 'the conversion of fine ideas into an action programme, and its realization.'[37] It seems reasonable to conclude that the permanent officials in the party, like most political bureaucrats, had some influence on policy formulation; and they presumably assisted members of the LCY executive in their trouble-shooting role in relation to particular political problems. But no evidence emerged at any stage to suggest that the permanent officials in the secretariat wielded considerable independent power.

One form of party control central to the operation of the Soviet Party is the '*nomenklatura*', whereby the party ensures that the important posts at all levels of political, economic and social life can only be filled with the agreement of the party secretariat at the relevant level, and top-level posts are vetted by the Central Committee Secretariat itself. This form of cadre control would of course have been in flagrant contradiction with the principle of self-management, and it appears that the League did not attempt to operate a comprehensive *nomenklatura* system. Nevertheless it is clear that the party did retain power over the appointment of key political and economic officials at federal, republican and commune level, and the main change in cadre policy during the 1960s was the decentralization of this power to republican and commune levels of the party, not the abandonment of party involvement in personnel policy.[38] There was no doubt at all that the allocation of government posts and of the key posts in the federal and republican assemblies was decided in advance by the party, despite the formality of the assemblies electing their presidents and the executive council. The nomination for the post of Prime Minister in 1969, Mitja Ribičić, who was duly elected by the new Assembly in May that year, was announced at the Ninth party Congress in March.[39]

Party Control Over the Assemblies

The League was able to exert considerable influence over the parliamentary assemblies in a number of ways. In the early 1960s there was a good deal of overlap between membership of the Federal Assembly and of the LCY Central Committee. The Central Committee Report to the Eighth Congress had noted that after the Seventh Congress sixty-three Central Committee members were also in the Federal Assembly.[40] Research on the accumulation of functions indicates that after the 1965 elections fifty-four of the LCY Central Committee were in the Federal Assembly — forty-five in the Federal Chamber, seven in the Economic Chamber and two in the Organizational and Socio-Political Chamber — but after the May 1967 elections only thirty-eight deputies in the Federal Assembly were on the League Central Committee.[41]

Assessment of the extent of party control over parliamentary assemblies raises the obvious question whether all or most deputies are members of the party. General statistics about the composition of the parliamentary assemblies tended to exclude clear statements about the percentage of communists in the assemblies, but on the evidence which is available, it is clear that all but a handful were members of the League. Scrutiny of the biographical details published for all members of republican assemblies elected in 1967 reveals very few who do not list party membership or party offices held, and since the entries are not wholly standardized some of those who failed to mention membership of the League were, on the evidence of other political posts held, almost certainly communists (this is particularly true of entries for the Bosnian assemblies). These data show that in the various Republican Chambers — each of which was composed of 120 deputies — all the deputies in Serbia were communists, one in Croatia was apparently not a party member and seven in Slovenia were not listed as League members. (The figure of eighteen members of the Bosnian Republican Chamber who did not explicitly list League membership is almost certainly very misleading.) It would be reasonable to expect the specialist chambers to include a slightly larger number of non-communists, and two members of the Serbian Economic Chamber failed to claim party membership, while six members of the Croatian Economic Chamber and nine members of the Social-Health Chamber were not listed as communists.[42] Representation of non-communists at republican level in the assemblies, even after an exceptionally liberal election in 1967, was therefore clearly token. It is reasonable to deduce that normally party membership and long party service was even more important in becoming a federal deputy, though in the 1969 elections there were instances of the League supporting a non-communist in preference to a party member of the partisan generation.[43] Bogdan Denitch found in a survey of the Yugoslav élite in the late 1960s that out of a sample of sixty-five federal deputies (chosen from the 243 members of the Federal Chamber and Chamber of Nationalities) 100 per cent were League members.[44]

It is in any case arguable that non-communists would not usually be any more independent than their communist colleagues, since they have normally been sponsored by the local party as reliable candidates, since any unorthodox behaviour would be likely to lead to the party promoting their 'recall' by their constituents, and since on the evidence of the 1967 and 1969 elections the most serious 'opposition' posed to the party leadership was by long-standing party members opposed to aspects of the liberal reform and appealing to their partisan past. (For details see next chapter.) Furthermore, it is relevant that if non-communists are not directly subject to party discipline (as opposed to forms of party pressure) they would normally be members of the Socialist Alliance and obligated by decisions of the Alliance. They are also open to public pressure by the Alliance.

The question of the relationship between the Socialist Alliance and deputies in the Federal Assembly was raised in the course of polemical disputes over the nature of the electoral law to be passed for the 1969 elections. The issue was whether elections to the federal and republican assemblies should be direct or indirect; the polemical tone stemmed from the fact that it was also a disagreement between republican parties, the Croats pressing for direct elections and the Serbian party arguing for the indirect procedure.[45] The role of the Alliance was brought into the dispute when a deputy, during a debate on the electoral law in the Federal Chamber of the Federal Assembly, attacked the General Secretary of the Socialist Alliance for making damaging allegations about deputies who supported direct elections. This attack was seconded by a woman deputy from Zagreb, who criticized remarks made in the Socialist Alliance and in the Serbian Central Committee, and complained that two deputies who sat in the Chamber failed to speak during the parliamentary debate, but 'took advantage of various political forums they belong to in order to speak about comrades who sit next to them'.[46] A *Borba* commentator took up the question, and argued that since deputies in the Federal Assembly tended to avoid the real issues and direct confrontation, the Socialist Alliance had filled this gap and clarified the issues for the public. The article also defended the right of the Socialist Alliance to criticize deputies, since it was 'the legitimate sponsor of free political activity by the widest sector of the population'.[47] The Presidium and Executive Committee of the Socialist Alliance reverted to the topic a few days later. One of the speakers observed that a serious political issue about the relation between the Alliance and the Assembly had been raised. He observed:

> It seems to me that the public, and a considerable part of the press, have tried to deny the right of the Socialist Alliance to assume a critical attitude towards what is being decided in the Assembly. One might conclude that deputies are freelancers, who can strive towards views which contradict the policy of the Socialist Alliance.

The Chairman of the Deputies' Club retorted that part of this exposition would lead to a new misunderstanding about the role of a deputy: 'We must clarify this matter or there will be no conflict of ideas.' He supported the proposal for a joint meeting between the Alliance executive and the Deputies' Club. The General Secretary of the Alliance, Beno Zupančić, joined the debate and claimed that he had not imputed dubious motives to any deputies, and went on to state the general position:

> 'It is quite clear' Zupančić declared, 'that it is essential that both the Socialist Alliance, and the Assembly, as well as the deputies, adopt their views freely. This, however, presupposes the need for all of them to bear political responsibility for the views they are striving for. There is, incidentally, a common platform from which no one can depart.'[48]

The desire to maintain overall party and Alliance control over the actions of deputies on crucial issues does not of course mean that the party wished the assemblies to act merely as rubber stamps for the government, and there was official encouragement to deputies to adopt a critical attitude and make a substantial contribution to legislation during the sixties. Rato Dugonjić lamented the fact that the introduction of new methods of inter-republican negotiation had pushed the Assembly into the background and undermined its control over the executive, in a speech at the eighteenth session of the Presidium in 1971.[49] The official position was stated by Kardelj in his farewell address as President of the Assembly in 1967, in a speech in which he celebrated the contribution made by the Assembly between 1963 and 1967, and the fact that deputies had developed into independent and responsible participants in the work of the Assembly. But Kardelj stressed the role of the League and Alliance in enabling deputies to adopt this role, and the fact that the independence of the

Federal Assembly depended on the 'mobilising and integrating activities of the League of Communists, Socialist Alliance, trade unions and other factors'.[50]

When a number of Slovenian parliamentary deputies decided to challenge the control the party had over nominations to the (governmental) Collective Presidency in 1971, the Slovenian party reacted sharply. Republican Deputy Matičić initiated an amendment in the Republican Chamber that nominations for the new Presidency should be valid if backed by twenty deputies. On the basis of this amendment he and two other deputies — Tone Remc and Ivan Kreft — approached Kardelj to stand as an alternative candidate to the nominees chosen through the Socialist Alliance. When Kardelj refused they put up another name. This initiative was supported by twenty-five deputies in all.

The party reaction was prompt and directed initially against Matičić. The Socialist Alliance organization in his constituency immediately called for his resignation and the Executive Committee of the Slovenian Socialist Alliance said Matičić had shattered the unity of the Alliance.[51] A few days later the party organization of his constituency expelled Matičić for violating the programmatic principles of the League and the Statute of the Socialist Alliance. Only one member at the party meeting opposed Matičić's expulsion.[52] The Executive Committee of the republican Alliance met on 11 August to condemn 'the action of the 25 deputies'. The meeting reaffirmed that the Socialist Alliance, which had conducted 'very broad consultations' was the correct vehicle for nominations for this high organ of state, and that the deputies had contravened 'the practice of the general mechanism of our self-management'. One of the supporters of the deputies' initiative, Vojan Rus, opposed the official stand and warned that if the deputies were politically condemned 'this will inflict great harm on the Assembly, because the deputies will lose their independence of initiative'. The meeting abstained from accepting a proposal to start proceedings for the recall of all three of the chief offenders on the grounds that this was the responsibility of the commune organizations.[53] The matter arose again at the Republican Conference of the Socialist Alliance in September, where the Chairman explained that the Executive Committee had condemned the deputies for acting without the knowledge of the Alliance. He added:

We must be aware that our democracy is not boundless . . . we are a society which has opened its doors to democracy, to a democratic climate, but on condition that the role of the working class and of its direct and historical interest prevails.[54]

The Conference endorsed the position taken by the Executive Committee.

The only group which stood up for the twenty-five deputies in defiance of the League and the Socialist Alliance was the Ljubljana University students. The Executive Committee of the Student Union, after listening to Tone Remc, who was a member of the Student International Committee, declared their support for the twenty-five deputies and criticized the proceedings being taken against them by the League and the Alliance.[55] The student representative at the SA Executive Committee meeting drew attention to 'the fact that the Executive Committee of the student community was not going to change its position which had already been presented to the public, and which involved a condemnation of the procedures used against the deputies'.[56]

The Slovenian party leadership could accuse the rebel deputies of having broken two of the fundamental principles which underlay the maintenance of control by the League over governmental bodies: the primary responsibility of individual communists to their 'socio-political organizations' and the implicitly accepted need to maintain party control over the process of electing candidates to political office at all levels. It is possible, as the newspaper reports seem to suggest, that the Slovenian party leadership was also angry at what they construed as a personal attack on one of the candidates for the Presidency, Mitja Ribičič. But it seems reasonable to view the severity of the party's response as an attempt to end a direct threat to the League's position.

Conclusion

The League failed to achieve any substantial alteration in its political role, partly because of lack of clarity about what was entailed, manifested in the 1966 discussions, partly because there was doubt among even the most consistent reformers about how far they should go in separating the party from power, and above all because of the inherent difficulties of maintaining overall political control by the party and simultaneously relaxing this control. The difficulty of securing a real division of functions between the party and government is inherent in the nature of this relationship, and could probably only be resolved if the League genuinely abandoned its basic hold on political power and limited its role to ideological persuasion. The restrictive attitude apparently adopted by the party and the Alliance to any independent action by parliamentary deputies does not seem to stem so directly from the logic of the situation and may have been prompted in part by the automatic hostility of many political functionaries to a challenge to their authority. There was certainly an interesting contrast between the comparative independence and initiative deputies were allowed and even encouraged to show *vis-à-vis* government proposals and legislation, and the strong reactions aroused by signs of independence from the Alliance and League. The former could be seen as a means of correcting policy and legislation which were badly thought out, allowing for expression of legitimate social interests which might have been over-looked, and of course of curbing the state bureaucracy. It was also a good advertisement for the distinctive and democratic nature of the Yugoslav experiment in socialist democracy. It was, therefore, analogous to encouraging greater debate and independence in the party Central Committee in relation to the Executive. The latter raised the spectre of a political opposition outside of the party.

The issue on which the party reformers could agree and could claim to have implemented with a fair degree of consistency after 1967, was the division of political functions, so that party executive members did not normally hold governmental posts. Although this policy may prevent individuals concentrating power in their own hands, widen the circle of power holders and make for greater efficiency, a system in which leading party members alternate between key political posts cannot be seen as a genuine separation of party and government.

Notes

1. *Naše Teme*, November 1966, p. 1890.
2. *NIN*, 18 October 1966.
3. Zoran Vidojević, 'Premises of avant-gardism and the vanguard responsibility to the working class', *Socialist Thought and Practice*, October–December 1968, p. 36.
4. Miko Tripalo, 'Još jedanput o reorganizaciji saveza komunista', *Naše Teme*, January 1968, p. 9.
5. *Komunist*, 17 November 1966.
6. *Borba*, 23 November 1966.
7. *Borba*, 18 October 1966.
8. Sources *RFE Research Report*, 3 July 1967; Dennison Rusinow, *The Yugoslav Experiment: 1948-1974*, Royal Institute of International Affairs, London, 1977, p. 226.
9. Source *Jubilarno Izdanje Društveno-Političke Zajednice*, Tom II, Beograd, 1968.
10. Jovan Raičević, 'The type of leadership we need', *Komunist*, 31 October 1968.
11. Source for governmental changes *Keesings Archives*, 2-9 August 1969, p. 23492.
12. Source for governmental bodies *Keesings Archives*, 31 July to 7 August 1971, p. 24733.
13. *Borba*, 22 June 1968.
14. *Borba*, 3 July 1970.
15. *NIN*, 18 October 1966.
16. *Yugoslav Survey*, October–December 1966, p. 3933.

17. *Politika*, 28 December 1969.
18. *NIN*, 23 August 1970.
19. *Komunist*, 15 October 1970.
20. *Komunist*, 12 August 1971.
21. See for example *Komunist*, 2 August 1969.
22. *Borba*, 9 August 1969.
23. *NIN*, 22 August 1971.
24. *Borba*, 19 September 1970.
25. *Politika*, 17 October 1970.
26. *Politika*, 21 October 1970.
27. See Ribičić interview in *Komunist*, 12 August 1971; Rusinow, op. cit. 1977 pp. 285-6.
28. *Gledišta*, July-August 1971, pp. 970-2.
29. *Borba*, 4 December 1970 cited by *RFE Research Report,* 9 December 1970.
30. *Politika*, 23 April 1970.
31. *Borba*, 3 July 1970.
32. *Politika*, 13 December 1966.
33. *Borba*, 16 December 1966.
34. *Borba*, 3 September 1969.
35. *Komunist*, 3 June 1965.
36. *Komunist*, 24 June 1965.
37. *Politika*, 18 May 1969.
38. See subsequent chapters on elections and on the party in enterprises.
39. See *Keesings Archives*, 2-9 August 1969, p. 23491.
40. *VIII Congress of the LCY, Practice and Theory of Socialist Development in Yugoslavia.* Medjunardona Politika, Beograd, 1965, p. 328.
41. Source unpublished research on cadre policy carried out at Glasgow University.
42. See *Jubilarno Izdanje Društveno-Politicke Zajednice*, Tome II, Beograd, 1968.
43. See Dennison Rusinow, *Yugoslav Elections 1969: Part I, American University Field Staff Report*, July 1969. No specific examples given.
44. A. H. Barton, B. Denitch and C. Kadushin, *Opinion-Making Elites in Yugoslavia*, Praeger, New York, 1973, pp. 9-11 and 98. The unpublished Glasgow University research found that all members of the Federal Chamber in 1963 were party members, that in other years there was a percentage of members whose party membership was not known (this category tends to indicate lack of data, but may also suggest that in some cases the deputies concerned were not in fact in the League): in 1965 the percentage unknown was 9.1 per cent, in 1967 2.1 per cent and in 1969 19.3 per cent.
45. The Croats argued that indirect elections increased the opportunities for political bureaucrats to manipulate the electoral process, the generally liberal Serbian leaders found that greater freedom in direct elections allowed their partisan opponents in the party to capture parliamentary seats from the liberal faction. For details see next chapter.
46. *Borba*, 16 January 1969.
47. *Borba*, 18 January 1969.
48. *Borba*, 22 January 1969.
49. *Politika*, 3 June 1971.
50. See *RFE Research Bulletin*, 11 May 1967 summarizing Kardelj's speech from *Vjesnik*, 10 May 1967.
51. *Politika*, 31 July 1971.
52. *Politika*, 5 August 1971.
53. *Borba*, 12 August 1971.
54. *Politika*, 18 September 1971.
55. *Politika*, 7 August 1971.
56. *Borba*, 12 August 1971.

8   Elections

Elections proved to be particularly important in the evolution of the role of the party in the reform period. They posed interesting problems for party leaders trying to define the precise role of the League, since there was a strong incentive to maintain overall political control of the selection of representatives to the federal, republican and communal assemblies and avoid any kind of 'opposition' emerging; but some of the reformers believed that this was an obvious area in which to increase democracy. The elections also provided an occasion for contending political factions within the party, or contending local personalities, to bid for power and position – this struggle became overt in 1967 and dramatized some of the political problems facing the reformers. A study of elections is especially rewarding because a good deal of evidence about electoral conflicts was published in the Yugoslav press.

The election procedures remained substantially the same for the 1963, 1965 and 1967 elections, but these elections differed considerably in style and in their political implications. The 1963 elections were carefully controlled and involved no public opposition or surprises, although they did apparently provide the reformers with an important opportunity to slip their men quietly into the assemblies, and in particular into the economic chambers.[1] The 1965 election reflected the public influence of the reformers: a much more democratic tone was adopted in official pronouncements and there was greater opportunity for citizen participation in the early stages of nominating candidates. It remained in general an orderly and unexciting election, however, and the only real complaint made by the party was that there were too few alternative candidates. There were by contrast a significant number of constituencies with multiple candidates in 1967, and quite a number of these were 'wild' candidates – mainly communists of the partisan generation challenging the new reformist leaderships and their candidates. A number of factional squabbles between rival local personalities, which did not necessarily have great political significance, also surfaced in the elections. These electoral scandals continued to reverberate in local parties for up to 9 months. The League therefore decided to restructure the election process before the 1969 elections and a new law was passed just in time. This did go a long way to achieving the desired result of eradicating 'wild' candidates — only a few managed to beat the system in competition for federal or republican seats. The new procedures had, however, several undesired results: a tendency to revert to single candidacies, and a reduction in the number of workers, women and young people elected to assemblies. There was also a further series of well publicized disputes over the allocation of seats, and some communal officials openly defied their republican party leaders. So the 1969 elections also ended in a proliferation of 'cases' and disciplinary proceedings. Under the new electoral law the assemblies were totally renewed, and no further elections were held until 1973.

The Electoral Process

The League exercised political control over elections partly through the official procedures, partly through the Socialist Alliance which was formally assigned a central role in organizing nominations, and partly by public (or more often behind the scenes) pressure to promote or rule out candidates. Since the legally determined procedures structured the whole process, and also provided specific institutional methods of eliminating undesirable candidates, it is necessary to start by explaining them.

Yugoslav electoral law was amended with great frequency, but the nature of elections was initially determined by the Constitution and by structure of the assemblies. The new Constitution passed in April 1963 set up one chamber representing the territorial constituencies, the Federal Chamber of the Federal Assembly, and four functional chambers: an economic chamber, a social-health chamber, an educational-cultural chamber and an organizational–political chamber. This pattern was followed at republican level. The 1963 Constitution provided that the commune assemblies must have one functional chamber representing 'work communities' and that republics could provide for several such chambers at communal level. All citizens voted directly for representatives to the chambers representing territorial constituencies at the federal, republican and communal level. In addition all those working in the social sector took part in elections organized at their place of work for the functional chambers representing their sphere of work.[2] Deputies to the functional chambers in the republican and federal assemblies were elected indirectly by the communal assemblies, from nominees put forward at voters' meetings in enterprises and other institutions. This system of indirect elections ensured that the process was less open to popular pressure — although this could sometimes manifest itself at voters' meetings to propose nominees. The main controversies arose in connection with elections to the (territorial) Federal and Republican Chambers and this chapter concentrates primarily on this aspect of the elections.

The first stage of the election procedure for all assemblies involved drawing up a preliminary list of possible candidates. This stage was organized by the Socialist Alliance, and the purpose was to ensure that the list took account of the criteria laid down by the party and Alliance for the desired social composition of the assemblies, and that promising individuals were not overlooked. In 1965 the preliminary listing of candidates was opened to a broader public at a meeting to 'register' nominations where any citizen could put forward suggestions. Secondly voters were given an opportunity to participate in the formal nominating process at voters' meetings. The primary role of these meetings was to endorse candidates proposed by the Socialist Alliance, but under the 1963 procedure citizens could nominate additional candidates. Nominees had to get support in a number of voters' meetings before they could get on to the official list of nominations. In 1963 they had to be endorsed by one-fifth of the total of registered voters in the constituency, in 1965 after amendments to the electoral law they required one-tenth of the registered votes and in 1967 the law was amended again to lower the requirement to one-twentieth of the total.[3] These electoral amendments had the desired effect of substantially increasing the number of nominations. In 1963 only 158 candidates were proposed and 142 formally nominated for 120 seats in the Federal Chamber. In 1965 there was 378 candidates proposed and 305 nominated for the 60 seats falling vacant in the Federal Chamber. (Deputies had a mandate for 4 years, but half the assembly was re-elected every 2 years.)

Increasing the scope for popular participation in the nominations process meant, however, that there had to be a more drastic reduction of candidates at the later stages of the election. There were two institutional devices designed to cut down numbers and to provide opportunities for political checks. The first was the electoral commission, an appointed body headed by a judge, set up in each constituency to check that all the legally required procedures had been followed and that candidates were qualified to stand. Although in principle this was a legal and not a political form of scrutiny, it seems likely that in practice political considerations also weighed with the commissions. Certainly the figures for 1965 and 1967 show a drastic drop in the number of candidates 'confirmed' by the electoral commissions: only 64 out of the 305 nominees for the Federal

Chamber in 1965 and 97 out of 455 nominees in 1967. There was also a dramatic reduction in the number of candidates confirmed for republican chambers and for the functional chambers of federal and republican assemblies. Many of those candidates were not however directly crossed off by the commissions. *Yugoslav Survey* explained that some withdrew voluntarily, due to lack of confidence or to avoid the burdens of being a professional deputy, but admitted frankly at the same time that others withdrew because of 'pressure on the part of high functionaries aimed at securing the planned election results'.[4]

The second, and more explicitly political, method of weeding out candidates was selection by the communal assembly. As Milosavlevski commented in *Gledišta*, this stage was effectively 'taken care of by the two leading socio-political organizations: the LCY and SAWPY'.[5] The assembly had, as noted earlier, total responsibility for electing representatives to the functional chambers. It also had a decisive voice in deciding which candidates should be put before the voters in the final election for the territorial chambers. In 1963 a candidate had to receive the support of half of the assembly in order to be put before the voters. The 1965 amendment to the electoral law tried to encourage assemblies to put more than one candidate before the voters by reducing the required support to one third. If, however, the assembly itself only had one candidate to consider, he still had to be endorsed by at least 50 per cent of the assembly.[6]

If voters at the final stage of the popular election for republican and federal deputies had only one candidate before them, as was normal before 1967, then the candidate had to be endorsed by over half the registered electors. The same rule applied in elections to communal assemblies, and until 1965 it was quite common for there to be no choice in these elections either. Cases did occur, however, when voters rebelled against a candidate whom they felt was imposed by the party, without due consultation of popular wishes. Koliševski cited such a case when he was being interviewed during 1966. A Comrade Panto, who was sole candidate for a commune assembly seat in Bogatić, failed to get 50 per cent of the votes in a 90 per cent poll. The election was cancelled and the League and Alliance insisted that in the new election two other candidates were also nominated, which led to rumours that the party had written Panto off. As a result he was elected second time round 'with an enormous majority'. Koliševski commented: 'The people in Bogatić then said "We do not want the LC Committee to impose our Comrade Panto on us, but we want to impose him upon the LC Committee instead." ' Koliševski added that examples of candidates being imposed from above had occurred in 1963 and 1965.[7]

Theoretical Problems about the Role of the Party

The electoral role formally assigned to the party and to the Socialist Alliance (assumed to be working closely in conjunction) was: to fix the criteria for choosing candidates bearing in mind the desired social composition of the assemblies; to take an active part in the process of nominating suitable candidates, and if necessary to exercise a veto power over any clearly undesirable nominees. Two methods of exercising control were in principle ruled out: deciding on criteria and possible candidates 'behind closed doors', instead of in the course of public debate in co-operation with other citizens; and deciding which individual should have what job and imposing this decision by all means to hand. These guidelines were not simple to operate, however, and the statements by party leaders often seemed to indicate that League members should, if in doubt, adopt the more restrictive role. In practice republican and communal parties did use the formally forbidden methods until 1967, as a party spokesman acknowledged, and many commune parties continued to do so in 1967.

One problem inherent in the party's approach to elections was the potential conflict between maintaining the agreed criteria and giving voters a free hand to nominate candidates, as the choice of the voters might unbalance the desired social composition. The official line on this question seemed to be quite clear in 1963.[8] *Komunist* explicitly told its readers that the political *aktivs* were expected to ensure that the criteria for candidates – age, sex, nationality and necessary qualifications – were not changed by meetings of voters. Alteration of individuals was in order, but only provided that they fitted all the required criteria.[9] In later elections there was some shift towards freedom of electoral choice, though even in 1967 the party was prepared to place the requirement of balancing national representation above freedom of choice.[10]

A second contradiction inherent in the party's view of its electoral role was that it wished simultaneously to promote popular participation and to ensure that such participation did not lead to a challenge to the party. The active role assigned to communists and the Socialist Alliance in the election meant that normally they could dominate the proceedings, while the right of citizens to put up their own nominees remained relatively ineffectual unless they had the organizational ability and personal contacts to get the required support at other voters' meetings and ultimately in the commune assembly. When partisan veterans were able to mobilize their own unofficial organizations in 1967, official comment made it clear that they had broken the rules of the game, which required that the party and Alliance should be the only organized political forces. Kardelj warned

in advance of the election that he had received the impression that all
organized activity to secure good candidates was being condemned as
'anti-democratic'. He continued:

> In my opinion, it is not only politically but also practically impossible
> to abandon the nomination of candidates to the blind workings of
> circumstance at meetings of constituents. If this were to happen,
> anarchy would prevail . . . either organized groups would surface who
> would work against the democratic resolutions endorsed by the Social-
> ist Alliance, or there would be careerist demagogy by people who
> would organize through personal friends. This could be anything but
> a democratic election.[11]

The course of the elections, which did throw up a number of challenges
to party control and internal party discipline, prompted an interesting and
reflective article in *Vjesnik* about the future role of the party. *Vjesnik*
suggested that one major question which arose was whether 'the LCY is
going to insist, within the framework of its organization and discipline, on
an understanding among communists on the choice of members to run in
the elections or not?' If the answer were 'yes', which might be regarded
as the natural answer for the League, then the writer considered that three
problems would ensue. First, who was going to make the decisions;
secondly, that individual party members would be deprived of their basic
rights as citizens; and thirdly, that party committees who did decide which
communists should stand and punished unauthorized rivals, 'could
practically dictate the majority of the elections in view of the reputation
and social activity of communists'.[12]

The 1965 Elections

Contradictions and problems in interpreting the electoral role of the party
become more explicit as moves to promote greater popular participation
were encouraged by party leaders. In 1965 the party and Alliance urged
the need for voters to play a more active part in the nomination process.
The amendments to the electoral law were tangible evidence of a desire
to increase participation at this level, and public exhortation underlined
the message. A *Borba* article attacked political *aktivs* who wanted to
maintain control over the lists of nominations and distrusted the ability
of citizens to take part. The article noted that voters were excluded
because of fears that the lists would be watered down, and that it would
not be possible to secure the right composition of assemblies and the
right kind of deputies. *Borba* commented: 'if such an attitude did indeed

prevail . . . it would be a step back.' The article also dismissed fears of 'uncontrolled action' and distrust of the maturity of the voters, citing the example of Maribor where voters had proposed over 100 candidates, all of whom were deemed suitable to be members of the assemblies.[13] The demand for more voter participation in nominations was logically linked to the demand that the Alliance open up discussions to the general public. Lidija Šentjurc, chairman of the Alliance Electoral Commission, made a speech at the beginning of February complaining that 'in a fairly large number of communes' preparations had been confined for too long to the *aktivs* of the Alliance, and that there was a danger that meetings of voters would simply be faced with the proposals from the *aktivs* and asked to endorse them.[14]

The party did not lay primary stress on the need for a choice of candidates in the final election. *Komunist* observed that the question, which was frequently being raised, whether to nominate one or several candidates, was not the essence of the problem, which was to ensure that the voters had real confidence in their representative. *Komunist* suggested that anxiety about the number of candidates reflected 'a reaction to the practice of proposing a single candidate without really consulting voters, and there have been such cases in our country.'[15] At the end of the formal nominating process (but before scrutiny by the electoral commissions) 359 candidates had emerged from voters' meetings for 300 Federal Assembly seats and 1779 republican candidates had been proposed for 1083 seats. All republics had multiple candidacies for republican seats, but there was much more variation in policy on federal nominations. Montenegro was the only republic to have nominated exactly the same number of candidates as there were seats, but Bosnia and Macedonia had only nominated one or two extra candidates, while in Serbia 170 candidates had been proposed for 125 seats.[16] The winnowing down of candidates at the electoral commission stage still left 482 standing for 327 seats in the republican chambers of the republican assemblies, but only 2 of the 60 seats falling vacant in the Federal Chamber of the Federal Assembly were contested in the final election.[17]

In practice there was resistance to multiple candidacies both among political *aktivs* trying to ensure the prearranged allocation of posts, and from some of the candidates themselves. Lidija Šentjurc referred in passing to this phenomenon in her report to the Socialist Alliance Executive Committee.[18] Milosavlevski writing in 1966 observed that in the last elections 'many candidates for representative bodies tried their hardest to prevent the nomination of other rival candidates in their constituencies, and stood down rather than compete with others'.[19]

During the 1965 elections there was a greater willingness than before to admit the existence of a conflict between the criteria set by the party and democratic choice of candidates by the voters. *Borba* raised this question with Zvonko Brkić, one of the Vice-Presidents of the Federal Assembly, and he readily admitted that a blueprint for the ideal social composition of the commune assemblies would, if rigidly maintained, violate democratic procedure and 'make it impossible for voters to exercise the necessary influence'.[20] *Komunist* also commented that excessive insistence on various 'keys' for selecting candidates (youth, women, workers) might suppress 'what is essential', sending to the assemblies the voters' choice.[21] An interesting example of the voters overturning the recommended social composition of their commune assembly occurred in the Serbian town of Niš, where the voters strongly favoured directors in preference to ordinary workers in elections to the Economic Chamber, and also gave preference to managers of cultural institutions for the newly formed Chamber of Social Activities over other categories of candidate. The Niš 'phenomenon' suggested that free electoral choice might be more élitist than party control, which was committed to broad social representation. It also indicated that a conflict between the party's criteria and popular choice could occur not only at the nomination stage but in the final election, and that multiple candidacies necessarily meant that the prescribed structure of the assembly could be upset. The President of the Niš Assembly observed: 'It is a matter for the citizens themselves who they elect, and no one can possibly influence them to make them cast their votes in a way which would accord with the desired structure of the commune assembly.'[22]

Despite such evidence of popular influence on elections, there was also a good deal of evidence to suggest that many party leaderships ran the election in the old way. Koliševski commented in a television interview in 1966 that some League committees found themselves trying to ensure at all costs the election of a specific individual for some post 'for the sake of their internal relations and of certain persons, of having to arrange the so-called personnel schemes and compromises'.[23]

A letter to *Komunist* provided an example of party leaders exerting pressure to get their man elected to the commune assembly with an eye to his then becoming president of the assembly. Communists in the Vračar commune in Belgrade were informed that the party members ought to try to elect Comrade N.N. 'because we communists are interested in who will hold responsible positions in the commune assembly'. They were told that this should not be interpreted as an order to canvass other voters, but 'that they should convey this to other communists who are not present, as well as to members of their families'. Comrade N.N. was elected with a comfortable majority. The writers of the letter complained that this party directive violated their freedom as voters, violated legality because it prejudiced the election results, and meant that some candidates were more equal than others.[24] Another complaint to *Komunist* came from a pensioner in Čačak, Serbia, who had been in the party for 20 years, and who claimed he had been expelled for speaking against the candidate proposed for the republican assembly, despite the fact that 80 per cent of those at the voters' meeting had been against the candidate.[25]

The main tenor of official comment about the 1965 election tended to criticize party leaderships for lack of trust in the voters, for making all key decisions in small circles and for striving to ensure the election of specific candidates. But Lidija Šentjurc made it clear in a speech immediately after the elections that in some cases the party and Alliance had adopted too passive a view of their role. She continued:

> A certain number of cases indicate that it is not wholly clear to the SAWPY organizations and to communists that democracy is not an end in itself . . . a broad procedure of selection and nomination requires 'intervention', quick and public reaction to irresponsibility in putting forward candidates, for example, to demagogy, etc; it requires . . . clear and public explanation of the reasons why it is opportune to nominate specific persons . . .[26]

The critical debate which flourished in 1966 indicated that most voters saw the party keeping a generally tight control over the election process. A television interviewer talking to Koliševski quoted from viewers' letters to make a number of critical points. He observed that the view was often expressed in letters that candidates were imposed on citizens – which Koliševski admitted to be partly true – and quoted from a letter that claimed: 'When persons are selected for certain posts, the question is first of all discussed in the League Committee and the LC Committee decides who is to be elected and who will occupy what posts.' Koliševski agreed this was true in some places, but condemned the practice.[27] At meetings of voters in the Banjaluka district strong criticisms were made of the way seats in the republican assembly were reserved for leading officials: presidents of commune assemblies, commune party secretaries and presidents of the Socialist Alliance. The voters were satisfied with their role in nominating candidates, but a large number of objections were made to the 'editing' of lists of candidates by the narrow circle of commune political leaders. Critics proposed that editing should take place in the Socialist Alliance Conference.[28]

Democracy and Disobedience in 1967

The 1967 elections, which took place in the aftermath of the public debate stimulated by the ousting of Ranković and in the context of a much stronger party commitment to promoting democratic choice, were the freest and liveliest elections yet held under the party. The party leaders gave much stronger emphasis to the principle of giving voters a choice of candidates in the final election. This policy had been especially strongly urged by the Macedonian radical, Slavko Milosavlevski, who argued that the final stage of the election had no meaning unless there was a choice of candidates, and that awareness of the voters' real influence in the election would be an important stimulus to deputies to be responsive to their electorate, whereas they had in the past been on average extremely negligent.[29] Further amendment to the electoral law before the elections made it easier for meetings of voters to nominate candidates. The party and Alliance also changed their policy to allow commune assemblies some independence in proposing candidates, according to Crvenkovski, who told *Borba* that previously 'these matters' had been more or less decided in higher bodies.[30] Though one of the post-election criticisms was that 'etatism' had simply moved from the federation and republic to the communes, as often the assembly only let in 'their man'.[31]

Despite these liberal gestures, official pronouncements in the run-up to the elections showed that the party leaders were nervous about the possible results of too much voter freedom. Kardelj's warning about the danger that anarchy would prevail was quoted earlier in this chapter. Milovan Dinić writing in *Komunist* struck the same note:

> We must not have illusions: to create opportunities for themselves, pseudo-democratic and various other anti-socialist forces are already trying to create the belief among the people that it will be the voters themselves who will be able to select the best candidates on impulse, without the organized activity of conscious political forces. They label any organized activity by the Socialist Alliance and other social forces 'non-democratic'.[32]

Later the same article referred to 'vestiges of bourgeois society', 'the class enemy' and 'bureaucratic etatist' forces trying to misuse the self-management process and to infiltrate their own cadres. The main target of this attack was the anti-reform wing of the party, who were included in the category of those pursuing anti-socialist goals.

The fears of the leadership were partially justified by the events of the 1967 campaign, which included examples of the voters stoutly resisting the Socialist Alliance, candidates refusing to stand down when ordered to do so by the party, and passionate rivalry between candidates fighting for the same seat leading in some cases to corruption or violence. In some multiple candidate constituencies the party had approved all the candidates, but in others partisan veterans were able to win more support than the officially approved reformers, and the Serbian republican party later claimed that there was clear cut evidence of pro-Ranković forces trying, in some places, to make a political comeback.

It is important, however, not to exaggerate the extent of voter freedom in 1967. Although Dobrivoje Radosavljević, President of the Serbian party, claimed categorically that all consultations about lists of Socialist Alliance candidates had been public, and 'no lists have been fixed in closed circles',[33] news stories suggested that the 'old methods' still persisted in places. Komunist reported on Socialist Alliance meetings to draw up final lists before the voters' meetings, and observed that it was an opportunity to repair any mistakes in registering of nominations, if these had either been too uncontrolled, or subject to 'administrative pressure'. But there were cases, Komunist noted, where all candidates were being eliminated under various pretexts except those planned by commune leaderships.[34] The Macedonian party Central Committee complained that there were still cases of political aktivs deciding unilaterally on candidates regardless of the wishes of the voters.[35]

There was, however, also interesting evidence that some voters' meetings had been taken aback by being allowed too much democratic initiative. A Politika article reported that in many places in Macedonia meetings had been surprised that Socialist Alliance representatives had not drawn up their official list, that in some cases the voters had asked for the official view, and if the representative said he had no such view asked for the meeting to be adjourned for some days.[36]

Where there was strong official political support for a particular candidate, press coverage indicated that in a few cases voters were prepared to assert their rights tenaciously. One example was the campaign mounted by the trade union organization and council of the Philosophy Faculty in Novi Sad to annul the nomination of a candidate for the Republican Chamber. The Republican Nominations Commission of the Socialist Alliance had chosen Rehak for a key republican post provided he was elected deputy. The Faculty trade union body met and expressed opposition to Rehak, on the grounds that he had made an inaccurate public statement about the university. Rehak had obviously been chosen as a representative of the Hungarian minority and the Faculty branch welcomed the principle that a Hungarian should hold high office in the republic, but suggested another suitable candidate could be found. The Novi Sad branch of the Alliance and the electoral commission nevertheless upheld Rehak's nomination, arguing that he had been supported at other political meetings and by the leaderships of the socio-political organizations.[37] The Novi Sad Faculty then started to collect signatures from voters in an attempt to nominate a rival candidate. *Borba* commented:

> This is the first time in our political practice that the candidacy of a man running for a high office in the republic has been challenged. And the voters are voicing opposition through a democratic procedure . . . It seems to be an important moment in our political life. The action of the members of the trade union organization of the Faculty of Philosophy therefore deserves congratulation.[38]

The university opposition proved effective. The Novi Sad commune assembly failed to give Rehak enough votes to stand for the final election. This was one of several cases where assemblies registered opposition to the officially backed candidate.[39]

Another well-publicized example of vigorous opposition to what the voters saw as the fixing of the election occurred in the small Herzegovina commune of Gruda. Voters at twenty-eight meetings had supported the nomination of Nikola Glavas, whilst the local political leadership favoured an older candidate for the post of republican deputy. The commune assembly had failed to put Glavas on the final list of candidates, but the secretary of the electoral commission later admitted 'ballot papers used by members of the commune assembly for voting were marked by various signs. This proves that certain assemblymen were forced to vote in the way someone had calculated to suit him best.' The commune political *aktiv* met after the assembly vote. Angry demonstrators broke into the hall and demanded condemnation of those who had ensured Glavas was deleted from the list. Glavas himself persuaded the demonstrators to leave the hall and listen to the proceedings relayed over loudspeakers. But when the secretary of the party committee ordered that the loudspeakers should be switched off, the demonstrators broke in again. A number of speakers at the *aktiv* meeting condemned the habit of 'fixing things' in the commune. The electoral commission met immediately after the session of the *aktiv* and cancelled the elections, giving as a reason the fact that one of those who had voted in the assembly should not have done so.[40]

Several communal assemblies voted against the wishes of the party committee, most often when they came to elect their president. One of the most interesting of these cases occurred in Dubrovnik and culminated in the collective resignation of the party committee. Despite its significance for internal party democracy (see Chapter 5), the Dubrovnik resignation seemed to illustrate an 'undemocratic' view of the political role of the party. The committee had backed a local leader of the reform wing of the League, who was the sole candidate for the post, but when the assembly came to vote he failed to win the required majority. The commune committee held a 2-day post-mortem on the event, and, after a discussion which revealed a background of factional struggle between the supporters and opponents of the reform, decided to resign. *Komunist* commented that although a failure to assess the political situation properly might be a good reason for resigning, the committee's action did not meet the real issue of the correct role of the party. *Komunist* commented:

> It is not tragic if communists sometimes lose a battle or remain in a minority, since this proves primarily that weaknesses should be sought in ourselves and not elsewhere. In fact, the illusion of numerous communists that their committees should win a majority at all costs is far more dangerous.[41]

The defiance of communal assemblies more often took the form of supporting individuals who disobeyed the party committee in a bid to secure or retain the post of assembly president. A typical example occurred in the Croatian commune of Vinkovci, where a former president of the assembly, who had promised the party not to run again, did stand and was re-elected president by a large majority despite the public campaign by the party against him.[42]

A number of election scandals concerned individuals ambitious for republican or federal office who refused to accept party discipline. The Beli Manastir commune party committee expelled from the League two deputies to the Croatian Assembly because, after agreeing the criteria for the election, they had broken their word and accepted candidacies for seats earmarked for women, whilst refusing nominations for other seats. They had thereby prevented the election of any women.[43] Soon afterwards the committee also expelled a candidate for the Economic Chamber of the Federal Assembly for publicly slandering a rival candidate on the eve of the elections.[44] The most notorious case relating to republican assembly seats was the long-running saga in Derventa, Bosnia. The first stage of the post-mortem on the Derventa elections took place in June 1967, when the party commune committee resigned after a 65-hour discussion about what had gone wrong in the elections, and dissociated themselves from the election results. The committee had decided to expel one of the newly elected republican deputies, former president of the commune assembly, and issued a final warning to the second deputy, who had been commune vice-president. Two others who had been candidates for the republican assembly were warned by the party. All the four men punished by the party had during the campaign operated their own personal headquarters and used canvassers and 'agitators'. There were also accusations that assemblymen had been corrupted and ballots forged.[45] A fortnight later the commune party conference met to elect a new committee and voted by a majority to recommend that the two deputies should resign their seats.[46] The deputies showed no inclination to bow to this request, and said that to do so would be a denial of the worth of their long political·service to the commune. The weekly Belgrade periodical, *NIN*, commenting on the case in December observed that there was no doubt that the deputies had flouted the party in pursuit of their personal careers, but that the campaign to recall them was being mounted by their rival candidates, the president of the veterans association and the editor of a local newspaper, and was of dubious validity. *NIN* criticized the local political leaders for failing to take up a clear stand either for or against recall, and attempting to reach a compromise solution by persuading the deputies to stand down voluntarily on the understanding they would be found jobs and flats elsewhere.[47] The Bosnian party executive finally closed the Derventa case in February 1968 when they presented a report, jointly with the Socialist Alliance; then the two deputies, unable to maintain their claim to republican support, resigned their seats.[48]

The elections threw up a number of cases of ballot rigging and illegality. Members of an electoral committee in a village in Banjaluka forged twenty-seven ballot papers for the communal assembly elections.[49] An aggrieved citizen in Sanski Most wrote to the Bosnian paper *Oslobodjenje* to complain that he and 1100 other voters had been denied the right to vote for the republican deputy and that complaints to the responsible organs in their commune had been met with abuse by Alliance activists and by the newly elected deputy himself.[50] At Sinj the elections had to be held again because there had been illegal pressure on members of the assembly in the votes for two deputies to Federal Chambers.[51]

Political Opposition in Multi-candidate Constituencies

But the most sensitive political issues were raised in Serbia, where retrospectively some candidates were accused of promoting Great Serbian chauvinism. These opposition candidates were naturally opposed by party-sponsored men, so the most contentious electoral battles were in multi-candidate constituencies. Even in 1967 only a minority of constituencies had two or more candidates for the final election: 45 out of 60 only had one candidate in elections for the Federal Chamber and 234 out of a total of 325 constituencies only had one candidate for the elections to the republican chambers. In some cases the competition took place between candidates who were equally acceptable to the party and who, as *Vjesnik* observed, 'expounded their views tolerantly'. It was the places – all in Serbia – where 'opposition candidates' managed to get support from voters' meetings and muster enough backing in the commune assembly that created excitement.

An early indication of possible controversial candidates appeared in *Borba* in late January. The article reported that a former partisan Colonel Mica Dinić, who lived in Belgrade, had been asked if he would accept nomination to stand for Prokuplje. Before he had decided whether to accept, representatives of the political committees in Prokuplje descended on Dinić in Belgrade to warn him off, and claimed that the people wanted another candidate. The *Borba* correspondent observed that opposition to Dinić standing was valid only if 'the people' did not really mean 'the political aktiv'; asked what 'wild' candidate really denoted; and raised indirectly the question whether the Socialist Alliance had the right to prohibit all candidates not on their own list.[52] Dinić was according to rumours using his war record and that of his family to win votes and he was therefore representative of the veterans who came to the fore in other Serbian constituencies to embarrass the party and to challenge the younger reform candidates.

One such candidate was the war hero Miloje Milojević-Čiča, former commander of the Požarevac Partisans, who stood for Veliko Gradište in the Požarevac area as a candidate for the republican chamber. A *Politika* journalist began a colourful account of the campaign with a résumé of one of Čiča's war exploits, and quoted the comment of a local admirer: 'When he puts on his decorations, he has as many as all the other officers of Požarevac put together. You must take your cap off to him.' Čiča was nominated by a group who collected signatures supporting him in the villages – some said up to 6000 signatures were collected. He was challenging the official nominee, a lawyer with a good local record, who was currently president of the commune assembly. Some local political notabilities tried to persuade Čiča to withdraw on the grounds that his rival was better informed about local issues and would be a more effective deputy. Apparently, Čiča considered refusing the nomination until intervention from the district party committee, who wanted their secretary to be the republican deputy. Čiča then concluded that the local officials had really been trying to pave the way for the district committee nominee, and angrily decided to remain a candidate. The secretary of the district committee, no doubt fearing possible defeat in a three-cornered fight with two strong local candidates, then changed his mind about standing, leaving the two original protagonists in the field. The *Politika* reporter asked a peasant whom he would support. The peasant said he would back Čiča, partly out of loyalty and a feeling that the other candidate had plenty of chances open to him in the future, and partly 'because of that land the Commune has taken away from us'. The reporter then reflected on the advantages accruing to a retired war veteran who could not be held accountable for unpopular local political decisions.[53] These considerations enabled Čiča to win the election by 24 778 votes to 19 914, although he only scraped through in the commune assembly vote with 72 votes.[54]

Miko Tripalo made a similar assessment of the causes of the popularity of the partisan candidates in a detached comment after the election:

> We had a number of cases where some old partisan hero who had held a bureaucratic post in Belgrade for the last 20 years and was being shuffled out, would go back to his village to run. Of course he hadn't been in his village except for holidays, so naturally he had made no enemies.[55]

At the time of the elections the party authorities took a surprisingly relaxed view of the partisan candidates. *Politika* reported that at an Executive Committee meeting of the Socialist Alliance:

> Some of the speakers, stressing that certain members of the Veterans Association who have been put up as candidates have been 'too strictly' treated, said that every individual action must be evaluated, whether it concerns a veteran or anyone else, and individuals must not irresponsibly be dubbed 'self-styled' candidates.[56]

But after the elections the Serbian party leaders indicated considerable disquiet about the political implications of the victory of some partisan candidates in their republic, and some of these cases later became notorious.

Partisan candidates were successful in three federal seats in Serbia: Toplica, Čačak and Lazarevac. In Toplica the veteran Obrad Lazović-Živko stood against the Federal Secretary for Trade and tried to discredit him by disparaging his war record and by attacking him for allowing the import of cheap apples to the detriment of local fruit growers. Živko also promised to win the struggle for a railway line.[57] The campaign in Toplica was interesting because Živko unseated a federal minister, but the other two campaigns proved to be of more lasting significance.

The victor in Čačak was retired general Sredoje Urošević, who challenged a member of the Serbian Central Committee. Initially there was a three-cornered contest in Čačak, but the third candidate withdrew on the eve of the elections on the ostensible grounds that the principles upon which he had been nominated had not been respected in the political campaign.[58] According to a *Guardian* report he had attracted the support of alien elements and been persuaded to stand down.[59] The Veterans' Association took an active part in the Čačak events, entered into public polemics with the political leaders of the party and Alliance and also attacked the commune assembly for the way voting in it had gone. *Politika* looking back on the Čačak campaign commented that it had brought to the surface 'what in Čačak is called the "war veterans question" ', with the veterans complaining that they had in recent years been 'constantly ousted from public life'.[60]

The veterans' organization was also active in the most notorious of the 1967 election 'cases', Lazarevac, where five candidates stood in the final stage of the election. By far the most important candidate was the man who won, former officer in the pre-war royalist army, former partisan and former member of the security service (UDBA), Radivoje Jovanović-Bradonja. At the time of the elections it was not clear that Bradonja differed from other partisan victors, but by the end of the year he had been singled out for special attack in the press and by the republican party leadership, and became a symbol for all the political forces that threatened the liberal reform leadership.

One reason why Lazarevac continued to be a source of political trouble after the elections was that Bradonja's electoral victory was accompanied by the triumph of two of his cronies, who became president and vice-president of the commune assembly, and proceeded to abuse their position. They were accused of removing machines from the local coal mine and using them for road repairs to please a section of the electorate, of improper allocation of building plots and flats, and of uttering threats against various local officials. Continuing conflict in the commune also meant that the veterans were drawn into further open defiance of the commune party committee.[61]

The central reason, however, why Lazarevac became a *cause célèbre* was that Bradonja was identified as an important figure in what the leadership dubbed the 'political underground': a phrase designating a curious coalition of pro-Ranković and anti-communist forces united by Greater Serbian nationalism. Bradonja himself complained that he, who was a People's Hero, was being accused of gathering Chetnik forces round himself and opposing the official party policy.[62] The Executive Committee of the Serbian party produced a report on Bradonja's political activity, and the Central Committee condemned him unanimously. The main charges against him were that he had opposed the policy adopted at the July 1966 Plenum unmasking Ranković, was therefore against the social and economic reform and that he was involved with diverse political forces responsible for propagating Serbian nationalism. Miloš Minić speaking at the Central Committee said that he had tried, as a former partisan comrade and friend, to dissuade Bradonja from standing as a candidate for the Federal Chamber, but that Bradonja seemed to have new friends who had talked him into joining a factional struggle against the policy of reform.[63] Latinka Perović observed in her opening speech that the Lazarevac case indicated the responsibility of political officials who 'after launching an unprincipled struggle, became willy-nilly the banner under which opposition forces, including open enemies, are being rallied'.[64]

Press reports indicated that towards the end of 1967 the party was uncovering a series of cases in which representatives of the pro-Ranković forces had emerged during the elections.[65] One example was reported from Savski Venac, where the commune party committee decided to expel Slobodan Krstić-Uca, who had been in the State Secretariat for Foreign Affairs (in which Ranković had been building up his personal 'party') until April 1966, and had then become a deputy in the Serbian Economic Chamber. Krstić had lobbied in the Topola constituency in an attempt to get himself nominated as a candidate. The commune committee also turned up allegations that Krstić had been less than enthusiastic about the economic reforms, and that it was not clear he had endorsed the decisions of the Fourth Plenum. He was expelled for 'defending the positions of individuals who were condemned at the Fourth Plenary Session of the CC LCY'.[66]

The Serbian party clearly made a distinction between Bradonja's activities in Lazarevac and those of Urošević in Čačak, since steps were taken to have Bradonja recalled from his post as deputy, but Urošević was allowed to keep his seat. He used it as a base for a triumphal campaign in 1969, when he was the only partisan candidate to win in the federal parliamentary elections. Local officials claimed, however, in talking to Dennison Rusinow in 1969, that Urošević was getting support from former Chetniks and other nationalists.[67]

Apart from the specific political problems posed for the Serbian party by the 1967 elections, the campaign did bring to the fore some of the more general issues raised by the existence of several candidates. *Politika* published an article early in January which raised the question whether each candidate ought to have his own programme.[68] Rival candidates were also prompted to what the leadership stigmatized as 'demagogy', making promises to secure local benefits for their constituents: for example building roads for the villages. In some communes candidates promised peasants to cut taxes by 30 per cent.[69]

Rivals for the same seat could arouse more dangerous political passions. The Montenegrin party Executive Committee noted that the election campaign was stimulating the revival of tribal, religious, territorial and other loyalties.[70] The Montenegrin Central Committee meeting after the elections considered a report on unprincipled electoral activity which laid special stress on the tribal and religious conflicts aroused in the election of the commune president of Plav.[71] Nationalism had flared into communal violence in Plav, where Montenegrins and Albanians backed different candidates for the president of the assembly, and the militia had to intervene to stop the two factions fighting.[72]

Compromise and Dissatisfaction in 1969

The problems posed by the 1967 elections prompted party leaders to consider changes in the electoral law, but the Serbian and Croatian parties disagreed bitterly about the best solution. The Serbian liberal reformers, who had discovered that greater electoral freedom gave an opening to their illiberal opponents inside the party, opposed the principle of direct elections. The Croatian reformers on the other hand, who had not experienced the same problems, argued strongly for direct elections to all chambers, on the grounds that indirect elections gave more power to political bureaucrats.[73] The law finally passed was a compromise: it maintained indirect elections for the functional chambers; eliminated the communal assembly as a filter for candidates for territorial constituencies (where direct elections were retained), but created a new device to block 'wild' candidates. This was the nominating conference, to be composed of delegates elected by the political organizations, with the task of scrutinizing the initial nominations and producing an authorized list to be placed before the voters' meetings.[74]

The nominating conferences were relatively successful in preventing opposition candidates from standing, though a few slipped through the net. General Urošević in Čačak was blacklisted by the nominating conference, but mustered enough support in voters' meetings to get his name on the ballot paper, and won a resounding victory. A genuine independent stood for the Serbian republican chamber in Niš, and won narrowly against two official candidates; and a Catholic priest in Slovenia was elected to a commune assembly, ousting a deputy who had failed to attend the assembly for 2 years.[75]

The conferences were less successful in promoting the other officially declared goals of the party leaders. They failed in many cases to provide the electoral choice promised to the voters, and to the dismay of Socialist Alliance spokesmen fixed the list by a process of internal bargaining which allocated each seat to one individual.[76] Naturally enough this process of horse trading in the nomination conference meant that the nominations for each seat usually went to an established local politician, and as a result the names of workers, women or young people were dropped. The elitist nature of the candidate lists was bitterly attacked by the youth paper *Mladost*:

> Stories for good and obedient children — it can now safely be said that this is what all those convincing promises made by the Socialist Alliance in January have amounted to: promises that a new chapter would open and room be found for more workers, youth and women.[77]

The 1969 elections confirmed the picture presented in 1967 that in many communes the League was riven by faction fighting between local politicians. The most notorious case occurred in the Macedonian commune of Prilep, where a man reputed to have been sacked from three director-ships won control of the key post of president of the Socialist Alliance, and where hostilities culminated in physical violence, though local officials complained the story had been blown up by the press.[78] One interesting feature of this power struggle in a number of communes was the active role of the Youth Federation, usually acting in opposition to old-time politicians seeking a further spell in office. This conflict between young and old sometimes became extremely bitter — veterans in Požarevac demanded that the youth leadership be called to account for 'conducting a campaign against honest old communists', and allegedly threatened them with call-up into the army.[79] The elections also provided ample evidence of the spirit of indiscipline prevailing in the party, with ambitious local officials defying the authority of their republican central committees. The best-known case occurred in the Croatian commune of Varaždin, where despite local and republican party pressure two local political officials disobeyed calls to stand down, and a third resisted demands to withdraw until the last minute.[80]

The elections also indicated a degree of voter apathy and discontent. There was a slight decline in voter turnout during the 1960s, and in 1969 88 per cent of the electorate voted for candidates to the Federal territorial chamber, and 87 per cent for the communal assemblies. This relatively low poll for a communist country may have been due in part to technical shortcomings in the electoral registers and understandable confusion about the complexities of the new law.[81] Abstention may also have reflected a greater sense of freedom simply to stay away from the polls. But there was positive evidence of passive resistance by the voters. New elections had to be held in some uncontested constituencies because the candidate failed to get the necessary minimum of votes; some villages boycotted the poll because of unfulfilled promises or because their candidate had been taken off the list; and in one federal constituency in Bosnia 80 per cent of the ballots were cast blank.[82] It was officially reported that there was a higher percentage of spoiled ballots than in earlier elections.[83]

The disillusion of the voters was also perhaps indicated by their readiness to back candidates opposed by the official party organs. This question was raised bluntly by *Ekonomska Politika*, which commented that it was 'extremely interesting' that 'wherever local political forums have publicly and officially come out against a candidate who had obtained the support of meetings of voters, this candidate won at the elections'. The paper added: 'It would be difficult to say that this was the result of some sort of "opposition" by the electorate', but concluded that it did reflect the ineptitude of the party's methods in such cases.[84]

Conclusion

The elections held in 1965, 1967 and 1969 involved so many colourful incidents and raised such a varied range of issues that it is not easy to draw a few neat conclusions. The party reformers themselves failed — partly because of the conflicting pressures upon them — to reach any clear agreement on the problems posed by allowing increased democracy in the electoral process or on the necessary limits to democracy. But press comment did draw out a number of key questions, and reflection on the experience of these three elections suggests four central dilemmas faced the League.

The first and most obvious question was whether any degree of real popular influence on the elections, as opposed to manipulated participation, was acceptable to the party. The evidence suggests that although the League did genuinely try to promote popular participation in the nomination process and to ensure some choice of candidates it also tried to ensure the practice of democracy was within a framework controlled by the party, so that the people's choice had to be party approved. Any indication of 'spontaneity' breaking through, or of the people insisting on their own candidates, aroused the anxiety of most of the reformist leadership, though they did not always speak with one voice and some individuals — most notably Milosavlevski — were prepared to take risks in the interests of promoting more genuine voter choice.

Secondly, the experience of the elections raised very clearly the question of the degree of individual freedom allowed to communists to exercise personal choice in their capacity as voters or to claim the right to stand as candidates. Clearly, if the League did exercise total control over the selection process to ensure that only approved candidates did stand there would in principle be no problem in allowing communists the same (limited) freedom of choice as other voters. Difficulties occurred in practice either because the League's control had slipped, or because commune party leaders wished to ensure a specific allocation of posts which could better be ensured by the obedience of party members voting as they were told — especially in the crucial stage of the commune assembly vote. There is no doubt that the latter practice officially transgressed against the rules of the game, but equally no doubt that it was very frequently practised and that even the liberal republican and federal leaders were probably guilty of advance planning of job distribution (see for example the Rehak case in 1967). Freedom of individual communists to stand as candidates was more obviously in conflict with standard ideas about party discipline, and might, as various election cases showed, conflict with the official party line on the qualifications required for deputies or with the desired social representation in the assemblies. There is no indication that the reformers did want to extend this degree of personal initiative to party members, though they did by implication support the right of individual communists to vote freely for approved candidates — as is suggested by the correspondence in *Komunist* on this issue.

Thirdly the elections showed that some of the party's fears about the results of relatively unfettered democracy were perfectly justifiable. The evidence strongly suggests that only strict central-party control could ensure the goal of broad social representation, particularly for the less privileged social groups. Popular choice tended to favour the managerial elite against workers, women or young people. If the aim was to secure experienced and forceful deputies it is possible that the voters' choice operated to increase parliamentary effectiveness and independence, but it did clearly conflict with egalitarian principles of representation and worked against the proportional representation of the interests of significant social groups. The bargaining between local elites at the nominating conference in 1969 (which may be seen as a form of local pluralism, certainly if contrasted with strict central-party control) had the same result of favouring the elites and disillusioning young people committed to the principle of broad social representation.

The elections also showed that competition between candidates for a coveted seat in an assembly led to practices normal in Western elections, but arguably in conflict with responsible and desirable political behaviour: promising to favour the local interests of constituents and to achieve (probably unattainable) results if elected. There was also a fair amount of more straightforward electoral bribery and corruption and illegal attacks on opponents; methods which are by no means uncommon in free elections, but understandably deprecated by the League. Above all the elections demonstrated that public competition for power encourages the mobilization of sectional interests — in the Yugoslav case the tribal and national conflicts which the League had tried to surmount, and which have always been cited as one of the main objections to allowing a multi-party system in Yugoslavia.

Finally, the elections posed the important question whether allowing multiple candidacies in a one-party state can promote any significant exercise of popular choice unless elements of political opposition are expressed by some of the candidates. Choice of candidates logically suggests different individual 'platforms', as in American party primaries; and indeed different policy emphases seem the obvious alternative to relying on promises to electors. As in Western elections candidates could obviously stand on their past records — and, as a minimum, choice in the final elections does allow electors to turn down a candidate they believe to be lazy or corrupt or a party hack. But where the party is itself divided on central issues of economic and political policy it would be natural for different candidates to reflect these policy conflicts within the party — as of course happened in the 1967 elections in Serbia, when the elections gave a platform to internal opposition in the League. It is also natural that some freedom for individuals to stand in elections may encourage other opposition candidates to stand, or opposition forces to crystalize around a candidate — as it was also alleged happened in 1967 in Serbia. Elections therefore pose particularly sharply the question of how far the party in a one-party state can relax its monopoly of power and political decision-making without allowing the creation of some kind of political opposition.

Notes

1. See Dennison Rusinow, 'Understanding the Yugoslav Reforms', *World Today*, February 1967, p. 72.
2. Those excluded from the social sector are private peasants and others engaged in small-scale private enterprises, and of course housewives, pensioners and the unemployed.
3. *Politika*, 12 January 1967.
4. See *Yugoslav Survey*, July–September 1965, p. 3176. The 1967 figures are given in *Yugoslav Survey*, November 1967.

5. *Gledišta*, April 1966, p. 485.
6. *Politika*, 12 February 1965.
7. *Borba*, 8 April 1966.
8. See for example speech by Jakopić explaining the responsibility of the Alliance to secure elections of more workers, young people and women, reported in *Borba*, 5 April 1963 and *Borba*'s own gloss on rights of voters' meetings to propose new names but not to alter the criteria decided by the Alliance (*Borba*, 17 April 1963).
9. *Komunist*, 18 April 1963.
10. The Bosnian party Executive Committee issued a directive that in multi-national constituencies individuals chosen to ensure a balanced representation of national groups should not be opposed and as a result seven candidates for federal and republican seats in Banjaluka obediently withdrew their names (*Borba*, 30 March 1967).
11. *Borba*, 31 December 1966.
12. *Vjesnik*, 28 May 1967.
13. *Borba*, 4 January 1965.
14. *Borba*, 3 February 1965.
15. *Komunist*, 11 February 1965.
16. *Borba*, 30 March 1965.
17. *Yugoslav Survey*, July–September 1965.
18. *Borba*, 5 June 1965.
19. *Gledišta*, April 1966.
20. *Borba*, 17 January 1965.
21. *Komunist*, 11 February 1965, p. 486.
22. *Borba*, 27 March 1965.
23. *Borba*, 8 April 1966.
24. *Komunist*, 1 April 1965.
25. *Komunist*, 8 April 1965. In its next issue of 15 April the commune party secretary from Čačak replied expatiating on the popularity of the proposed candidate and accused the expelled comrade of spreading political confusion among the voters and other communists.
26. *Politika*, 1–3 May 1965.
27. *Borba*, 8 April 1966.
28. *Borba*, 29 October 1966.
29. See especially 'Problemi izbornog sistema', *Gledišta*, April 1966, and also 'Reforma i evolucija izbornog sistema', *Socijalizam*, September 1967.
30. *Borba*, 14 May 1967.
31. *Borba*, 3 December 1967.
32. *Komunist*, 22 December 1966.
33. *Borba*, 17 February 1967.
34. *Komunist*, 2 March 1967.
35. *Politika*, 11 February 1967.
36. *Politika*, 19 March 1967.
37. *Borba*, 7 March 1967.
38. *Borba*, 11 March 1967.
39. *Le Monde*, 5 and 11 April 1967.
40. *Borba*, 17 April 1967.
41. *Komunist*, 8 June 1967.
42. *Politika*, 11 June 1967. See also *RFE Reseach Report*, 21 June 1967.
43. *Borba*, 29 April 1967.
44. *Borba*, 29 July 1967.
45. *Borba*, 23 June 1967.
46. *Borba*, 11 July 1967.

SEPARATING THE PARTY FROM POWER

47. *NIN*, 10 December 1967.
48. *Borba*, 17 and 18 February 1968.
49. *Borba*, 5 May 1967.
50. *Oslobodjenje*, 21 June 1967.
51. *Vjesnik*, 28 May 1967.
52. *Borba*, 26 January 1967.
53. *Politika*, 2 April 1967.
54. *RFE Research Report*, 27 April 1967.
55. *New York Times*, 16 July 1967.
56. *Politika*, 15 March 1967.
57. *Politika*, 19 March 1967.
58. *Borba*, 18 April 1967.
59. *Guardian*, 21 April 1967.
60. *Politika*, 27 May 1967.
61. *Politika*, 20 November 1967.
62. *Borba*, 16 November 1967.
63. *Politika*, 23 November 1967.
64. Ibid.
65. See Dennison Rusinow, *Yugoslav Elections 1969, Part III, American University Field Staff Report*, July 1969, who notes that his file on cases similar to Lazarevac continued to grow.
66. *Borba*, 19 December 1967.
67. Rusinow op. cit.
68. *Politika*, 9 January 1967.
69. *Komunist*, 8 June 1967.
70. *Borba*, 2 March 1967.
71. *Politika*, 13 May 1967.
72. *VUS*, 14 June 1967, cited in *RFE Research Report*, 21 June 1967.
73. *Politika*, 12 December 1968.
74. For details of the nominating conferences and when they could be overruled by voters' meetings see *Yugoslav Survey*, November 1969, and Rusinow op. cit.
75. For details of Čačak and Niš see Rusinow op. cit, and also the *Financial Times*, 15 April 1969. *Večernje Novosti*, 15 April 1969 reported on the election of the Catholic priest.
76. Rusinow suggests plausibly that this result was partly due to the numerous ballots needed to obtain an absolute majority for a candidate, and partly to bargains struck between various territorial and professional interest groups to ensure representation for them all.
77. *Mladost*, 27 March 1969.
78. *Politika*, 26 March 1969 and Rusinow op. cit.
79. See *Mladost*, 10 April 1969 and specifically on Požarevac see *Večernje Novosti*, 8 April 1969.
80. For details see Rusinow op. cit. The remarkably mild party reaction to this indiscipline — a decision to overlook it altogether — is reported in *Borba*, 23 May 1969.
81. *Yugoslav Survey*, November 1969.
82. *The Times*, 17 April 1969.
83. *Yugoslav Survey*, November 1969, p. 25.
84. *Ekonomska Politika*, 28 April 1969.

PART IV

THE PARTY'S CONFLICTING ATTITUDES
TO LIBERAL REFORM

9   Problems and Possibilities of Pluralism

One major question which arose as part of the theoretical debate carried on by party theorists and political scientists after 1966 was whether the party could recognize the validity of divergent social and economic interests, and secondly what forms the political expression of pluralism could take. The debate was complicated by the fact that pluralist theories derive from Western liberal thought and not from Marxism, and the considerable ambiguity of the idea of pluralism. The Yugoslavs were constrained, however, to accept the reality of divergent interests in a multinational society with its contrast between developed and underdeveloped economic regions; and the evolution of a market economy highlighted conflicting interests between various social groups and between various industries, and therefore even between different groups of workers.

Najdan Pašić posed the issue in a series of articles in *NIN* as follows:

the dilemma of socialist democracy does not consist in making a choice between political monopoly and political pluralism, but what sort of pluralism and in whose interests; is it a question of pluralism of political parties and factions in a struggle for power or pluralism of self-managing subjects in a directly democratic process of decision-making?[1]

The question was of course rhetorical since a multi-party system and factional organization within the League had been ruled out of the area of legitimate debate. The real question was rather what kinds of pluralism within the ideological framework of guided self-management were either possible or permissible. The most obvious answer, and one which was suggested by the formal commitment by the party to stop using the mass organizations as transmission belts, was to allow genuine autonomy to trade union, youth and student bodies to promote the interests of their members. This was the answer given by Milosavlevski in his relatively radical reflections in the book *Revolucija i Anti Revolucija*, in which he argues the desirability of socialist pluralism and pays particular attention to the role of trade unions and the right to strike.[2] It was an answer the party reformers were prepared to give in principle, although in practice achievement of autonomy was hampered both by the inherited centralism and political style of the mass organizations, and by the usual party ambivalence about how much real freedom it could afford to grant.

One general point should be made here. The model of a communist party that uses other political bodies as transmission belts implicitly assumes a united and highly centralized party. Yugoslav political reality throughout the sixties was a good deal more complex. Factional differences at the top meant that leaders of various federal and republican bodies might disagree on particular policy issues, and the party could therefore appear to come into conflict with another 'socio-political organization'.

It is, therefore, important to distinguish an *ad hoc* and fluctuating pluralism, which may arise out of factional differences in the party finding an organizational outlet, from an institutionalized and recognized right to autonomy from party control. This would imply a certain separation from inner-party disputes, and would depend upon a degree of genuine internal democracy enabling the organization to elect its independent leadership and to formulate its own policies. The role played by the trade unions up to 1967 was a good example of factional pluralism, though given impetus by rank and file pressure. After 1967 trade union militants at lower levels began to state openly what was required for trade union independence, but were unable to transform their organization in order to achieve it.

This chapter concentrates on examining what happened to three of the main mass organizations: the Trade Union Federation, the Youth Federation and the Student Union. The role of the Socialist Alliance, a more explicitly political body, was considered earlier. The only other organization of real political importance is the Veterans' Association, which emerged as a political opposition in some Serbian constituencies in the 1967 elections and took a hand in the complex political machinations inside Croatia and at federal level during the 1971 Croatian crisis. The Veterans' Association however, acted primarily as a power base for the conservative faction inside the party, backing Ranković up to 1966, when it was headed by one of his close supporters, and giving an organizational base to opposition to the liberal reformers after 1966. It was, therefore, of primary importance in the power struggles within the League, and though there were certain issues like veterans' pensions, on which it acted to represent the collective interests of its members, it cannot be seen in the Yugoslav context primarily as an interest group. Nor was it thinkable that the Veterans' Association, which was so intimately linked with the triumph of the party in the liberation war and with the post-war developments in the party, should seek to separate itself from the League and pursue an autonomous course.

The Trade Unions

There is agreement among a number of Western and Yugoslav commentators on Yugoslav politics that during the early 1960s the trade unions did play a political role of some importance in the determination of economic policy. Ionescu views the unions as having become during the economic and political crises of the 1960s the 'spokesmen, and the organisers, of the positive opposition of the workers to the plans, budgets and industrial legislation of the government'.[3] This interpretation is generally supported by Dennison Rusinow, who charts the assertive role played by the Federal trade union organization betwen 1959 and 1965 in pressing its own proposals on income distribution and taxation policy. The Yugoslav economist Rudolf Bićanić notes that in 1963 the Federation of Trade Unions was asked by the government to agree with the Federal Secretariat of Labour and the Chamber of Commerce on indicators to be applied by workers councils when distributing internal revenue in the enterprise. He adds: 'This tripartite agreement is the first instance where the Trade Union Federation openly stood as an independent and separate representative of the workers' interests, side by side with the state authority and the representatives of the management of socialist enterprises'.[4] Dušan Bilandžić assigns the Trade Union Congress of April 1964 an important role in promoting the pressure for economic and political reforms and so implies that it was a forum of some political significance.[5]

It is arguable, however, that, as Rusinow suggests, one of the primary reasons for the relatively independent and energetic policy pursued by the Trade Union Federation was due to the personality of its President, Svetozar Vukmanović-Tempo, who had been one of Tito's close partisan colleagues, a prominent figure in the party leadership since 1945, and whose well-known single-mindedness and lack of political tact suited him for a relatively independent role. It is also relevant that the trade union leadership was working in the same direction as one, reformist, faction of the party against another faction, not opposing a united party leadership. There were certainly objective factors making for trade union assertiveness, for example the increasing number of token strikes by workers which demonstrated that nominal workers control did not in practice eliminate conflict between the workforce and the managers, and indicated the need for unions to defend worker interests. According to Tempo's own account,

Tito pressed him to take on the job as Trade Union President after the two-day strike of the Trbovlje miners in January 1958 had shaken the party, sent Kardelj, Ranković and Todorović hurrying to Slovenia and shown up the weakness of the trade union leadership. Tempo's account also makes clear that the trade unions were, at the beginning of 1958, treated entirely as a wing of the party. When Tempo objected that he would have preferred to work in the Central Committee, Tito told him briskly that working in the party and in the trade unions were the same thing 'in self-management conditions' and the decision to appoint Tempo as the new trade union head was made at a meeting of the party Executive Committee.[6] It is therefore the more interesting that he increased trade union independence. But a militancy which depends on the personality of an individual trade union leader is very different from the independence which flows from a trade union organization which genuinely represents the discontent of rank and file workers — a fact publicly recognized by dissenting delegates at the Trade Union Congress of 1968 dissatisfied both with the workers' lot and with the then cautious and subservient-seeming union leaders.

Tempo was ousted from his position as head of the Trade Union Federation in April 1967. It is possible to see his dismissal as a move by the new reformist party leadership to curb tendencies towards excessive trade union independence. A contributor to *Naše Teme* in May 1968 commented that the tendencies towards broadening the role of the working class in the trade unions had become very strong:

> but we dare not foster the illusion that this will be achieved at once. We recall how Tempo had to go when he tried to intensify this process. His efforts to bring the trade unions closer to the working class met not only with criticism, but with a regular campaign in the press, in public utterances and in political bodies.[7]

Certainly after losing his job Tempo was prepared to say publicly that trade union leaders ought to stand up for workers' rights. He told *VUS*: 'A trade union leader . . . must have the courage to act, regardless of whether he provokes the wrath of this or that functionary. . . .' Tempo revealed in the same interview that Ranković had accused him of trying to create a shadow cabinet, 'while some other people claimed we wanted to create a new Central Committee'.[8] He also blamed the inadequacies of the trade unions partly on lack of democracy in the organization: 'there are still remnants of the old party and trade union structures'.

Rank and file trade union discontent was openly expressed and reported in the discussions prior to the Sixth Trade Union Congress in June 1968, and was voiced forcefully on the floor of Congress. The workers made a number of specific complaints both about the economic situation, the role played by the trade unions, and the lack of internal democracy in the Trade Union Federation.

One problem arose from the fact that whereas prior to 1966 the trade union leadership had been acting as a pressure group in conjunction with the reformist wing of the party, by 1968 workers' grievances sprang from the perceived effects of the economic reforms. As a result trade unions which reflected the attitudes of their members could come into conflict with the new liberal party leaders and the government. Official trade union leaders acknowledged at the Congress that there were good grounds for worker discontent. Milan Vukasović, Secretary to the Central Council of the Trade Union Federation observed:

> In the present situation, the brunt of the reform is being borne by the direct producers . . . The differences in the earned incomes between various economic groups have created unjustified differences in the living standard of the workers, which is creating economic, social and political problems.[9]

A delegate speaking in a Congress Commission urged that one of the priorities for the trade unions was to solve the problem of unemployment on behalf of a million workers who would be looking for a job by 1970. 'So far, not even the trade unions have been particularly active in this respect. Their function of developing workers' solidarity has been neglected. . . .'[10]

Many delegates urged the trade unions to represent the interests of workers more forcefully. A Belgrade delegate said in plenary session:

> The membership of the Trade Union Federation, especially the workers directly engaged in production, demand of the Federation that it exerts stronger influence than it has so far on the making of decisions which are of vital interest for the working class.[11]

Miloš Kicević, a metal worker from the Rakovica motor industry, made a militant speech which was received by the Congress with stormy applause and widely quoted in both the Yugoslav and Western press, in the course of which he said:

> A trade union organization as a substitute for workers' management is no longer necessary to us at this stage of development — a TU organization as a shock-absorber of conflicts, which only puts off solution of problems, is not what we need. Let the TU forums remember

that we are not satisfied when they say: 'Yes, we have put forward propositions, but "some person" has not been willing to consider them, so, you see, we have not even been able to talk.'[12]

A number of critical comments about the Trade Union Federation blamed its ineffectiveness both on its internal organization and on its lack of genuine independence. A Belgrade delegate said at the Congress that trade unions were still organized in the old way 'and are really operating as if decisions about them were still being taken at the centre'. He added that by trying to represent differing groups of workers with differing aims they ended up by being 'tepid, inefficient, and often opportunist'. Therefore they should be reorganized.[13] A Split delegate complained that full-time paid trade union officials at commune level were not sufficiently militant.

> Volunteers elected directly from among the workers would be better interpreters of the interests of the workers, of their desires and aspirations; they would be more militant and less ready to make any concessions. In that way, it seems to me, the TU organization would be more energetic, more effective, more militant and more revolutionary.[14]

Miloš Kicević urged in the course of his speech that the trade union organization 'must in the future be much more independent in the programming and carrying out of its actions, bearing a full share of its responsibility for its actions'. He went on to call for internal democracy:

> The membership demands much greater consultation and a more direct influence on the formation of the policy of the trade union organization. It demands that officers be responsible for their actions and that they can be recalled. It demands election of the most capable cadres who have proved their worth in the practical work of the trade unions. If the trade union organization is fighting for direct democracy, it must further democratise itself.[15]

The aptness of these criticisms about the organizational style of the trade union leadership was demonstrated on the last day of the Congress when the delegates were asked to vote by public ballot for 107 candidates for 107 places on the Central Committee. *Komunist* commented afterwards on the unsuitability of this 'old practice' of selecting a leadership and asked: 'why are congresses held if not to make it possible for various people to be nominated for candidates, for lists to be expanded and supplemented by the names of people who earlier remained unnoticed for various reasons'.[16] The Congress delegates who were by the last day in a militant mood — expressed by demands for prolonging the Congress — greeted this electoral procedure with uproar, although a majority initially voted to uphold the proposal for a public ballot. But immediately after-wards (as a result of discussion among the delegates meeting in the lobby, circulation of a petition and a threatened walk out by the delegates from Dalmatia) the Chairman was forced to put the issue again to the Congress and advocate a secret ballot, which was accepted. A delegate then proposed from the floor that five or six names should be added to the list of candi-dates. Others seconded this move to nominate more candidates, and Miloš Kicević was proposed as a candidate becase he had 'described in the best possible way our wishes and feelings'. These attempts were, however, voted down.[17]

It is debatable how significant the rank and file rebellion demonstrated at the Congress was. Despite vocal approval of rousing speeches, the majority refused to support the more radical demands — for example an attempt on the penultimate day to interrupt the discussion in commissions, reconvene the plenary session and to summon members of the government and the Assembly to attend. The challenge to the leadership was unsuccessful. Moreover, the most prominent spokesman for the rank and file opposition, Kicević, was able to present his demands as support for the speech made by Tito to the Congress, in which he castigated those who got rich by dishonest means and attacked officials who were blocking self-management and the economic reforms.[18] The general tenor of most of the criticisms from the delegates was that the Trade Union organization had lagged behind in the movement for reform. It was therefore possible to interpret the protests of the delegates as consonant with the programme of the party leadership. *Borba* in a commentary on the Congress was sympathetic to the vision of the trade unions as 'a militant, omnipresent, effective and powerful organization of the working class' although it entered a caveat about 'statements made by some of the speakers'.[19]

The criticisms made on the floor of the Congress were also compatible with the position adopted by the President of the Republican Party in Bosnia and Hercegovina, Cvijetin Mijatović, when he spoke to the Republican Trade Union Council in mid-June. Mijatović noted that the recently published LCY Presidium Guidelines on economic policy had paid particular attention to the role of the trade unions, stressed the need for greater democracy in the trade unions and for independence for trade union personnel, and defended the need for trade union autonomy within certain limits. 'Starting from the uniform platform of the League of Communists they must be able freely to solve various problems on their own initiative taking into consideration primarily the interests of the working class.'[20] On the other hand, Mijatović made clear in the same speech that the trade unions were expected to exercise this independence responsibly in the context of the agreed economic policy. Noting that the problem of unemployment was often considered in an oversimplified way, Mijatović continued:

> If we one-sidedly emphasise that the Trade Unions are against dismissals of workers, and if we fail to explain the essence of the reform which is based on an increased productivity, such an attitude might then resemble the slogan of full employment, which cannot be achieved at today's level of our development.

It is therefore likely that a trade union organization genuinely acting autonomously and responding to rank and file pressure would have found itself in opposition to the party leadership.

In practice the Sixth Trade Union Congress did not constitute the 'charter Congress' and turning point in Yugoslav trade unionism heralded by Miloš Kicević, but it did nevertheless usher in a period of continuing rank and file pressure for specific economic policies, divisions in the top trade union leadership and signs of a rather more independent stance by the Federation of Trade Unions and some of its republican organizations.

One issue that had aroused strong feelings at the Sixth Congress was the question of the length of service required to make men and women eligible for a pension, and the Congress demand for a reduction in length of service and a lowering of the age limit for a pension was endorsed by the subsequent plenary session of the Trade Union Council. The federal government minister for labour responded to the trade union demand with an uncompromising statement to the Federal Assembly that 'one should not nurture any illusion whatsoever as to the possibility of reducing the length of service required for pensioning'.[21] Several deputies in the debate, however, supported the trade union demand and the government gave way on the reduction of length of service but contested the trade union proposal that the pension should be 75 per cent of earned income.[22] The federal union leadership according to Borba 'refused to express their views decisively' but stood by official Congress and Council decisions.[23] The leadership was under strong pressure from its rank and file. Radio Belgrade reported on a stormy debate at a meeting of fourteen commune trade union council representatives in the Serbian town of Niš on 7 January 1969, where the government draft pension plan was criticized bitterly. Radio Belgrade also reported that the trade unions in Požarevac had demanded that the Presidium of the Federal Trade Union Council should resign unless they managed to secure the Sixth Congress demands on pensions.[24] On this issue Serbian and Croatian workers were clearly united, and a conference of Zagreb trade unionists in February demanded that the Federation of Trade Unions should maintain the struggle for the Sixth Congress demands despite the fact that their own republican trade union executive was well known to oppose reducing the length of pension service.[25] The Secretary of the Federation of Trade Unions, Milan Vukasović, told a press conference on 26 February that the Federation leadership was caught between the conflicting pressures of their own rank and file and the government. 'Our organizations reprimand us for lack of combativeness, and the government for supporting inflationary trends.'[26]

There was also evidence early in 1969 of rank and file militancy on other issues. Workers in several Belgrade factories and the City Trade Union Council protested against the proposal to increase the salaries of deputies in the assemblies. The city trade union officials explained that the workers were not especially opposed to deputies getting a rise, but wanted to raise the broader problem of the discrepancy between those on fixed salaries and the wages of workers in factories.[27] Later in the year worker discontent with the performance of the trade union leadership was expressed by printing workers in Titograd who withdrew from their trade union in disgust. Top-level support for this discontent with the federal leadership was given by the FTU Vice-President, Vajo Skendžić, who resigned in protest against the way the Federation of Trade Unions was run and its ineffectiveness. He said he had exhausted all possibilities of trying to introduce new methods of work at the top, and that while the republican and commune organizations had changed, the Federal Council had not.[28] These two events prompted *VUS* to print a polemical article by a Zagreb printer, who complained bitterly about the failure of the Congress nominating commission to respond to delegates demands to put forward a printer as candidate for the Trade Union Council, about the ignorance of the trade union leadership about the printing industry, and the general inadequacy of the existing trade union organization:

We should not wonder at the decision of printers from Titograd to withdraw from the trade union. We should not be deluded into believing that it will not happen in other environments and branches. The working class can reach the conclusion that the present leadership of the trade unions does not correspond to it. For what has been done so far to implement the Conclusions of the Sixth Congress? What about our textile industry? And what about the mines and miners?[29]

The author also expressed warm support for Skendžić's resignation, which he said should be a warning to the trade union leaders, who now resembled 'generals without an army'.

A less committed commentary on the condition of the trade unions appearing in *Ekonomska Politika* in August 1969 indicated the extent to which radical views on the trade unions had become normal, but also assigned the official union leadership more credit for its achievements. The author noted:

> Last summer, many read with surprise and disbelief in the review *Pregled* . . . that the TUs in Yugoslavia are facing two alternatives: either to 'syndicalize' the Party and the State; or else the TUs must fight for the legal right to strike, for the institution of referenda, and for the right to veto all major decisions of the Government and the LCY. Judging by the present-day state of affairs, the TUs are rather far from playing such a decisive role, but if somebody brought up a similar proposal today, hardly anybody would find anything fantastic in it.[30]

The author concluded, however, that the Trade Unions had been increasingly active since the Sixth Congress, and had moved on from acting as 'a partner in talks with the government, with the assemblies, economic forums' where they had more or less represented the workers' interests, to trying in addition to improve communication with the union rank and file. The article said that the Trade Unions had been more successful at exerting influence in the bodies of the Assembly than at the shop floor level. The Trade Union Council meeting in June 1969 had therefore sent a letter to trade union organizations in enterprises offering advice and proposals about the 1971 Five Year Plan.

Between 1969 and 1971 the readiness of groups of workers to challenge the federal trade union leadership and the willingness of the party and government to recognize the right of the unions to represent working-class interests in economic policy making were both demonstrated, though the picture was complicated by increasing pressure from Slovenian unions for the autonomy of republican trade unions. Rank and file opposition to the Federal Trade Unions was demonstrated by the Bosnian miners who attacked the Federal Council in an open letter for not supporting the miners in a dispute with Yugoslav Railways over provision of freight cars to carry coal. The letter said: 'The TU Council of Yugoslavia does not understand the producers' needs and economic burdens which are caused by the crisis in coal transportation. We demand that members of the Council resign from their posts.'[31] This letter was prompted by criticism in the union paper, *Rad*, of local unions that had organized protest meetings and threatened to cut off coal supplies to Yugoslav Railways in retaliation for failure to supply enough freight trains. *Rad* and some federal union leaders opposed this form of pressure on the Railways and federal government. But the Bosnian Republican Miners Union President came out in favour of the miners,[32] and the Presidium of the Trade Union Federation then dissociated itself from the criticism in *Rad* and declared its support for the miners.[33]

There were some indications in the Yugoslav press that the TU Federal Council was adopting a fairly active and critical role in policy-making. *Borba* reported on a meeting between two commissions of the Federal Council and a representative of the Federal Institute for Planning on the Five Year Plan. The report said that the Institute's projections for development of living standards were 'the target for fierce criticisms' by trade unionists and most of them 'raised very specific objections to the proposed estimates'.[34]

Debate about the unions — whether it covered issues of organizational structure or the role of the unions in general — tended to raise what *Politika* described as 'certain old dilemmas' about the extent of trade union independence and its limitations.

> On the basis of objections to certain actions of the Government, some individuals have concluded that the TU organization is gradually becoming an opposition. However, in the explanation of the Trade Union's role it is explicitly stated that it is neither a replica nor an opposition.[35]

The position taken by the Federation of Trade Unions leadership was to admit continuing worker discontent with the performance of the Federation of Trade Unions, but to blame this lack of effectiveness partly on bureaucratic groups at various levels, and to align the unions with the party leadership in combating them. Milan Vukasović, a former organizational secretary of the Montenegrin party who had become Secretary of the Federation of Trade Unions, formulated this position to *Borba* in March 1970. In the course of his statement he admitted that trade union members were dissatisfied because: 'although we are making a considerable contribution to our general social development, we sometimes fail to do our duty when we are expected to assume the function of protecting the interests of our membership'. Commenting on areas where the workers tended to criticize the unions — dismissals, bureaucratic attitudes to democratic forces in collectives, and infringements of individual rights — he commented: 'I think that in questions of that kind the trade unions, as a social force, are not in a position to realize certain tasks without their allies, that is, the League of Communists, law courts and representative organs.' He also claimed that the unions had come into conflict with managerial groups, for example on the question of the 1968 Constitutional Amendment XV, which had allowed enterprises the option of transferring managerial responsibility to organs other than the workers council. The Trade Union leadership had formally opposed this diminution of workers control. Vukasović observed that 'Forums and various leading officials stated their views about that Amendment even before the Trade Unions did so' but 'certain managerial groups' had attacked the Federation of Trade Unions as a guise for attacking 'other forums, organs or individuals'.[36]

In conclusion, it appears that, despite the cautious approach adopted by the leadership of the Federation of Trade Unions, the general trend until 1972 was towards greater union autonomy, a trend promoted by continuing rank and file militancy and by the support of the liberal wing of the party for the relative autonomy of the unions and for the right to strike. Although trade unions got caught up in the demands for republican independence and the nationalist conflicts of the period 1970–1, this did not result in the extreme organizational hostilities that paralysed the Student Union. Moreover, the workers could, unlike the students and intellectuals, count on support from the more orthodox sections of the party who relied on the workers to combat the 'non-socialist' tendencies of the managerial elite and the 'anarcho-liberalism' of the intellectuals, as Tito's speech to the 1968 Congress made clear. After the about-turn in the policy of the League at the beginning of 1972, however, the party leaders tried to promote the interests of the workers not through the unions, but by strengthening their role in the self-management mechanisms through the implementation of Constitutional Amendment XXI and through a recentralized and disciplined party. The President of the Macedonian Party when interviewed in May 1972 about current political and economic problems stressed the role of the League of Communists in implementing the decentralized forms of self-management agreements envisaged in the Constitutional Amendments, and did not refer at all to the role of the trade unions.[37] One corollary of returning to a centralist style of party organization and discipline was abandonment of belief in the desirability of 'pluralism' for the mass organizations.

Youth Federation

The Youth Federation suffered from three major problems in seeking to establish itself as an organization with an independent role to play in

Yugoslav society. First, its constituency — youth — was too broad to have one definable set of interests, and therefore the press reported frequent complaints that the Federation had no clear cut programme or aims. Secondly, the organizational structure of the Federation had, like the League itself, become increasingly bureaucratic; by the early 1960s it was employing large numbers of full-time professional youth organizers, and the Federation was not under strong rank and file pressure to democratize itself. Thirdly, the Youth Federation was widely seen as a junior branch of the League of Communists, the channel through which young people should be attracted into the League and an avenue of promotion to top political jobs in the party. Therefore, despite the election of an unusually young and energetic President of the Youth Federation at its 1968 Congress, the most notable issue for the Federation between 1966 and 1971 was the move by the republican and federal student unions to dissociate themselves totally from their role in the Youth Federation.

Criticism of the Youth Federation for its lack of purpose and inactivity was voiced by party officials, the press and by opinion polls. Critics noted that the Boy Scouts, Mountaineers and holiday groups did more than the Youth Federation, which largely confined its activities to holding meetings and passing resolutions.[38] A Central Committee Plenum of the Bosnian party complained that the Youth Federation was not seen as a significant body in settling problems in schools, enterprises and the commune, and that it had restricted its sphere to cultural and recreational activities.[39] At a Presidium meeting of the Youth Federation in March 1966 one member said despairingly that 'We are now in such an embarrassing situation that we must debate why the Youth Federation exists at all, we are searching for reasons, causes, ideas for its survival.'[40] When the Slovenian Chairman of the Youth Federation talked to NIN about a poll of young people the paper had conducted he admitted:

> I am sure that a large number of youths do not know, and do not really care, what the youth organization in fact is . . . At the moment when the youth organization stopped being a pendent, or part, of the political structure . . . at that moment the youth organization remained speechless . . . It retained the traditional forms of political activity . . . One must reckon with the fact that our youth has some kind of aversion to such forms, that it is suspicious, that it demands results, and that the times of mass meetings have gone.[41]

The inability of the Youth Federation to play a vigorous role in representing the interests of young people was often blamed on its organizational forms. Janez Kocijančić, elected President in February 1968, commented on its shortcomings in *Gledišta* in December 1965 and observed that the Youth Federation had been modelled on the League, Socialist Alliance and Trade Unions as a political organization with central political bodies and professional staff and could not adapt to the differentiated interests of youth.[42] The Youth Federation did, like the League itself, make some progress in cutting down the number of full-time officials — *Borba* reported that the number had dropped from 464 at the end of 1964 to 373 at the end of 1965[43] — but not in more fundamental changes. A Youth Federation official admitted at a joint meeting with Party and Socialist Alliance Executive Committees that:

> In its very essence, the Youth Federation remained a conventional type of political organization with a pronounced hierarchical structure, an organization with a more or less influential part to play in social–political authority, and with very characteristic methods of party activity.[44]

The Slovenian Chairman interviewed by *NIN* commented that generations of youth leaders had tried to break down the hierarchical political structure of the Federation without much success.[45]

Commentators were prepared openly to attribute some of the failings of the youth organization to its inherited role as transmission belt for the party. *Borba* noted in February 1965 that the youth organizations often acted as mouth-pieces for others: 'it is believed that this is precisely the reason why youth organizations most often took up obsequious and timid attitudes, losing initiative and the ability to act in self-managing relations and processes.'[46] The Central Committee of the Federation, meeting in November 1966, voiced criticisms of the organization, including its lack of independence: 'It is well-known that the youth leadership has just to fulfil the role and objectives provided by somebody else and not those of the youth organization.'[47] The Federation spokesman already quoted for his strictures on internal hierarchy concluded his speech by stressing its subordination in the past to the League: 'the Youth Federation was not an independent socio-political organization. It was not independent in the fulfilment of its programme which was judged by the Programme of the League of Communists.'[48] An article in *Gledišta* criticizing the relationship between the League and young people commented on the domination of the Youth Federation by the party: 'Its ideological leadership of the Youth Federation . . . has not been exercised predominantly by political means, but predominantly by the bureaucratic practice of dominant influence on cadre selection, formulation of policy positions, etc.'[49]

There is little evidence of any subsequent move towards a genuinely independent policy by the Youth Federation. One exception was the activity of the Youth Federation in many communes in the 1969 Assembly elections, backed vigorously by the youth paper *Mladost*. The Federation was not opposing official League policy — to promote elections of young people and to encourage selection of several candidates per seat. On the contrary, it was being much more vocal on behalf of these principles than party leaders at local or republican level; and *Mladost* expressed disillusion about the failure of the party to promote these aims consistently. The Federation did therefore seem at some levels briefly to be emerging as a pressure group on behalf of youth. (For further details see Chapter 8.)

At the time of the June 1968 student protests, the Belgrade City and Serbian Youth Federation Committees came out strongly in support of the Belgrade students during the early days of the demonstration, but the Federal Committee refused to comment, and Kocijančić apparently was willing to condemn the protests. (For further details see Chapter 12.) It appears that what independence the youth organization was prepared to claim was initiated at local and republican levels and not reflected at the top. When party attitudes later swung more decisively against the student protest the Youth Federation did not stand out against the accepted line.

It is possible to argue that the moves by the student unions in Macedonia, Serbia and Slovenia at the end of 1968 to dissociate themselves from the republican bodies of the Youth Federation, by refusing to send official delegates to Youth Federation congresses, demonstrated the growing impatience of the students with the caution of the official youth organization. The federal leaders of both organizations agreed a formal separation in February 1969 but pledged themselves to a joint programme of action. By July 1970 that goal was publicly abandoned by the Student Union which brought out its own programme, marking its independence of the Youth Federation by the declaration that 'students are not youth but working people'. The *Borba* article reporting this final severance of relations noted that in practice the two bodies had not carried out any joint action since the beginning of 1969 and often failed to send observers to each other's conferences.[50]

It is debatable, however, how far the Youth Federation's caution was due to continuing direct party control, and how far it was due rather to a hangover of traditional organizational forms and attitudes plus a lack of rank and file pressure for any particular policy stand. Kocijančić's claim in May 1968 that the League had 'long ago "withdrawn" from the position of tutor to the Youth Federation' and was out of touch with the organization and the problems of youth may have been partially true.

There is some evidence that the Youth Federation had achieved a degree of organizational autonomy in the moves made by the League after its Second Conference in January 1972 to intervene directly in the affairs of the youth organization, and in the public resistance of the Federation President, Vladimir Maksimović, to these moves. Maksimović told *NIN* that Tito's comment at the Conference that the youth organization 'the way it is today, is not worth much' had been understood by many as a signal for 'some sort of a witch hunt against the youth organization'. Maksimović had earlier been quoted in the youth paper *Mladost* as saying that it would be a disaster if the suggestion 'to extend "fraternal assistance" to the Youth Federation is adopted now . . . Every intervention on the part of the LC could only be conducive to a demoralisation of communists who work in the YF.'[51]

Student Union

The Student Union moved into a position of more open conflict with the League of Communists than any other political organization during the period 1966–71. Unlike the Youth Federation it had a specific section of the community with common interests to represent. It also had an articulate and often militant membership. Students are traditionally disposed to engage in political activity and to protest against the existing regime – the party had itself drawn heavily on student activists in its pre-war struggles, as a number of commentators on the June events of 1968 wrily noted. In the late 1960s in Yugoslavia this natural tendency to student protest was enhanced not only by a number of specific student grievances – including the lack of self-management within the universities, but also by the exhilarating example of student movements in France, West Germany and the United States, and in Poland and Czechoslovakia within the socialist bloc. In light of the relatively sustained student dissent between 1968 and 1971, the student unions had either to try to represent the students or admit their own irrelevance.

The Student Union was in an analogous position to the trade union organization in so far as it was under pressure from its own rank and file. The League was, however, less willing to tolerate the 'anarchist' tendencies of student protest than it was to recognize the economic and political grievances of the workers. At the federal level the student leadership also appears to have been more independently minded than the trade union hierarchy and more willing to clash with the party. By 1971, however, conflict between the Student Union and the League was diverted into the more acute nationalist conflicts within both organizations.

The major source of nationalist conflict in the Student Union was the Croatian Student Union which was, from April 1971, under the control of the Croatian nationalist movement and blocking all action at the federal level. The first major conflict between the party and the students had in fact occurred in Croatia in 1967, but at this stage the Student Union leadership espoused a new left, not a nationalist ideology. *Borba* reporting on the Zagreb University Student Union annual conference in January 1968 made it clear that this was a meeting to restore party discipline in the Student Union after disputes the previous year, when the previous Chairman of the Student Union in the university had been expelled from the party. *Borba* commented:

> The student organization at Zagreb University was in a serious crisis especially after the two assemblies of last year. The newly chosen committee of the Union made several moves pretending to be the champion of student rights, but those moves unambiguously showed the wish to carry out an activity disregarding all other social-political forces and even acting against them.[52]

It is arguable that the conformist and unimaginative nature of the leadership imposed on the Zagreb University Student Union in the wake of the 1967 disputes made it easier for the Croatian nationalists to oust them early in 1971.[53]

The most publicized student protests occurred in Belgrade in June 1968. These events had a direct impact on the subsequent role played by the Belgrade University Student Union which in 1969 came into direct conflict with the University Committee of the League of Communists over proposals to hold public meetings to commemorate the anniversary of the June 1968 events and over proposals to boycott the election for rector and pro-rector of the university unless all groups in the university had equal rights in the election.[54] The Student Union Committee within the Faculty of Philosophy took an even more militant stand, complaining about the list of candidates for the April 1969 federal elections, and organizing a hunger strike in support of Bosnian miners in June 1970. The regime resorted to drastic action against the Chairman of this Committee, Vladimir Mijanović, in August 1970 and sent him to gaol on the grounds of conducting 'hostile anti-state propaganda', an action which prompted 5000 students at the University to go on strike. Even after the clamp down signalled by Karadjordjevo and the League's Second Conference there were moves to restore Mijanović to the Student Union Committee after his release from prison.[55]

The federal Student Union did not go as far as some of its constituent branches but reports appearing in the press in 1969 and 1970 indicated it was asserting a degree of independence troubling to at least the more orthodox in the party. *Borba* interviewed the President of the federal Student Union, Djuro Kovačević, in October 1969 and posed as an opening question: 'What do you think about the accusations that the Student Union wants to become a special centre of political power?' The paper reported that Kovačević had replied rather angrily that no one — except students — had found any fault with the Student Union when it was passive. 'Relations between the League of Communists and the Student Union are clearly defined', Kovačević went on to say. 'The League of Communists must develop a policy which the Student Union will be able to support.'[56] A row which blew up over the draft programmatic principles of the Student Union led to postponement of its Ninth Conference. The most violent reaction, according to *Politika*, came from Niš University at which local political officials said that the draft was 'non-Marxist', 'non-scientific' and involved criticism of the whole of existing society.[57] At a joint meeting between the federal leaders of the Student Union and the Socialist Alliance the latter spoke tactfully about the draft, and confirmed their readiness to 'help the students'. A Socialist Alliance spokesman said that:

> It was perfectly clear to him why certain forums of the League of Communists had opposed the drafting of a document like the Draft Programmatic Principles. 'As soon as someone enters the area of ideology he runs the risk of a confrontation with the League of Communists.'

He went on to query whether 'it would be opportune for the Student Union to be transformed into an ideological organization. As far as the SA is concerned, it would not be profitable.'[58]

There is, however, a qualitative difference between the kind of 'autonomy' being exercised by the federal Student Union, which occurred broadly within the limits set by the League itself (even if there was some uncertainty among party leaders about how wide those limits were), and the autonomy achieved by the Zagreb and Croatian Student Unions when the nationalist movement took over control from the previous communist leadership. The sense of shock experienced by many communists faced with this coup suggested the decisive difference between autonomy exercised under the aegis of the party and between organized political opposition. The more orthodox party leaders feared that granting the first would pave the way for the second — a fear which perhaps had some substance in the case of the new left student activists. The subsequent evolution of Croatian nationalism served to reinforce the fears of the orthodox and to alarm even some of the liberal leaders into retreating from their attempt to grant a limited degree of pluralism under party guidance.

Conclusion

The discussion so far has centred on three main factors in promoting or discouraging pressure group organizations to be independent of the party: the strength of formal and centralist styles of political activity; the extent to which there are identifiable social interests to be represented; and the willingness of the rank and file membership to exert pressure from below. The example of the Youth Federation suggests that orthodox and hierarchical organizational attitudes were more likely to prevail where there were no genuine interests to be represented. Conversely the existence of such interests tended to stimulate the rank and file as in the trade unions to press for more internal democracy and for greater autonomy. The other conclusion that can be drawn is that lower level committees were more likely to be responsive to grass roots feelings and to depart from a cautious official stance than republican, and especially federal, committees. This was true of all three organizations.

The other side of the coin is the question of how far the League was willing to relax its hold, so it is necessary to consider briefly to what extent the party continued to use standard techniques to try to maintain overall party control. The most obvious means of subordinating other political organizations to the party was to stack their executive committees with high-ranking League officials. This tactic was less appropriate to the trade union and youth organizations than it was to the Socialist Alliance, but was used up to 1966.[59]

After 1966 the general tendency was to separate personnel at the top of the party and other political organizations, although the new trade union head, Dušan Petrović, was a member of the LCY Presidium. But it is debatable whether in itself that policy of separation did conduce to greater independence. It is arguable that the kind of autonomy which flows from inner-party factionalism and the strength of respective personalities may actually be greater if the top men have, like Tempo, considerable standing in the party. Only if separation of personnel resulted in a total divorce between pressure group officials and professional party politicians would it significantly promote independence.

After Brioni the League continued to use other established methods of asserting general party supremacy: formal joint meetings between party leaders and executives of the other organizations; co-ordinating all the political organizations through republican and local *aktivs*; and by mobilizing the mass organizations in the party-sponsored policy discussion and activity before party congresses, or after official Central Committee policy statements. It is arguable that these joint activities allowed for a degree of reciprocal influence, enabling trade unions to press their particular interests and problems on the party, for example, but it seems clear that they would tend to perpetuate the traditional primacy of the party and to define the permitted scope of activity of the mass organizations. The party underlined its expectation that the other political organizations would follow the lead given by the party in issuing a number of public exhortations and reprimands to organizations showing insufficient zeal. For example the Executive Committee of the Croatian Party meeting in December 1969 stressed that the Youth Federation should take an active part in implementing the conclusion of the Croatian Party Conference and criticized the youth press for not publicizing these conclusions.[60] So that while displaying a certain degree of tolerance of moves towards pressure group autonomy, the general tendency of the League was to indicate the existence of clear limits to the exercise of this autonomy.

Notes

1. *NIN*, 6 April 1969.
2. Slavko Milosavlevski, *Revolucija i Anti Revolucija*, Revija, Beograd, 1971.
3. Ghita Ionescu, *The Politics of European Communist States,* Weidenfeld, London, 1967, p. 119.
4. Rudolf Bićanić, *Economic Policy in Socialist Yugoslavia*, Cambridge University Press, Cambridge, 1973, p. 113.
5. Dušan Bilandžić, *Ideje i Praksa Drustvenog Razvoja Jugoslavije 1945-1973*, Komunist, Beograd, 1973, p. 229.
6. Svetozar Vukmanović Tempo, *Revolucija Koja Teče, Memoari*, Komunist, Beograd, 1971, pp. 318-19.
7. Milan Skrbić, 'Dezintegracija radničke klase — uzrok neuspjeha u provodenju reforme', *Naše Teme*, May 1968, p. 786.
8. *VUS*, 26 April 1967.
9. *Borba*, 28 June 1968.
10. *Borba*, 29 June 1968.
11. *Borba*, 27 June 1968.
12. *VUS*, 10 July 1968.
13. Speech by Branko Vuksa reported in *Borba*, 28 June 1968.
14. *Borba*, 28 June 1968.
15. *VUS*, 10 July 1968.
16. *Komunist*, 4 July 1968.
17. *Borba*, 30 June 1968.
18. Tito's speech was printed in *Borba*, 27 June 1968.

19. *Borba*, 2 July 1968.
20. *Borba*, 16 June 1968.
21. *Borba*, 14 February 1969.
22. *Borba*, 25 February 1969.
23. *Borba*, 14 February 1969.
24. *RFE Research Report*, 27 February 1969.
25. *Borba*, 14 February 1969.
26. *RFE Research Report*, 27 February 1969.
27. *Borba*, 11 February 1969.
28. *Politika*, 17 July 1969.
29. *VUS*, 3 September 1969.
30. *Ekonomska Politika*, 4 August 1969.
31. *Vjesnik*, 8 August 1970.
32. *Borba*, 8 August 1970.
33. *RFE Research Report*, 10 August 1970 citing Radio Belgrade.
34. *Borba*, 26 March 1970.
35. *Politika*, 13 December 1970.
36. *Borba*, 22 March 1970.
37. *NIN*, 11 May 1972.
38. *Borba*, 7 May 1965; *Politika*, 27 July 1966.
39. *Borba*, 3 November 1965.
40. *Borba*, 23 March 1966.
41. *NIN*, 9 August 1970.
42. *Gledišta*, December 1965, p. 1707.
43. *Borba*, 1 March 1966.
44. *Mladost*, 12 October 1967.
45. *NIN*, 9 August 1970.
46. *Borba*, 11 February 1965.
47. *Borba*, 25 November 1966.
48. *Mladost*, 12 October 1967.
49. Manojlo Bročić, 'Omladina i Politika', *Gledišta*, February 1967, p. 177.
50. *Borba*, 13 July 1970.
51. *NIN*, 5 March 1972.
52. *Borba*, 17 January 1968.
53. See Dennison Rusinow, *Crisis in Croatia, Part II, American University Field Staff Reports*, 1972.
54. *Politika*, 1 June 1969; *Borba*, 17 October 1969.
55. *NIN*, 26 March 1972.
56. *Borba*, 23 October 1969.
57. *Politika*, 16 December 1970.
58. *Borba*, 24 December 1970.
59. There were eight members of the LCY Central Committee on the nineteen-member Trade Union Federation executive, including Tempo himself and one of the two vice-presidents, Vajo Skendžić, who was to resign in protest in 1969. Two other members of the Trade Union Executive were on the LCY Control Commission and Revision Commission respectively. The President of the Youth Federation, Tomislav Badinovac, was also on the League Central Committee. (Source for composition of Federation of Trade Unions Executive Committee before Brioni is *Joint Translation Service Supplement*, 12 February 1964.)
60. *Borba*, 11 December 1969.

10 Freedom Under the Law?

Changing Party Attitudes to the Rule of Law

Most communist parties striving to rid themselves of the terrors of Stalinism have laid considerable stress on the restoration of legality. In the Soviet case this meant legal reform but strict party control of the legal process; this was a considerable improvement upon police tyranny which subordinated the party and bypassed the courts, but the dominance of the party over the courts undermines legality and denies political rights. East European reform movements, in particular the Prague Spring, have aspired to move much further towards the liberal conception of judicial independence. It is, therefore, interesting that the Yugoslavs in their initial repudiation of Stalinism did not lay great ideological emphasis on the importance of legality, though they did denounce Stalinist terror.

There were two reasons why the rule of law did not figure very high on the agenda of the Yugoslav party. One was the political fact that in the early years after the break with Stalin the security service under Ranković helped Tito to crush the pro-Moscow opposition, the Cominformists within the Yugoslav party, and so to maintain the independence from Moscow which was the basis for reform. It has also been suggested by a Slovene judge that because the party loosened its direct control over the state apparatus the security police had stepped in to fill this vacuum and so became 'a state over a state'.[1] The second reason was ideological. In the early fifties the Yugoslav leaders looked for inspiration to Marxism–Leninism uncontaminated by Stalinism. Worker control of factories and a new role for the party arose much more naturally as socialist alternatives to what the Yugoslavs diagnosed as the repressive state bureaucracy and monolithic bureaucratic party of Stalinism, than Western liberal concerns with law as a safeguard of freedom, which had been dismissed by Marx as bourgeois hypocrisy.

Nevertheless the party did take an important step towards asserting respect for legality and renouncing its own previous excesses in 1951, when Ranković made a 15 000 word report to the Central Committee in which he criticized maladministration and abuse of power by the security police, especially the large number of unjustified arrests. He revealed that 47 per cent of those arrested in 1949 had subsequently been found innocent and had been released.[2] During 1951 an amnesty was also declared for many 'misled' by the Cominform, and the Yugoslav National Assembly debated a new criminal code, which was more liberal than the 1947 Soviet-style code though still biased in favour of the police.[3] Bakarić criticized public prosecutors for turning ordinary crimes into political offences.[4]

There was a temporary campaign against the assertion of Western liberal freedoms in Yugoslav life during 1952, which attacked claims to freedom by the press and universities, and extended to a denunciation of judges who were under the mistaken belief that the courts should act independently, and a decision to purge politically unreliable judges.[5]

The government proceeded with judicial reform, however, and a new act regulating the operation of the courts was passed in July 1954. The intention of the act was to improve the professional qualifications of judges and enhance their independence.[6] Despite the implementation of legal reforms during 1954, the Djilas affair at the beginning of that year marked a move away from political tolerance of debate and dissent. Although Djilas escaped legal action at the time, he was sentenced to imprisonment at the end of 1956 for his criticism of Soviet suppression of the Hungarian uprising and Yugoslav policy on this issue, and sentenced to a further 10 years in 1957 for publishing *The New Class* abroad. The willingness of the party to clamp down severely on political opponents was further illustrated by a trial of Social Democrats early in 1958.

The increasingly liberal atmosphere in the early sixties resulted in an amnesty for political offenders in March 1962 and about 1000 prisoners were released.[7] Despite the brief period of party vigilance signified by Tito's Split speech in May 1962, and by Djilas' second imprisonment for publication of his *Conversations with Stalin*, political trends encouraged a greater independence by the courts. But even more than in the case of party and government reform, significant legal reform resulted after the Brioni Plenum of 1966 exposed the excesses of the security police.

The first measures were naturally enough directed against the security service itself. Top officials were systematically purged at federal, republican, city and commune level and replaced by reliable party members. There was also a general reduction in the number of UDBA officials as an indication of their more restricted role, and measures were adopted to make the security service more directly accountable to governmental and assembly organs. Party bodies within the Secretariat of the Interior met to confess their errors and denounce some of their colleagues, who were duly expelled from the party. But perhaps more important if less tangible was the fact that party committees at every level publicly revealed the corruption and abuses of the security service in their area and promised it would not happen again. It is not possible to assess how successful this campaign was in making the security police fully accountable in checking all abuses, and the stringency of the controls imposed must have been moderated by the desire for the party to maintain the effectiveness of the service. Nevertheless it seems reasonable to claim that in the period 1967–71 the police were subject to the rule of law.

Secondly, there was a general awareness after Brioni of the need for judicial reform. This issue was raised explicitly by the President of the Slovene Supreme Court, Vladimir Krivić, at the Slovene Central Committee Plenum in September 1966. He claimed that the Slovene Court had been trying to promote judicial reform unsuccessfully since 1957, but especially in the run-up to the Eighth Congress; and noted that while the President of the Supreme Court of Yugoslavia was at this time debarred from candidature to the LCY Central Committee in the name of separating state and party functions, the Secretary of Internal Affairs was put on the Central Committee.[8]

Government sponsored amendments to the criminal code were introduced into the Federal Assembly in February 1967. These amendments were designed to restrict the powers of both the security service and the ordinary police (the people's militia), and the right to cross-examine suspects and to decide on detention was vested solely in the courts, whereas previously the public prosecutor had enjoyed considerable power and discretion at this stage. The amendments also reduced the period of detention for questioning from a maximum of 21 days to 24 hours, required the presence of a defence lawyer and enhanced the powers of the defence lawyer to have access to evidence and to communicate freely with his client.[9]

Party Influence on the Legal Process

Unfortunately the evidence available on the role of the party at all stages of the judicial process is too fragmentary to produce a comprehensive picture, but it is possible to find some clues. In certain cases Tito himself, or a small group at the top, almost certainly took the main decisions: to prosecute Djilas, to halt the proceedings against Ranković in December 1966 and grant him a presidential pardon and to release Djilas early in

1967. Tito also appears to have taken the initiative to prosecute Mihajlo Mihajlov for his critical articles on the cultural scene in the Soviet Union published in *Delo* early in 1965. The articles included references to the existence of labour camps under Lenin and led to an official protest by the Soviet ambassador, which presumably prompted Tito to take action, though around this time Tito criticized a delegation of public prosecutors for not acting promptly on their own initiative to ban articles like Mihajlov's and for waiting for a political cue.[10]

At a more routine level there is some evidence that public prosecutors sought political advice, at least in tricky cases. *Borba* observed in relation to a case of economic crime reported in 1965 that because of the ambiguous attitudes to this particular type of crime the public prosecutors 'dials the number of the commune assembly or of the party committee in order to "consult" them' before taking action.[11] After 1966 prosecutors may have become more independent, but it seems likely they still sought political advice on what were the limits of acceptable criticism and dissent. Indeed an interesting example of prosecutors accepting general policy guidance from the party was a consultative meeting of prosecutors held in Croatia in mid-1971, at which the prosecutors considered their obligations 'in connection with the decisions of the Seventeenth Plenum of the LCY Presidium and the Tenth and Twentieth Sessions of the Croatian Central Committee'.[12] In this instance the prosecutors were obviously trying to decide what expressions of Croatian nationalism were in the view of the Croatian party to be tolerated and what forms of nationalism should be met by legal penalties.

There were individual cases where local party bodies publicly called on the prosecutors to take action, particularly on the banning of publications, and this public political pressure does in some cases seem to have been automatically effective. One case where legal action *seemed* to follow directly from a public party statement occurred in August 1971. The Belgrade City Committee condemned an article in *Kniževne Novine* for being 'nationalist' and the Belgrade public prosecutor instituted proceedings against the paper immediately afterwards.[13] Sometimes, however, local party bodies had to go to some lengths to achieve a judicial response. For example a dispute involving Albanian nationalism occurred in a timber combine in Kosovo, where a worker accused of taking part in hostile nationalist demonstrations attacked his accuser with a knife. The attacker was only arrested after the party conference in the enterprise had made representations to the commune and Provincial party committees. In this case the main issue seems to have been concern that the prosecutors were turning a blind eye to nationalist intimidation, and the party itself did not act until after a protest strike by some of the workers against the failure to arrest the attacker.[14] It is therefore arguable that the party intervention in this instance was designed to ensure the objectivity of the judicial process against other political pressures.

An interesting example both of the extent to which judicial organs were prepared to condone illegal action by high-ranking party figures, and of the willingness of party committees to intervene to promote the impartiality of the judicial process, arose in Croatia in the autumn of 1968. A scandal concerning fraudulent activities by a publishing enterprise, in which top political figures like the President of the Republican Veterans' Association were involved, was apparently uncovered by a young lawyer during the summer recess when his superiors were on holiday. Pressure was obviously exerted to hush the matter up. The Executive Committee and Central Committee of the Croatian party, however, came out in support of a full investigation by the public prosecutor and the court 'irrespective of the individuals who may be involved in the case'. The *Večernje Novosti* report on the case noted wrily that while optimists expressed satisfaction with the attitudes of the party committees, pessimists observed that it was a bad sign that after Brioni 'political forums' should have to intervene to uphold principles which should have been basic. The paper itself concluded that it indicated the strength of old habits of deferring to prestigious political figures who had in the past by virtue of their executive position in the party been above the law.[15]

The crucial test of the independence of the judiciary is not whether the prosecution could be influenced by the party, however, since the decision to prosecute in political cases is likely in most regimes to be a political as well as a judicial decision. What is of central importance is that the party should avoid intervention in the processes of the law after the decision to prosecute has been made, that defence lawyers should be able to put up an independent defence and that the courts themselves should feel free to reject the prosecution case and to impose sentences at their own discretion.

In practice of course when a top-level party decision has been made to start legal proceedings against an individual it is unlikely that the party will abstain from indicating what results it expects from the court. It must be assumed that the courts handed down agreed sentences not only on Djilas but also on Mihajlov. The fact that Mihajlov escaped from the charge of slandering the Soviet Union with only a one-year suspended sentence seems to have been due to countervailing political considerations: the desire to avoid diplomatic embarrassment at a time when PEN, the international writers' club, was due to hold a conference in Slovenia. On the other hand, in less sensitive political trials, for example in many of the banning cases considered in Chapter 11, the local party bodies do seem to have avoided direct involvement and the defence could win their case.

The evidence on how far defence lawyers felt free to conduct a vigorous defence and how far the party would sanction such independence is sketchy and points in different directions. Apparently defence lawyers would sometimes cover themselves by consulting the party, at least before Brioni. The defence lawyer in the case of 'economic crime' cited earlier called the local party committee to enquire whether the comrades thought his client should be punished. According to *Borba*, which deplored the lawyer's action, the committee told him it was not their business and they had no wish to be involved.[16] On the other hand, even before 1966 the defence could put up a strong fight. The court case over the novel *Canga* in 1963 showed the defence able to muster a formidable range of academic and literary experts to speak against banning the novel.[17]

It would seem likely that after Brioni defence lawyers not only enjoyed greater legal rights under the 1967 Amendments to the Code but greater freedom from political pressure. Nevertheless two cases, well reported in the Yugoslav press, both occurring in Mostar, indicated the kind of political trouble lawyers could run into if they stirred nationalist passions. A defence lawyer who claimed during the trial of a group of terrorists in 1968 that Serbs and Croats committing the same offence received different treatment from the courts was expelled from the party for his remarks, and another lawyer at the trial who made the same point was deprived of his right to practice by the Bar Association of Bosnia and Herzogovina.[18] Two years later nine defence lawyers in a case involving charges of Croatian nationalism were attacked by the President of the Republican Alliance for being part of a reactionary political plot and later censured for unprofessional activity by the Mostar branch of the Bar Association. The lawyers had asked for members of the security service to be excluded from the trial and challenged the composition and impartiality of the court, and were apparently proposing publication of a 'white book' on the trial, based on tape recordings and photographs they had taken in court. The political passions surrounding this case were obviously inflamed by the active interest taken by the Croatian press and radio, who were seen by Herzogovina officials to be casting a slur on the courts and other institutions in their republic.[19] Nevertheless these two cases do show that the party was prepared to bring pressure to bear on lawyers because of the way they conducted the defence, and also strongly suggested the subservience of the Bar Association to party wishes.

Against these examples implying limitation of the rights of the defence lawyer should be set the freedom to pursue the rights of the defence apparently allowed to Yugoslavia's main 'civil rights lawyer', Jovan Barović, who acted on behalf of Mihajlov and of Albanians demonstrating in the Macedonian town of Tetovo in 1968. Despite the fact that Barović himself had supported Djilas and had been harrassed up to 1964, when he was allowed to pass the bar examinations, he seems to have been free to conduct an uninhibited defence for his controversial political clients. While the main credit clearly belongs to Barović himself, who has continued to take up political cases most defence lawyers would hesitate to touch, the fact that the party did not try to curb his controversial legal career indicates some respect for legal forms. There was no attempt to intimidate defence lawyers by preferring legal charges against them until a well-publicized case in 1975.[20]

There was after 1966 publicly expressed concern to improve the professional qualifications of judges, and at the same time to ensure their judicial independence. Both issues were raised in connection with the election of new judges by the assemblies in February 1967. Just before the elections the President of the Supreme Court urged that those elected should be people: 'who will abide by the letter of the law in their work, stand firmly by their decisions, and reject interventions no matter which side they come from. . . .'[21]

How adequately judges lived up to these expectations is impossible to assess, but it is suggestive that Tito complained often and publicly in 1972 that judges had been too soft on political offenders, and attacked the idea of judicial independence. A campaign requiring the courts to act as instruments of 'class justice' began in Serbia in December 1971 with a hardline speech by the President of the Serbian Assembly and ended in December 1972 with members of the Serbian judiciary meeting to hear a member of the Serbian Constitutional Court condemn 'hesitation and liberalism within the system of justice'.[22] December 1972 also saw the announcement of a new law to strengthen the powers of the security service and reduce the rights of defence lawyers to make investigations on behalf of their clients in political cases.[23] The comparative degree of judicial independence which was allowed by the party and asserted by the courts themselves can be partially gauged by the 1972 measures to restore party control.

Notes

1. See speech by Vladimir Krivić, Slovene party Central Committee Plenum, reported by *Borba*, 1 October 1966.
2. *New York Times*, 4 June 1951.

3. See *RFE Research Report*, 20 February 1967, which refers back to 1951 Code.
4. *New York Times*, 27 February 1951.
5. *New York Times*, 4 March 1952.
6. Fritz W. Hondius, *The Yugoslav Community of Nations*, Mouton, The Hague, 1968, pp. 217-18.
7. *New Yugoslav Law*, March 1962. The amnesty also extended to the thousands of Yugoslavs who had belonged to various political groups opposed to the partisan liberation movement during the war and so covered about 130 000 émigrées.
8. *Borba*, 1 October 1966.
9. *RFE Research Report*, 20 February 1967.
10. *Komunist*, 4 March 1965.
11. *Borba*, 5 November 1965.
12. *Borba*, 26 June 1971.
13. *Politika*, 19 August 1971; *Borba*, 20 August 1971.
14. *Borba*, 3 January 1969.
15. *Večernje Novosti*, 12 October 1968.
16. *Borba*, 5 November 1965.
17. *Politika*, 17, 19, 21 and 27 December 1963.
18. *Borba*, 6 March 1968.
19. *Borba*, 30 September 1970; *Politika*, 10 October 1979. The case concerned a Professor Alilović, who had publicized the underprivileged position of Croatians in Bosnia and Herzogovina, implying this was due to Moslem domination. He was sentenced to 3 years' imprisonment for hostile propaganda and 'undermining the brotherhood and unity of the peoples of Yugoslavia'.
20. For a colourful summary of Barović's career and also for details of the 1975 case against defence lawyer Srdja Popović (which ended in his receiving a one-year suspended sentence) see Dusko Doder, *The Yugoslavs*, Allen and Unwin, London, 1978, pp. 162-9 and p. 161.
21. *RFE Research Report*, 20 February 1967.
22. *RFE Research Report*, 8 January 1973.
23. Ibid.

11   Freedom of the Press

No study of the League's interpretation of its role, and of the degree of liberalism achieved in society, would be complete without some analysis of the party's attitude to the press, and of how much freedom the media enjoyed in gathering and publishing information and in commenting on social and political issues. The press undoubtedly did have greater leeway during the latter part of the sixties, although by 1969 party leaders were expressing some concern about the use of that freedom and moves to curb it were introduced in the early seventies.

General consideration of the degree of party control over the official press leads naturally to questions about the scope of debate allowed to the unofficial literary, intellectual and student periodicals which flourished in the sixties, but quite often found themselves in trouble with either the party hierarchy or the courts. The problems the League experienced in setting limits to comment and criticism in these periodicals overlap with broader issues of cultural, intellectual and student dissent. These issues are only touched on here as they arise in relation to the press and other journals.

The Legal Position

The legal position of the Yugoslav press was defined in 1960 by a press law which abolished all advance censorship (except in case of war or mobilization) but did allow for prohibition of the distribution of papers. All publications had to be sent to the public prosecutor, who could order a temporary ban on distribution, but the ban then had to be upheld in the courts. The limits on press freedom were set out in the nine clauses of Article 52, which were the legal basis for invoking a ban on distribution.[1] The clauses included provisions against publication of military secrets and confidential government information. An important clause forbade material disturbing to friendly relations between Yugoslavia and other countries or slandering foreign governments, which in practice was invoked for criticism of the Soviet Union. Another provision which led to many prosecutions, and according to *NIN* led to a good deal of unnecessary trouble,[2] prohibited circulation of 'false, distorted, or alarming pieces of news or allegations'. The prosecutors also sometimes invoked the clause prohibiting 'grave injury to morals', despite the proliferation of soft pornography on Yugoslav bookstalls.

The frequency with which the press code was used to ban individual issues of papers may have depended partly on the attitudes of local prosecutors. *NIN*, commenting on the large number of temporary bans ordered in Belgrade in the period 1969–71, observed in a sarcastic aside that the public prosecutor had 'while trying to learn how to impose bans' denounced two Picasso drawings as pornography.[3] It is debatable how serious a sanction the banning order was to the unofficial press. As *NIN* noted, because of the administrative difficulties of confiscating all copies of a banned issue, the advertising value of a banning order often meant that the issue was sold out before the police could seize it. There was also a fairly good chance that the courts would support the periodical when the case was heard. In the space of 3 months in 1971 the Supreme Courts in Serbia and Croatia refused to uphold seven out of ten cases where the prosecutor had applied for a banning order,[4] and the fact that the republican courts were involved meant that local courts had already found against the prosecutor who had later decided to press his case. Nevertheless frequent banning of individual issues clearly did mean a journal was being harrassed by the authorities, and might be the prelude to closure.

Occasionally writers or editors faced the more serious hazard of being charged under the Criminal Code and sent to prison, as Mihajlo Mihajlov was. Zoran Gluščević, editor-in-chief of the literary journal *Kniževne Novine*, was almost imprisoned for a critical article on the anniversary of the Soviet invasion of Czechoslovakia.[5]

Party Methods of Control

Quite apart from legal penalties the League had at its disposal a number of methods of exercising control over journalists and writers. First it could of course demand party discipline from its own members. A survey of journalists showed that in 1965 about 65 per cent of the 3600 professional journalists in the Yugoslav Journalists' Association were in the League.[6] Where individuals stepped too far out of line they might be disciplined by their colleagues. The *Politika* basic party organization decided in March 1969 to expel one of its members, Dragoljub Golubović, who had sent a letter of complaint to the Ninth Congress, but had it published in the controversial paper *Student*, instead of confining himself to representations through the approved party channels, and had also been guilty of complaining that 'pressure is brought to bear on the press and reprisals are carried out against journalists which resemble absolutely the Stalinist epoch'. Golubović had been in trouble before for writing excessively critical articles 'with negative political consequences' soon after the 1966 Brioni Plenum. Nevertheless the communist journalists of *Politika* were not unanimous in their assessment of the gravity of his errors: fifty-seven voted for expulsion, nineteen voted for a party warning and three abstained.[7] *Politika* communists also took a severe line towards the editorial board of *NIN* on the issue of 'Yugoslavism'.[8] In both cases the *Politika* basic organization may have been responding to pressure from above – in some of the more notorious cases where editors were dismissed (see below) journalists were clearly under strong pressure from higher party bodies.

A second method of party pressure was to make public attacks against an individual writer or periodical. Attacks by individual party leaders were not always very serious and writers were willing to hit back at this form of intimidation. For example, when a Slovenian Central Committee member criticized a writer of humorous television serials at a Committee plenum the writer sent a letter to *Borba* complaining that his critic had no right to use a privileged position in a party forum when he had failed to object at the time to the director general of Ljubljana television.[9] If Tito himself singled out a writer or his work for criticism the results were likely to be more serious, and often led to a banning order or prosecution.[10] Sometimes there was a concerted attack by party bodies at a lower level. When the editorial boards of Serbian periodicals met in the town of Leskovac, the commune committee of the party after some delay decided to criticize the nature of the meeting. There was a follow-up in *Komunist* in the form of a strong attack on the meeting by the editor, who also deplored the 'belated reaction' of the Leskovac party committee.[11] Several of those present at the meeting responded in sharply worded letters to *Komunist*. Dobrica Ćosić, the well-known Serbian novelist, protested that the allegation made in *Komunist* that the Leskovac meeting was 'an obviously planned political diversion' was 'politically and morally despicable and untrue, and characteristic of the backward, bureaucratic and Stalinist method of squaring accounts with people who had different opinions . . . '.[12]

It is sometimes difficult when assessing the types of party pressure applied to journalists and writers to distinguish between official top level condemnation by the League and the pressure exercised by groups disposed to take a hardline on the limits of freedom in the press and culture. The League by no means always spoke with one voice (even within a particular republic) and, as we shall see when looking at party reactions to the 1968 student movement, hardliners were more entrenched in some committees than on others. The Belgrade City Committee for example could be relied on in this period to be tough with dissenters. It was the Belgrade Committee that called on communists in the satirical paper *Jez* to discipline the editorial board in connection with an offending article on Skoplje.[13]

When the case was judged to be really serious there was of course concerted party activity, initiated at the highest levels and implemented by the relevant basic organization, as in the case of the *Tanjug* editor-in-chief, who was forced to resign in June 1969 for allowing publication of critical comments on the international consultation of communist parties in Moscow.[14] The Serbian literary journal *Kniževne Novine* was the target of this treatment not only in 1969 on the Czechoslovak issue, but for less clear-cut political reasons early in 1968. The editors were suspect by 1968 for their political commentaries critical of the political and economic reforms − *Kniževne Novine* took a somewhat similar line to *Praxis* − and for their comments on the Croatian Language Declaration of 1967. But their crowning sin was to print a letter from a Zagreb political scientist stating that Serbs in Croatia were in a subordinate position and criticizing LCY Central Committee member Kiro Hadživasilev for creating confusion on this issue.[15] Hadživasilev reacted angrily and the repercussions for *Kniževne Novine* illustrated why attacks on party leaders were normally regarded as taboo. The campaign against *Kniževne Novine* was waged with vigour by the Belgrade City Committee, who met several times on the issue and noted with satisfaction that nearly 200 party organizations had duly convened to pass judgement.[16] The journal published an outspoken defence of its record, arguing that it was only carrying out the process of enquiry and criticism initiated at Brioni to promote the struggle against old-style relations in all walks of life, especially in the League itself. *Kniževne Novine* quoted Crvenkovski, who had said in a recent interview that no theme should be excluded from debate, and that although in the past criticism of individuals had presaged punitive action, there was now 'nobody, no individual including the most prominent functionaries, who should not be criticised'. They had expected Kiro Hadživasilev to react by writing to them, or to some other paper, or even by filing a suit in court. But, *Kniževne Novine* continued bitterly, they had not expected that he would shield behind and be shielded by the Executive Committee of

the LCY.[17] At the culmination of the campaign against *Kniževne Novine*
party sanctions were invoked, the Belgrade Radio organization expelled
one member of the editorial board, and communists in *Jez* met to take
action against the *Kniževne Novine* editor-in-chief and another editor, but
refused to do more than pronounce warnings against them both. The
Stari Grad Commune Committee overrode the basic party organization
and insisted on expulsion, a decision later upheld by the Serbian Control
Commission.[18]

The effectiveness of both legal and political methods of control in
deterring the press from adopting a critical stance or from independent
reporting and comment depended in part on the attitudes of journalists
and editors. In assessing the success of papers and periodicals in resisting
pressures towards conformity it is useful to distinguish between the
official and unofficial press.

The Official Press

The major daily, evening and weekly newspapers represent the 'official'
press in Yugoslavia, as opposed to the much more independent literary,
intellectual and youth journals; but the official press did enjoy some
degree of autonomy in institutional terms and this relative autonomy was
sometimes reflected in their contents, so this press is in a different category
from the specific party organs *Komunist* and *Socijalizam*. The most
'official' of the daily papers is *Borba*, formally owned by the federal
Socialist Alliance, which circulates throughout the country. The other
all-Yugoslav paper is the much livelier *Politika*, although as it is Belgrade
based it may be regarded as primarily a Serbian newspaper, and was seen
in those terms during the inter-republican disputes of the period 1967–71.
The *Politika* chain includes the weekly news magazine *Nedejne Informativne
Novine* (*NIN*) which was sometimes criticized for its critical stand. The
editors of both *Politika* and *NIN* were sacked in the 1972 purge of liberals
in Serbia. Croatia has seven dailies, of which the most important is *Vjesnik*,
which has the largest circulation and is officially the organ of the Croatian
Socialist Alliance.[19] The *Vjesnik* enterprise also issues an evening paper
and the important news and cultural weekly paper *Vjesnik U Srijedu*
(*VUS*). *Vjesnik* and *VUS* have in practice been closely linked with the
Croatian party leadership and the editors of both fell at the time of the
purge in Croatia. Every republic except Montenegro has its own daily
newspapers and the provinces of Vojvodina and Kosovo also have Hungarian
and Albanian language papers.[20] The readership of the daily papers, even

in the more developed republics, is (as noted in Chapter 2) quite small, so the republican radio and television stations are an important source of news.

There were relatively strict party controls over the staffing of the official newspapers until the early 1960s, when the appointment of directors and editors was assigned to the workers' councils. This does not necessarily mean there was no party influence on subsequent appointments, but Gertrude Joch Robinson notes that *Borba* and *Vjesnik* both appointed directors who were professional journalists in the 1960s in place of the previous party professional politicians.[21] The papers also acquired greater financial independence, acquiring control over 70 per cent of their profits as other enterprises did through economic reforms.

As a result of these changes, and probably due even more to the general change in the political climate, the official press was given more scope in its news gathering and its commentaries after 1966. Stipe Šuvar had condemned the press in the Ranković era for being 'very conformist, sycophantic, faceless and apologetic'.[22] By January 1967 a symposium on the media was calling for changes in the press law, which 'lagged behind' constitutional norms, and *Politika* urged that the press should be freed from all controls.[23]

How far the press made use of its comparative autonomy is open to debate. Two surveys of those working in the media suggest that journalists were rather timid in testing the limits of freedom to report and comment. A study by Allan Barton contrasted the views of 101 professional communicators with other élites and found that the media men were less willing to call for more press criticism not only than intellectuals but also than party and trade union officials. As Barton suggests, this finding may be partly explained by unwillingness to criticize their own past performance, though the media group also seemed to be less willing to sanction attacks on public personalities. The second survey was carried out by the Yugoslav Journalists' Association in 1969, and discovered that some of the respondents hesitated to write critical articles, whilst others had experienced suppression of critical articles or other harassment. The sample of those answering was much too small to be representative, only 139 out of 4206 circularized, but did indicate the political difficulties of journalistic independence.[24] Further interesting evidence is provided by a *Politika* commentator, who noted in an article on the press that there was a sporadic tendency to impose controls on the spread of information, and that although the methods of bans and censorship were rarely used, there were 'less conspicuous' methods, for instance stigmatizing the publication of a piece of information as 'malicious', and due to a desire to dramatize events and to disturb relations between cities or areas. The writer also complained about the pressure to publish reports by 'our leading functionaries' on the pretext of giving the reader 'the best information as to what is going on in our country'.[25]

Selective reading of the official press in the late sixties suggests that the papers did often echo official standpoints: for example *Politika* attacked *NIN* for an article on the contentious issue of 'Yugoslavism' and attacked *Kniževne Novine* for its article, which was banned, on the anniversary of the invasion of Czechoslovakia.[26] The press naturally tended to give prominence and support to party meetings and policy documents, and papers usually abstained from criticizing party or government officials by name, though they might do so indirectly.[27] One exception to this rule was a polemical exchange between Svetozar Vukmanović Tempo and *Ekonomska Politika* after Tempo had attacked the paper on television. *Ekonomska Politika* listed 'the brief story of our misunderstandings with the President of the Yugoslav Trade Union Federation' and went on to discuss the policy differences between them: the case for autonomy of enterprises and rights of managers, against the predominant rights of workers and the right of political organizations to intervene on their behalf.[28] *Ekonomska Politika* may have felt emboldened as the spokesman for managerial interests to oppose the trade union boss who had his opponents in the party.[29]

If the press did often play safe, nevertheless there was also evidence that it was prepared to criticize, and to report freely. There were numerous reports of economic shortcomings and cases of corruption, but these may be regarded as coming within the scope of permitted journalism, and as evidence of the openness of the party about the shortcomings of Yugoslav society, rather than the crusading zeal of the press to assert its autonomy. But some press frankness may have been less welcome, for example the airing of election tangles and the sometimes caustic comments on the election policy of the party already quoted in Chapter 8. It is also worth noting *Borba*'s commentary on the affair of the Tanjug criticism of the Moscow meeting of world communist parties. The paper observed that the official repudiation of Tanjug's position by the League should not cause surprise, as the habit of regarding press commentaries as expressions of the official position was a legacy from the past. This statement might be read as a reiteration of an orthodox line, which had been adopted by the Socialist Alliance in 1966, were it not for the timing (communists in Tanjug were busily pressurizing the editor-in-chief to resign for his error in political judgement) and for *Borba*'s own references to 'an unpleasant legacy' of a practice 'unfortunately still with us', and its assertion of the need for political independence of the press in Yugoslavia tempered 'of course by due political and social responsibility'.[30]

One indication of the relative independence of the press is that there was obviously pressure to tighten up controls by the Socialist Alliance and the League over the main newspapers. An important debate about relations between *Borba* and the Alliance took place in January 1968. *VUS* commented on the stormy session of the Alliance Presidium, which threw out prepared draft decisions advocating formal Alliance appointment of editorial staff of *Borba*. *VUS* noted the decision of the Presidium with approval, and suggested the importance of establishing 'new links' between the press and party now that the old system of the press being an 'instrument of transmission' had ended. The League Presidium devoted half its agenda to problems of the media in November 1969, and speakers urged the need for communists and the Alliance to be more vigilant in this sphere. The Presidium did not, however, endorse some of the more restrictive proposals in the Executive Bureau Draft (the formation of political bodies in federal and republican secretariats of information), and these proposals were apparently edited out of the text before it was published 10 days later. Savka Dabčević-Kučar and Slavko Milosavlevski had both raised objections in the meeting.[31] The party seemed to be more sensitive to criticism in the aftermath of the June 1968 demonstrations and the Soviet occupation of Czechoslovakia. The Presidium debate had been intended to usher in a new press law, but in the event this was delayed until early in 1972 when the government attempted to rush it through. The media resistance to the new bill indicates that journalists were prepared to assert a degree of independence; they protested publicly against the more stringent controls included in the draft law, and the President of the Serbian Journalists' Association attacked the tendency of the League, after Karadjordjevo, to make the press scapegoats.

Dissenting Periodicals

One of the best indices of the extent and limits of dissent is the chequered career of the various intellectual periodicals which flourished in the 1960s in Yugoslavia. There was in law almost total freedom for any group of five or more individuals to found a paper or journal, provided the promoters registered officially with the authorities. Overt flaunting of the limits tacitly set by the party — like Mihajlov's gesture in 1966 of trying to start an opposition journal advocating a multi-party system — could land those responsible in serious trouble, and established journals like *Perspektive* could go too far and be totally suppressed. But many journals survived for years to wage continuing battles with the public prosecutor and the party leaders without bringing down on themselves either the closure of the journal or the gaoling of the editors. The best known of these periodicals in the West is *Praxis*, which survived intermittent harrassment until the spring of 1975, when the party closed down the journal by the indirect means of ensuring that the printers' union would refuse to handle it.

Praxis, which was founded in 1964 during the movement towards liberalization, represented the limits of what was tolerable even to the liberal section of the League. It was frequently under fire from party spokesmen, including top Croatian officials and Tito himself.[32] It was also the target of a concerted party campaign in 1966. *Komunist* wrote critically about the award of a cultural prize to two *Praxis* staff members and observed that *Praxis* had been criticized by a city conference of Zagreb communists, in the Executive Committee and Central Committee of the Croatian League and at the Third Plenum of the LCY Central Committee; as a result of the controversy over the prize it had in addition been attacked in the Republican Chamber of the Croatian Assembly.[33] *Praxis* had to suspend publication in 1966, partly because of an internal editorial conflict, but no issue was actually banned until 1971, and then the Supreme Court refused to uphold the ban.[34] *Praxis* provoked stronger reactions than independent academic journals like *Naše Teme*, which ran a wide range of interesting academic surveys and political commentaries, or even the more explicitly oppositional *Gledišta*, despite the fact that *Gledišta* published in 1966 a much quoted, if tentative, proposal for a multi-party system in an article by Stevan Vračar.[35] One reason for the alarm *Praxis* aroused in party officials was perhaps, as Gerson Sher suggests in his study of the journal, that in contrast to the more eclectic *Naše Teme* the editors of *Praxis* promoted a specific ideological outlook of Marxist humanism.[36] It also became a symbol of the dissenting 'humanist intelligentsia'. *Praxis* devoted a good deal of space in its pages to discussing problems of method and content in Marxism, promoting the conception of Marxism as a radical and humanist approach to understanding the social world, and stressing the young Marx and the theory of alienation as against mechanistic versions of dialectical materialism. While these philosophical speculations aroused some distaste in official party ideologists, the real threat was posed by the practical political implications of these philosophical views: the *Praxis* critique of bureaucracy and of the authoritarian role of the party, which went further than the liberal leaders wished — for example in calls for 'minority rights' within the party, and the egalitarian critique of the inegalitarian results of the market economy.

Given these cogent reaons for disliking *Praxis*, it is worth asking why in fact the party limited itself until 1975 to criticism and financial pressure by removing subsidies. It is surprising, not that official subsidies were sometimes withheld, but that they were ever given. When, during the Croatian Assembly debate, one speaker demanded 'who subsidises this rag?', Bakarić replied, in the course of his own highly critical speech, that 'we have been and are subsidising *Praxis*'.[37] One possible reason for this comparative tolerance of *Praxis* is, as Rusinow suggests, that many of the party liberals were genuinely sincere in their espousal of greater freedom of criticism and were prepared to allow a journal which operated broadly within an acceptable ideological context. This may have been particularly true in 1966-7, when – despite a tendency to 'balance' the attack on Ranković ism by criticizing its opposite and to draw the limits of liberal reform – there was a heady atmosphere of free and experimental debate. After mid-1968 as various economic and political difficulties closed in on the liberal leadership they became less tolerant of 'elitist' intellectuals, new-left platforms and 'anarcho-liberalism', and the *Praxis* board began to diverge more sharply from official party liberalism. Nevertheless it appears that the Serbian party leaders refused to countenance severe sanctions against the Belgrade *Praxis* members, who were in a vulnerable position after the June 1968 student protests, for which they were held partly responsible, and after personal attacks by Tito. A number of factors operated in favour of *Praxis*, including a fair degree of editorial caution in the period 1968-9, the relative eminence of the international board of editors of the selective international edition and international standing of Yugoslav *Praxis* editors, and the fact that more serious enemies were threatening the relevant republican party leaders in Serbia and Croatia. One of the strengths of *Praxis* was that, during the period of growing republican nationalism, it was opposed to these developments and could therefore be seen as an ally against Serbian chauvinism and Croatian nationalism. The 1971 ban had in fact been prompted partly by *Praxis* taking a firm stand against rising nationalism. After the 1971 crisis Stipe Šuvar, the new president of the Croatian party Ideological Commission, explicitly told the Commission that *Praxis* and the Korčula summer school (founded in 1963 and associated with *Praxis* members and their intellectual concerns) should continue to be financed.[38] Šuvar's position undoubtedly reflected in part his own academic and political liberalism, he had been a contributor to *Praxis*; but it must also have reflected the search for allies by the new Croatian party leadership in the aftermath of the purge of the party and intellectual community affected by nationalism. The fact that *Praxis* editors were based on both Zagreb and Belgrade also made it more difficult for republican parties facing different political problems to co-ordinate action against the journal as *Praxis* editor Mihajlo Marković argues in his account of the *Praxis* affair.[39]

The genuine freedom which existed for groups to found their own papers in the 1960s and the tendency to dissent were both well illustrated by the youth and student press which flourished in this period. *NIN* devoted an article to the 'extraordinary phenomenon' of the youth press, and calculated (in the absence of any official figures) that sixty-eight different youth papers appeared during 1969, published variously by commune, city or republican organs of the Youth Federation, by youth centres and secondary schools, and by student bodies. While some were very localized school journals others were nationally known.[40] Most which achieved public recognition or notoriety were student papers, but the Belgrade-based *Susret* was an organ of the City Youth Federation, whose committee sharply attacked the contents of *Susret* in May 1969, and decided a year later that the paper should be regarded as the mouth-piece of its editors, not of the organization.[41] *Susret* had very actively defended the June 1968 student protests and programme.[42] The Slovenian Youth Federation Presidium passed a rather similar motion of dissociation from its journal *Problemi*, arguing that it had no control or responsibility for its contents and that the formal ownership by the Federation of the journal was anachronistic.[43]

A number of student papers became the target of party attacks, legal bans, and in some cases of moves by the Student Union to dissolve the editorial board. The best known was the Belgrade University paper *Student*, which became central to the June 1968 demonstrations and remained a focus for student dissent for the subsequent 3 years. At the end of 1969 *Student* came under sustained fire from the University Committee of the League, and after internal dissent and interrupted meetings the Student Union in the University finally implemented the Committee's call for the dissolution of the editorial board. The University League Committee drew up an eight-point indictment of *Student*, which condemned it for showing too little interest in student affairs, for failure to support the Committee's policy and for exaggerated criticism. The more substantial political indict-ment concerned *Student*'s 'demagogic' attacks on social inequalities, its inciting of factional activity and its support for the party branch (then disbanded) in the Philosophical Faculty.[44] *Student* continued to run into trouble, however; ironically, it was banned in August 1971 for an article complaining about the banning of reviews, papers and films. The legal charge was for issuing 'false, alarming and distorted statements'. The Belgrade Student Union complained that two bans on *Student*, one on

Stradija and one on *Vidik* had cost them a lot of money, and that the political effect of successive bans on student papers was dangerous and tended to limit information within the student organization. The Union therefore planned to campaign to amend the Press Law.[45] By the end of the year the Student Union had nevertheless withdrawn its support from *Student*, which was permanently banned at the end of November for a letter from a Dutch anarchist to Tito and a cover picture about his visit to Iran which were regarded as insulting. The Student Union dissociated itself from this issue.[46]

Other student papers ran into almost as many difficulties with the party, university and legal authorities. The Zagreb Student Centre literary review *Razlog* shared with *Praxis* the honour of being singled out for condemnation by the Zagreb party City Conference in 1968 and was banned at the same time, though the Zagreb Court refused to confirm the ban.[47] The prosecutor claimed that certain articles denied that the League was still a leading social force and encouraged unconstitutional action to achieve illegitimate goals, while the defence successfully urged that the paper was trying to analyse trends among students in Europe and not to attack self-management or the role of the party. Despite their legal victory the editors of *Razlog* were in due course penalized by the party. The basic organization in the Student Centre met in October in the presence of the President of the Zagreb City Ideological Commission and voted by forty to nine (with two abstentions) to expel the editor-in-chief and a member of the editorial board.[48]

Amongst the student papers which ran into trouble was the Sarajevo paper *Naši Dani*, which published an article entitled 'Comrade Boss' in the spring of 1969 claiming that the working class was exploited. The public prosecutor banned the article, which went to trial in the regional court that confirmed the ban. The University Committee of the League condemned the paper and called for party organizations to take action against the editors, while the Presidium of the republican Student Union decided to dissolve the editorial board and council.[49]

The Vojvodina student paper, *Indeks* aroused a similar storm in mid-1970 when the prosecutor banned an issue on the grounds that it slandered the Montenegrin government in connection with the building of the Njegoš Mausoleum. The University party Committee moved in and criticized other articles in the same issue fiercely. But the Student Union in this instance refused to align itself with the University Committee. On the contrary the Executive Committee of the Vojvodina Student Union stated their support for *Indeks*, said the position of the party Committee was 'unacceptable' and that its claim that *Indeks* had become a stronghold of destructive forces was 'sheer nonsense' and not worth discussing. A meeting between the University Committee and the Student Union Executive failed to budge the latter. The youth paper *Mladost*, which complained that 'our obliging information media' had fully publicized the condemnation by the University Committee but had failed to publish the response from the Student Union, retailed these events with gusto.[50] *Indeks* also received some surprising indirect support in the columns of *Komunist*, where a contributor castigated the habit of issuing general denunciations unsupported by facts or arguments, suggested the League had done this in the case of *Indeks*, and concluded: 'Perhaps those who have found incriminating views in the pages of *Indeks* are right; but they are not at all convincing in their public accusations.'[51]

Party pressure against *Indeks* was maintained, however, and ultimately successful. Mirko Čanadanović, provincial party President, lent his authority to the attack on the paper at a meeting of the University League Conference in November 1970, and in December the editorial board was finally dismissed and some members expelled from the party.[52] The Student Union leaders apparently carried on a rearguard action, however, since in March 1971 the President of the Vojvodina Union resigned over criticism in the paper of the Student Union Plenum, and *Politika* commented that the student leaders who had backed the previous editorial board of *Indeks* seemed unwilling to support the new one.[53]

Despite the punitive action encouraged by party officials and committees against the more outspoken student periodicals, not all party leaders were convinced of the desirability of resorting to such measures. When Marko Nikezić was interviewed in Niš in 1969 and asked what he thought of the student press, he replied that he did not have much faith in the methods of replacing editorial boards and banning papers, which showed that the party had not been able to settle matters by political methods. He did urge the need for editorial boards to be more aware of the limits of social tolerance, but continued that the right measures to delimit what was acceptable could not be prescribed 'even by youth committees, and least of all by the Central Committee. The right measures should be found by the readers and the editorial boards.'[54] Nikezić was in effect urging a degree of self-censorship to avoid heavy handed party or legal repression.

Conclusion

If one looks at the pattern of press cases which aroused the greatest ire in party circles it is possible to see where the League generally drew the line in allowing public comment and criticism. The picture which emerges is consistent with the broader evidence concerning political offences which warranted penal or political sanctions. There were three clearly dangerous and highly sensitive areas where frank comment was usually taboo. The first, ironically enough in view of the Yugoslav party's celebrated independence from Moscow, was criticism of Soviet domestic or foreign policies. Two of Djilas' prison sentences and Mihajlov's first brush with the authorities were due to such criticism, and the troubles encountered by the editors of Tanjug and *Kniževne Novine* for commenting on the invasion of Czechoslovakia were recounted earlier in this chapter. Attacking the Soviet Union was not of course always taboo, but in the oscillating diplomatic relationship between Belgrade and Moscow it required a cautious sense of political timing. The second danger zone arose naturally out of Yugoslavia's troubled history of national conflicts and legacy of mutual distrust and hatred. A number of novels and journals were banned on the grounds that they promoted reactionary forms of nationalism or insulted the national sentiments of some section of the Yugoslav population. Censorship on these grounds was understandable, but clearly could be, and sometimes was, used as well to suppress all searching and uncomfortable social comment touching on nationalist issues. The third subject which was proscribed was open or provocative advocacy of a multi-party system, as the Djilas and Mihajlov cases and the banning of *Perspektive* demonstrated. It is arguable that this proscription arises naturally from the logic of a one-party state, and raises the clearest questions about the necessary limits of free speech and publication in a one-party system. In this connection it is important to note that not only the subject matter but the political context influenced the strength of party reaction: who advocated the need for multiple parties, how and when were material to the gravity of the offence. Both Djilas and Mihajlov were established as controversial and dissident figures, and the *Perspektive* affair occurred during the struggle for reform before the battle against Ranković had been won.

There were two lesser political offences which were unlikely to lead to penal action in the courts but could and did provoke the righteous wrath of the party. One was to draw attention to the illiberalism of the Yugoslav authorities or to suggest that Stalinist attitudes persisted within the League. The much publicized meeting of Belgrade philosophers in November 1969 to protest about a spate of bannings prompted denunciations in the columns of *Borba* and *Politika*, the former entitled 'Where is Zhdanovism?'[55] *Praxis* was also condemned for finding Stalinism to be alive and well and inhabiting the Yugoslav League. The second type of offence was of course to criticize the principles of the programme of economic reform, one of the key issues which divided the 'true reformers' from the unreconstructed conservatives, or to imply the working class in Yugoslavia was exploited. *Praxis* and various student journals brought themselves into disfavour on these issues.

The final offence which prompted summary retribution was that of *lèse-majesté*: criticism of Tito himself was completely taboo; criticism of other high-ranking political functionaries was not sacrilegious, but as the *Kniževne Novine* affair in 1968 illustrated it was risky. If freedom to criticize powerful political figures is seen as one touchstone of a free press and a liberal society, then Yugoslavia fell far short of both. But as the account of the unofficial and even at times the official press suggests, journalists and writers often did show considerable independence of mind and the party leaders were far from united in the desire to impose timid conformity.

Notes

1. For the 1960 Press Law see *Yugoslav Survey*, October 1960.
2. *NIN*, 26 September 1971.
3. Ibid.
4. Gertrude Joch Robinson, *Tito's Maverick Media*, University of Illinois Press, Urbana, 1977, p. 62.
5. *Kniževne Novine*, 13 September 1969; *Borba*, 30 September 1969.
6. *Komunist*, 4 November 1965.
7. Full details of resolution published in *Student*, 15 April 1969.
8. *Politika*, 15 September 1969.
9. *Borba*, 8 October 1966.
10. Note Tito's intervention in the Mihajlov case in 1965 and against the play *When the Pumpkins were Blooming* banned in 1969.
11. *Komunist*, 1 February 1968.
12. *Komunist*, 29 February 1968.
13. *Borba*, 15 April 1969.
14. See *Komunist*, 12 June 1969; *Borba*, 25 June 1969.
15. *Politika*, 10 December 1967.
16. *Borba*, 9 January 1968, 21 February 1968.
17. *Kniževne Novine*, 23 December 1967.
18. *Borba*, 21 February 1968; *Politika Ekspres*, 19 October 1968.
19. See *Borba*, 22 April 1970.
20. For details of the press see Robinson op. cit. and *Komunist*, 4 November 1965.
21. Robinson op. cit. p. 45.
22. *Naše Teme*, November 1965.
23. *Politika*, 12 January 1967; *Komunist*, 19 January 1967.
24. Sources for both surveys Robinson op. cit. pp. 125-7.
25. *Politika*, 6 June 1971.
26. *Politika*, 6 September 1969; *Kniževne Novine*, 13 September 1969.
27. See Robinson op. cit. p. 122.
28. *Ekonomska Politika*, 12 November 1966.
29. Tempo comments in his memoirs that he was not surprised by the reaction of *Ekonomska Politika* because he knew it supported managerial autonomy.

(Svetozar Vukmanović Tempo, *Revolucija Koja Teče, Memoari*, Komunist, Beograd, 1971, p. 496.)

30. *Borba*, 10 June 1969.
31. *Borba*, 18 November 1969; *Radio Free Europe Research Report*, 4 December 1969.
32. Gerson S. Sher, Praxis: *Marxist Criticism and Dissent in Socialist Yugoslavia*, Indiana University Press, Bloomington, 1977, p. 315 on 1966 attack and p. 213 on 1968 attack.
33. *Komunist*, 30 June 1966.
34. Sher op. cit. p. 216.
35. Stevan Vračar, 'Partijski monopolizam i politički moć drustvenih grupa', *Gledišta*, August-September, 1967.
36. Sher op. cit. p. 37.
37. Ibid. p. 207. See also Dennison Rusinow, *The Yugoslav Experiment 1948-1974*, Royal Institute of International Affairs, London, 1977, p. 219.
38. Sher op. cit. p. 221.
39. M. Marković and R. S. Cohen, *The Rise and Fall of Socialist Humanism*, Spokesman Books, Nottingham, 1975, p. 28.
40. *NIN*, 17 May 1970.
41. *Komunist*, 22 May 1969; *Borba*, 7 March 1970.
42. *Politika Ekspres*, 20 October 1968 attacked *Susret* jointly with *Student*. *Susret*, April 1969, carried a sarcastic comment on 'How one should write about the June events'.
43. *Politika*, 26 May 1969.
44. *Borba*, 27 November 1969, 26 December 1969; *Politika*, 11 January 1970.
45. *Borba*, 26 and 28 August 1971.
46. *Borba*, 3 and 25 November 1971, 19 December 1971.
47. *Politika*, 9 and 10 July 1968.
48. *Borba*, 10 October 1968.
49. *Borba*, 18, 19 and 20 April 1969; *Politika*, 12 April 1969.
50. *Mladost*, 18-25 June 1970.
51. *Komunist*, 4 June 1970.
52. *Borba*, 26 November 1970, 22 December 1970.
53. *Politika*, 4 March 1971.
54. *Politika*, 15 May 1969.
55. *Politika*, 28-30 November 1969; *Borba*, 5 December 1969.

12   The Party and Political Dissent

Previous chapters have explored how far the League was prepared to allow autonomy to interest group organizations, and what limits it set to public criticism and political comment. It is now necessary to consider what attitudes the party adopted towards the active expression of dissent in popular demonstrations and strikes or in political movements outside party control.

Yugoslav citizens did not enjoy a definite right to demonstrate — this was indeed one of the demands made by the Belgrade students in June 1968. In practice certain local protests against maladministration seem to have been tolerated. The local authorities effectively gave in to demonstrators' demands, for example, when the citizens of Gruda besieged the town hall to complain about the electoral results. On the other hand, the party naturally tended to react sharply when political attitudes, whose expression in print was effectively banned, found more tumultuous expression in the streets. Nationalist demonstrations in Slovenia over the failure to allocate World Bank funds for road building in the republic were treated as a major crisis by the League, and widespread Albanian nationalist demonstrations and riots in Kosovo in 1968 were met with legal reprisals. The Albanian eruption did involve acts of violence and a genuine disturbance of public order, as well as promoting inter-communal hatreds which had led to Serbs and Montenegrins being forced by harassment to leave their homes in Kosovo. In addition the Yugoslav authorities were alarmed by the political demands associated with the protests, which had been timed to take place on Albania's national day and which implied secessionist aspirations. Desire to be united with Albania probably remained a minority movement, but Albanian demands for full republican status, thus denying Serbian rights to the historic and symbolic land of medieval Serbia, were almost equally unacceptable in terms in internal Yugoslav politics.

This chapter examines two types of protest which posed a political challenge to the party in the way purely localized demonstrations did not, but which also came within the sphere of potentially legitimate political action: strikes by workers and demonstrations by students. The third and most important case study of the attitude of the party to dissent is provided by the Croatian nationalist movement in the period 1970-1. Given the history of Croatian nationalism in the Second World War, and given the growing evidence during 1971 of discrimination against the Serbian minority in Croatia and of demands for Croatian separatism, logically the Croatian movement might appear to fall into the same taboo category as Albanian nationalism. In practice it did not (until December 1971) because the Croatian party was itself pursuing nationalist economic goals and extended tolerance and in effect a degree of protection to the movement. Moreover, the Croatian movement concentrated on political organization and mobilization and eschewed the direct challenge of public demonstrations until the student strike in November 1971, which the students (wrongly) hoped would inspire a general strike in Croatia, and which in fact prompted Tito's intervention to curb the movement.

Worker Dissent

The League's attitude to rank and file workers dissent as manifested by strikes was much more sympathetic than it was to intellectual criticism or to student dissent. Nevertheless the party leaders found themselves somewhat puzzled and divided over whether strikes were legitimate in a country where the party officially represented workers' interests and where in addition the workers had been given the right of self-management.

The first strike took place in January 1958 at Trbovlje, involving all the employees at the coal mines, and supported by a sympathy strike in a nearby town. After that 'work stoppages', often on a smaller scale than Trbovlje, became a fairly common method for workers to express their frustration, and 1657 strikes took place between January 1958 and September 1969.[1]

The main reason for going on strike was discontent with the level of wages and the principles for deciding on distribution of income within the enterprise. A *Borba* article on work stoppages between 1964 and 1966 found that out of 231 stoppages in 1965, 165 were due to 'incorrect distribution of personal incomes', sometimes because funds had been siphoned off from one plant to another. A factory spokesman observed that the main problem was that workers' incomes depended directly on the results of their work and the success of the enterprise, whereas the incomes of the administrative staff were fixed and not dependent on enterprise performance.[2] The second cause of strikes was resentment among workers at lack of information and at the arbitrary behaviour of leading officials in the enterprise. One reason for the comparative frequency of stoppages was that workers in enterprises who had resorted to this method once, and found it led to effective action to remedy their grievances, turned to it again. A post-mortem by the party organization in the Rakovica car factory, after a strike by 500 workers in 1969, revealed that it was the twelfth stoppage in the enterprise.[3]

The majority of strikes were purely token. A survey of stoppages between 1958 and 1963 showed that 175 lasted under 3 hours, 106 lasted 2-6 hours. 111 were 1-day stoppages and only 23 continued for 4 days or more. A later survey of strikes in Serbia between 1964 and 1967 found that over 60 per cent took place within the workplace and did not involve a walk out or demonstrations in the streets.[4] By 1969 the position appeared to be rather more serious from the standpoint of the League. The number of strikes each year had not increased but the numbers involved in strikes had. Of greater political significance was the fact that whereas the earlier strikes were unorganized, and this fact was cited as one reason for their brief duration, there was by 1969 a tendency for unofficial strike committees to spring up. There was also a tendency for the strike to be directed not against the management inside enterprises but against the political authorities, and for workers to demonstrate their grievances in the streets.[5] All these factors suggested a dangerous politicization of what had been localized expressions of economic grievances. In addition the workers' anger quite often spilled over into minor violence. Crvenkovski, despite his opposition to making strikes illegal, commented in 1969 on the 'anarchism, anarcho-syndicalism' and 'forms of violence' manifested in recent strikes and on the 'inimical elements' who had been involved in some strikes.[6] The Rijeka dock strike which took place in June 1969 illustrated the tendencies towards unofficial organization and violent demonstrations. The strike began on 1 June when 300 workers walked out in protest against measures which would mean a cut in wages. Very shortly 1500 out of a total work force of 4600 joined the strike. There was a demonstration outside the head offices of the docks, and workers broke into the building and assaulted top managerial and political officials. An unofficial strike committee was formed and met with trade union officials. After further negotiations with political officials in Rijeka and elaboration of the workers' demands, a meeting of 3000 agreed to end the strike and expressed regret for the use of violence. Later seven strikers were arrested for assault.[7]

The fact that workers did often air their grievances by going on strike, even if briefly, was a curious anomaly in a system of self-management which ostensibly gave workers a decisive voice in running their enterprises and deciding their own wages. Party officials tended to argue that the fact stoppages took place must be seen as an indication of a failure to achieve proper self-management. This analysis provided a plausible explanation of how workers could come to 'strike against themselves' and at the same time pointed to the approved long-term solution — realization of self-management. It also implied a general tolerance of work stoppages. This formula did not, however, give specific guidance on how strikers, and in particular communists who joined in strikes, should be treated. The official line propagated in 1964 and afterwards was that although strikes were not strictly legal, they were not specifically illegal, which implied that they should not be met with legal sanctions.

In practice there seems to have been some divergence between the attitudes of top party leaders and local party committees. A tolerant view of strikes was indicated by Bakarić answering a question on this issue. He observed that if a strike occurred it was a sign that the party should investigate what was wrong, since strikes should not really take place. 'It is abnormal, although I do not condemn strikes.'[8] *Komunist* carried a brief article on work stoppages which noted that this method was strictly 'anachronistic', but sometimes the only way of getting swift action from management and political bodies.[9] Some local parties did apparently apply sanctions against communists who took part in stoppages. The Vojvodina Control Commission commented unfavourably on the tendency to punish workers for their action, whilst professional staff who were often responsible for provoking stoppages got off scot-free. The Commission added that communists who fought for the statutory rights of workers should not be blamed.[10]

The extent of worker dissatisfaction by 1969, which had been demonstrated at the June 1968 Congress, and the political evolution of strikes, meant that they had to be treated as an important factor. The federal and republican organs of the League debated the problem during 1969, and it appeared there was an important division of opinion on the best way to respond to strikes. The Executive Committee of the Croatian party noted that two diametrically opposed views had been voiced: that stoppages should be made legal, and that they should be banned. The Committee sidestepped this issue by urging that everything should be done to prevent stoppages taking place.[11] Miko Tripalo said at a LCY Presidium meeting in November that the dilemma over whether to legalize strikes was 'senseless' since strikes were a 'realistic reflection' of the stage reached in self-management and of the maturity of the working class. Strikes were not the best method of settling disputes, however, and the only reasonable conclusion was 'that it is necessary to create a mechanism which would eradicate the causes of strikes'. The Trade Union President speaking at the same meeting commented that recent debate about work stoppages had created unnecessary alarm: 'for both the number of stoppages and of those taking part have indeed been small so far'. He also denied that the unions were obliged to take up an attitude for or against strikes in the abstract, but said that many stoppages were justified and had been a way of resisting bureaucratic arbitrariness. He also claimed that 'all the analyses so far show that stoppages of work in our country do not have an anti-socialist character, with certain exceptions when a hostile activity is subsequently introduced'.[12] The LCY Presidium reverted to the problem of strikes in December 1969, and recommended that if a strike did occur, then the trade union in the enterprise should take the initiative to settle it, and if necessary resort to use of a referendum or outside arbitration. Where an enterprise failed to resolve a dispute the commune assembly should intervene.[13]

Some party officials were prepared to suggest publicly that strikes should be legalized while at the same time the law should set limits to permissible forms of behaviour by strikers. Neda Krmpotić from Croatia suggested that strikes should be made legal on condition that there was no violence and 'no diminishing of the value of social property'.[14] The idea of legalizing strikes within strict conditions was taken up by the Draft Self Managers' Code submitted to the Second Congress of Self Managers in 1971. *NIN* reported on the draft code, singling out Article 8, which provided for the right to strike. *NIN* also listed the limiting conditions: that the decision to strike must be adopted at a formal meeting and should be the last step after trying all the regular channels. The Code therefore specifically aimed to exclude wild-cat strikes. The Draft Code also required workers to inform management and the commune assembly a week before the beginning of the strike, so that an arbitration commission could meet.[15] The Self Managers' Congress in May agreed the Code should be adopted as soon as possible, but in practice this move towards formal legalization of strikes got lost in subsequent political upheavals and was never implemented.

It is arguable that the willingness of the party to consider legalizing strikes was prompted by a desire to harness and channel worker discontent, which might otherwise become more militant and find its own organizational expression, thus posing a more direct threat to the regime. A commune trade union organization in Maribor had frankly admitted that the union expressed its readiness to organize a 4-hour 'work stoppage' in support of workers at the Maribor car factory in order to direct the protest. 'Certainly it is far better that the TU be an organizer of the protest stoppage of work, than observer of a strike and demonstrations' the trade union commune president told *Nedeljne Novosti*.[16] The general nervousness of the party of spontaneous mass protests and of unofficial action committees operating outside the approved organizational framework were both manifested in the responses to the June 1968 student demonstrations. The active steps taken by the party at that time to isolate the Belgrade workers from the students suggested a very real fear that the workers might support and act on the political demands being made by the students.

Nevertheless it would be unreasonable to deny the very considerable concession being made by the Yugoslav party in contemplating a policy of making strikes legal. It was for a long time a radical demand within the Yugoslav context, voiced for example by Belgrade philosophers, by the students themselves during the June days and put forward by Milosavlevski in his book *Revolucija i Anti-Revolucija*. Until the success of the workers' strikes in Poland in the summer of 1980 it was a policy unthinkable in any other communist party state.

Student Dissent

The first known example of student protest in communist Yugoslavia occurred in 1958 in Zagreb, by an interesting coincidence soon after the first workers' strike at Trbovlje. The cause of the demonstration was apparently the bad food in the student canteen. Peter Jambrek says in his brief account of these events that press coverage outside Zagreb was virtually non-existent: 'relevant information was either transmitted through confidential channels linking together top-ranking political officials, or by means of rumours which informally spread among the population at large'.[17]

During the early 1960s a much more explicitly political movement developed at Ljubljana around the dissenting intellectual journal *Perspektive*. According to Jambrek, speaking here from inside knowledge, this movement in conjunction with dissenting intellectuals 'partly transformed, partly penetrated and partly evolved out of the official student organizations', and took control of student committees in the Economics and Philosophy Faculties and of the student paper. This movement embraced large numbers of students in critical debate and open activity in 1964, but was effectively suppressed when *Perspektive* was closed down by the Slovene party leaders in the spring of 1965.

There were other signs of student activism after Brioni. Belgrade students clashed with the police in December 1966 when they tried to march through the streets in a protest that would seem to be ideologically unexceptionable, against American bombing of Hanoi during the Vietnam War.[18] There were also student strikes, in 1966, over the more parochial issue of inadequate student accommodation.[19] By early 1968 there was plenty of evidence that Yugoslav students were being affected by the ferment of student protests and new-left ideas in other parts of Europe. They expressed solidarity with the demands of West German and Polish students, and in Belgrade debated hotly the issue of university reform. Most significant of all was the fact that new-left ideas had apparently been taken up by official student leaders at Zagreb who were purged in the spring of 1968.[20] Press coverage was unfortunately sketchy, but the Zagreb Student Union officials seem to have been influenced by their contemporaries abroad, and there is no indication at all that the Zagreb students linked up with *Praxis* in the way the Slovene students had rallied round *Perspektive*. In fact the Croatian editors of *Praxis* seemed during 1968 to be keeping their distance from the student movement, though the Belgrade philosophers were much more directly involved.

The controversial life of the student press in such university centres as Belgrade, Novi Sad, Niš, Zagreb, Ljubljana and Sarajevo was of course closely associated with the relatively high level of political independence and activity among a section of students in the period 1968–71. This dissent sometimes took the form of demonstrations and strikes, staged for a variety of objectives. Belgrade students for example took part in a hunger strike in sympathy with striking Bosnian miners in the summer of 1970, and 6000 of them went on strike when Vladimir Mijanović, Chairman of the Student Union Committee in their faculty, was sentenced to 18 months in jail for 'hostile propaganda' in September 1970.[21] The Belgrade University Committee of the League condemned the student strike, but also criticized the sentence passed on Mijanović. The Ljubljana University party Committee gave surprisingly strong support to a local student demonstration in Askerceva Street in protest against the failure of the city authorities to reduce the noise which was disturbing their studies, arguing that 'self-managing methods' of trying to stop the noise had been exhausted, and demonstrations which pointed up the existence of social problems and the inability of responsible organs to deal with them 'contribute to the strengthening of democracy based on self-management principles'.[22]

By far the most important student demonstrations, however (at least until the pro-nationalist Croatian student strike of 1971), were those which occurred in June 1968 in Belgrade and spread to Zagreb, Ljubljana and

Sarajevo. The June events were widely agreed to have had important political repercussions at a crucial period in the development of the party's thinking on its new economic policy, and to have posed a serious challenge to the League. The evolution of the June days suggested how party liberals tried to 'guide' the students in the desired political direction, while simultaneously steps were taken to head off the dangers of a link-up between students and workers. Top party bodies indicated early on the general line to be taken towards the student protests – support for 'progressive' demands whilst warning against hostile elements trying to use the student movement and against use of 'violent' methods – and the press, and other political bodies, took up this cue. But newspaper reports and the statement of various political organizations revealed interesting divergences in their reactions to the demonstrations, suggesting a split within the party. The student movement also posed dramatically the important question of how far the League could tolerate spontaneous political dissent and the attendant likelihood that new and organized forms of political opposition would emerge from such a movement.

The account below focuses on the Belgrade protests, which were the most central and were the best documented. This movement started, as significant movements often do, largely by accident; although its political evolution was of course determined by the discontents and ideals of the student population and by the explosive context in which it took place. The protest movement was triggered off on Sunday 2 June by a street fight between students and youth-brigade workers over entrance to a free entertainment, and was launched by the violence used by the police to break up the fight. Later that night the students, already beginning to produce a range of political demands, began a march of protest towards the Federal Parliament, and the police reacted with even greater violence, arresting many students and firing at the demonstrators. Next day the students assembled in a mass meeting and began another protest march into the city. They were halted by the police, but met by a number of party and government representatives who started to negotiate with them. According to *Borba*'s account Veljko Vlahović, whose opening remarks were: 'I led many demonstrations before the war, but we knew exactly what we wanted. What do you want?', had a friendly debate with students around him.[23] Whilst the discussions were still in progress the police charged the assembly using truncheons and tear gas and injured at least a hundred students. The reasons for the police charge were disputed at the time, and the official commission set up to investigate the incidents never reached agreement. The Serbian government statement, which backed the police action throughout Sunday night and Monday, blamed student extremists who tried to force their way through into the city centre by truck.[24] The student version, published in *Student*, was that the police assault was entirely unprovoked; *Student* also criticized the politicians present for their failure to stop the police — only Miloš Minić, President of the Serbian Parliament, tried (unavailingly) to do so, and was himself attacked by the police.[25] The *Borba* report (in general quite sympathetic to the students) suggested that there was general confusion, with students at the back pressing forward and wondering what was happening in front, and that the police reacted to a group of students who were calling for the right to demonstrate in Belgrade. The students responded to this further experience of police violence by going on strike and occupying the university, initiating a sustained debate in mass meetings in the various faculties, and promulgating a series of appeals, demands and policy statements addressed to factory workers, the party leadership, the press and the general public. The student occupation and mass dialogue was reminiscent of the events in France the month before, but there the similarities ended. After the initial confrontation with the police the students managed to avoid further violence; despite a ban on demonstrations and a police blockade of the university there was an understanding that the students would not attempt to enter Belgrade if left free to control their territory. The general conduct of the occupation was peaceful and disciplined, carefully policed by the students themselves, and the tenor of the students' demands was relatively moderate and based on declared loyalty to Tito and the policy goals of the party. The response from the regime was also generally moderate, though somewhat uncertain during the week of the demonstration. The uncertainty apparently ended with Tito's broadcast on Sunday night, 9 June, which indicated a good deal of sympathy for the students' goals and a promise of action. The students responded by calling off the strike, though they kept in being the Action Committees set up during the protest and planned to continue holding regular mass meetings. A fortnight later the party leaders began to take a much harder line against the students and those who had supported them too unconditionally.

The relative moderation of the students' demands was undoubtedly influenced by the role played by individual communists, both students and lecturers, and by the University Committee of the League during the crucial week of the strike. Instead of the normal tendency for a movement to make more extreme and radical demands as the protest continues, the Belgrade students voted for policies which were towards the end of the week formulated in a way more acceptable to the League than the initial policy slogans and demands. There were some signs that certain faculties, in particular the philosophy faculty later to become notorious as the centre of dissent, were not content with compromise formulae, but Tito's broadcast pre-empted any escalation of the student movement.

The first set of demands, issued on Monday 3 June were put forward primarily by the *ad hoc* Student Action Committee of the demonstrators, although the document was also signed by the editorial board of *Student* and the University Council of the Belgrade Student Union. This statement denied press and radio reports that the demonstrators were 'bullies, rioters and insolent idlers' who had attacked police and youth brigadists, summarized their main policy concerns – social inequality, unemployment and lack of democracy – and made three specific short-term demands: immediate release of those arrested and destruction of their dossiers; the convening of the Federal Assembly to discuss the students' views; and the dismissal of the directors and staff members of 'the Belgrade daily papers, of the Belgrade Radio and the Tanjug Agency' which the students thought had slandered them.[26] The Student Union issued a separate statement glossing the contentious demand for more equality, claiming it was not a demand for 'levelling', thus seeking to bring the students' aims into line with the official liberal party position on economic reform.[27] Another early document, signed simply 'The Students of Belgrade University', listed eleven long-term demands: five were concerned with educational questions and six with economic and political reforms, including 'abolition of all social privileges and an end to individuals enriching themselves at the expense of the working class', 'radical change in political cadres in all spheres of social life' and 'freedom of strikes and demonstrations'. The University Committee of the League began to take an active part in policy formulation on the Tuesday, when it agreed with the Student Union and the Student Action Committee a formal 'Political Action Programme', which was then endorsed by the students' faculty meetings with some additions. The influence of the party activists resulted in both a moderation and an elaboration of the initial demands. It dropped the demands for freedom of strikes and demonstrations and for 'freedom and impartiality of the means of information' in the earlier eleven-point programme. The demand for more social and economic equality was translated into a series of more specific and less radical points: the need to establish the socialist principle of distribution according to work, to set criteria for minimum and maximum incomes, impose high progressive taxation on incomes over the maximum, eliminate differences due to 'monopolistic, unsocialist and other privileged positions' and nationalization of unjustly gained property. The clause on unemployment noted the need to link this goal to long-term economic planning and an adequate investment policy.[28] The official desire to view the students' programme as a slightly more radical version of the League's own policy was indicated by a *Politika* comment on 8 June, which noted that the Serbian party Central Committee and the University had drawn up, on the same day, two documents with the same ideas and standpoints, though the student document reflected 'youthful enthusiasm and impatience'.[29]

The Serbian party Executive Committee had in the early days of the protests stressed the responsibility of communists, especially those at the university, to 'prevent events taking a course which would jeopardise efforts to promote democratic relations and equality among nations since the Fourth Plenum of the CC LCY'.[30] The university communists took up this responsibility. The University Committee of the League adopted a strong line in favour of the students from the outset, associating themselves (as the university authorities had done) with the protest against police brutality and the call for an enquiry. They therefore won the students' trust. Dennison Rusinow has made the very interesting point that the university communists 'were behaving — almost for the first time in this society — as contemporary communist theory says they should . . . exerting a decisive influence over the course of events, not through power in the stricter sense, which they temporarily lacked as a minority in a fluid situation, but through persuasion'.[31] He assigns their success to the lack of any other well-organized group. The Student Union appears at this stage to have been acting in concert with the party Committee, although subsequently it was to show more sympathy for student dissidence than the party. There were the *ad hoc* Action Committees whose existence as a potential alternative leadership alarmed many in the League, and who were being pressed to disband by the end of the week. But their membership was rotating and the committees less cohesive and less politically experienced than the party organizations.

When later the University Committee of the party was under fire for its active sympathy with the students and its toleration of the Action Committees, a defence of the Committee's position was put forward by Professor Žarko Bulajić, who pointed to the justified nature of the student demands, natural sympathy with the students attacked by the police, and to the Committee's desire to channel the movement in a positive direction. He added:

> I am sure that the party organization would have gone to pieces, and the University Committee would have found itself isolated if it had failed to assume this attitude of sympathy with the students. It is a serious question — who would then have assumed leadership of the movement?[32]

Official statements and press reports suggested a number of political

candidates for the role of infiltrating the movement – the most absurd
being agents from the French Embassy. Some alarm was also raised about
'emissaries' from Djilas trying to address the students. Much more serious
were the allegations by a number of official sources, including the Serbian
Presidium and Executive Committee, that Rankovićist and Cominformist
forces were at work. The Serbian leadership was at this stage, in the
aftermath of the 1967 elections, genuinely concerned about the activities
of the 'political underground' and it was also a handy stick with which
to beat the students. Although official comment in the first week tended
to distinguish between the progressive views of the great majority of
students and the forces trying to use them, later such distinctions were
not made so carefully. Svetozar Stojanović says in his retrospective
analysis of the June Days in *Praxis* that 'rumours about the Stalinist-statist
background of the student movement were spread on all sides'.[33] Accusations that became more popular in later assessments, and were rather more
plausible in terms of the policy content of student documents, were that
students espoused a form of primitive communism or Maoism (Stojanović
comments that in so far as this had any validity the primitive communism
was that of the Yugoslav partisans rather than of Chairman Mao) or that
they had come under pernicious influence of the Western New Left, in
particular Professor Marcuse. It was also alleged that the students were
being unduly influenced by the brand of intellectual elitism propagated
by the *Praxis* group.

During the first week there were varied responses from the political
committees which met to discuss and pass judgement on the student
movement. The strongest backing for the students came from the Belgrade
and Serbian Committees of the Youth Federation; the former praised
the 'dignity and maturity' of the students and the latter expressed
sympathy for student demands and condemned police violence
unequivocally.[34] The Federal Executive of the Youth Federation played
safe and refused to comment. The Federal Presidium of the Student Union
expressed support for the Belgrade students with rather more caution than
the lower level Youth Federation bodies, condemning individual attempts
to set students against police; but it also criticized the 'incredibly brutal
action' of the police and blamed the press and media for misinforming
the public.[35] All these committees gave more wholehearted support to
the students, especially in their appraisal of the initial demonstrations,
than any party organ (excepting of course the University Committee
of the League). How far this divergence was due to a feeling of youth solidarity, how far to willingness to claim autonomy from the party, and how
far to the lack of agreement within top party circles which made some

differences in emphasis easier, is unclear. Probably all three factors were involved.

The fiercest party criticism of the students came from the Secretariat of the Belgrade City Committee, though it paid ritual tribute to the justified nature of some of the students' demands it condemned their methods; the University Committee later criticized its assessments. The Executive Committee of the Serbian League met on 3 June and issued a statement expressing sympathy with the students' demands for educational reform and reorganization of the university and their concern about unemployment, but deploring use of 'disorder and pressure' and pointing to hostile forces trying to use the movement.[36] A broader meeting of the Executive and Presidium a day later reiterated selective support for dealing with specific student problems, but seemed more hostile in tone.[37] The Serbian Socialist Alliance Presidium met at the end of the week and also commented in fairly hostile terms, expressing distrust of the mass meetings and fear the students would be misled by demagogy.[38] The attitudes of the Serbian party organs may have been influenced by the fact that the Belgrade and Serbian government authorities were directly responsible for the police and for the general maintenance of public order, so the party was unlikely to take the students' side publicly on issues arising from the early demonstrations. The Socialist Alliance meeting may also have been influenced by the fact that most observers detected a hardening of the party line towards the students at the end of the first week and the League was anxious that the students were still on strike and that some faculties were pressing for the resignation of the Belgrade police chief and the Serbian and Federal Ministers of the Interior.[39] But the most important consideration was probably the influence of party conservatives in Belgrade and in the broader League and Alliance committees. The only Serbian political official who appeared from his actions on 3 June, from his radio and television address, and from informal rumours, to be clearly sympathetic to the students was the President of the Serbian Parliament, Miloš Minić.

The position of the top bodies of the LCY itself was interesting. The Executive Committee met on 4 June and issued a statement supporting university reform along self-management lines and 'socialist principles of pay in accordance to work done', and urging the mobilization of citizens to solve outstanding questions 'more democratically', noting 'that excludes methods of violence and street riots'. The statement was couched at a level of theoretical abstraction dear to the hearts of Yugoslav party draftsmen in all circumstances, but which had here the advantage of sounding neither sympathetic nor hostile.[40] Although the impression conveyed was on balance one of cautious support, the party at federal level could be seen to have reserved its position at this stage. The Executive Committee met again on the Sunday, together with the LCY Presidium, in advance of Tito's broadcast scheduled for the evening. We have interesting inside information about the evolution of that meeting from Tempo, who had earlier been involved in debate with Belgrade students about their policies. Tempo told *Delo*, in the course of an interview about his memoirs, that: 'the session of the Presidium began in a fairly strained atmosphere, because many felt that this was a counter-revolution and evaluated the event negatively, even young Kocijančić [the Youth Federation President]'. When he could stand these comments no longer, Tempo exclaimed 'it's our children who are there'; Tito then apparently adjourned the session to ask Tempo about his talk with the students, and when the Presidium resumed its meeting Tempo outlined the student concerns.[41] Whether or not Tempo's account is wholly accurate, the outcome of the meeting was the television speech made by Tito, in which he promised to take action on the 'majority' of student demands which he said he had always supported, admitted the delays by the party in tackling economic and social problems, and declared his belief in the spontaneity of the student movement despite some attempts to infiltrate it.

Press coverage of the student movement may be interpreted at least partly in terms of oscillations in the official attitude during the first week and the influence of different forces within the League. The initial coverage of the student demonstrations was mostly hostile. The students themselves complained bitterly about the bias in reporting the events of Sunday night and Monday in the Belgrade press and radio, but *Student* praised the television coverage of Sunday night – though not of the Monday confrontation.[42] The Belgrade evening paper *Večernje Novosti* was hostile throughout to the students and alleged 'foreign agents' were at work. The attitude taken by *Borba* was more interesting. The 4 June issue carried a long story on the 'great student demonstration in Belgrade' which seemed a very fair and detailed account and quite sympathetic in tone, and news reports in later issues continued to present a favourable picture of the students' self-discipline and their support for the Political Action Programme. *Borba*'s editorial comment on 5 June was critical, however, stressing the warning given by the Serbian Executive Committee regarding 'hostile forces' and expressing alarm about the 'inflammable' turn taken by the student movement despite the support for their main demands by the party. Milan Bajec wrote in the 8 June issue another editorial polemic, especially attacking the 'self-styled avant garde' and 'new left' who were chiefly concerned with slogans and destined to become the tool of anti-socialist forces. The most violent and surprising attack by *Borba* came, however, in an editorial entitled 'Young wheat and chaff' printed on 10 June, after Tito's broadcast, and contrasting strongly with the tone of Tito's address. *Borba* on 11 June maintained a generally hostile tone in comment on the student protests, so its much resented and often cited 'wheat and chaff' editorial was not simply a miscalculation written in advance of Tito's broadcast. This editorial was not, however, directed primarily at the students themselves, but blamed the University Committee in the League for its previous 'alienated' and 'bureaucratic' position and the resulting political inexperience of the students. Above all the editorial was directed against 'certain politicians' who were 'confused and panic stricken' by the student disorders, and therefore were ready to accept 'all student slogans, even the most abstract, but simultaneously failed to dissociate themselves from everything smuggled in from abroad or imparted by the political underground . . . '.[43] *Borba* therefore seemed to be taking sides in an inner-party vendetta.

The line taken by *Politika* roughly followed that of *Borba*, printing a number of fair reports but making some critical, though less extreme, comments on the student movement. Not all the daily press, however, was antagonistic to the students. The Bosnian League Executive and Presidium condemned the Sarajevo dailies for being too sympathetic to the student protests in the early days. The Director of *Oslobodjenje* argued back that Tito and 'all forums' had endorsed the programmatic demands of the students.[44] Another interesting ally of the students was the trade union paper *Rad*, which printed several articles favouring student demands, despite the obvious party moves to promote worker hostility to student demonstrators and their slogans favouring equality and the right to work. The Council of the Trade Union Federation strongly criticized *Rad* for a serious political mistake which could serve the purposes of 'various hostile elements'.[45]

The hesitancy within the League during the first week was due not only to the conflicting impulses of liberal and conservative groups at various levels, but also to the fact that the radically democratic and egalitarian demands of the students in the first days cut across the policy divisions separating the two factions in the party. Those liberals in the League genuinely sympathetic to calls for greater freedom and democracy could hope to capitalize on the student movement to bring pressure on their more conservative colleagues. On the other hand, the egalitarian emphasis of the movement ran counter to some of the requirements of the economic reform and seemed in danger of playing into the hands of those who had always opposed the reform. In practice the more conservative figures showed more sustained hostility to the students throughout, no doubt influenced by their dislike of the bulk of the student demands and instinctive distrust of any spontaneous movement and the methods adopted in the student protest, while the liberals tried to use and direct the movement though expressing some alarm about its possible repercussions.

The position of both factions in subsequent weeks is less clear. Two weeks after his television address Tito made a speech at the Trade Union Congress, which has generally been interpreted as the signal for a much harder line against the student activists and the staff members who supported them. Although Tito mentioned more than once that the 'riots' had 'aroused us from lethargy', which could have positive results, and reiterated support for giving students equal self-managing rights, he laid much more stress on the attempts made to infiltrate the movement, singling out for mention 'philosophers, *Praxis* people' along with 'various dogmatists' and former UDBA officials amongst those who must be dealt with.[46] The purpose of Tito's second speech was to defuse worker unrest and he appealed to natural hostility among the workers to privileged and troublesome intellectuals, while speaking sympathetically about their economic grievances. The policy content of Tito's two speeches was not substantially different, but the tone of the second did suggest the desirability of tougher methods by the party.

Certainly after his second speech liberals and conservatives in the League appeared to unite in bringing the student movement into line – for example insisting on the dissolution of the Action Committees and penalizing rebellious academics: the party organizations in the philosophy and sociology departments were disbanded, and the University Committee of the League retracted its previous position under pressure from above. The question remains why the League should now unite behind a hard line policy towards the student movement. The most obvious answer is that the conservative faction won on this issue. The fact that there were still a number of prominent conservatives in the Serbian League, and the conservative tendencies of the Belgrade City Committee, give some support to this argument, but it is not entirely convincing. The liberals showed themselves to be in control of cadre allocation later in the year, and it is unlikely they could be forced to give in on an important policy issue. While Tito's influence may have helped to tip the balance, it is not at all clear that in practice he could at this stage control the increasingly independent republican parties. The most persuasive explanation therefore is that the liberals, particularly in the Serbian Central Committee, had agreed on the necessity of defusing the situation during the summer vacation. It is also reasonable to point to the events in Czechoslovakia as an additional influence on the thinking of the party liberals. On the one hand the rapid evolution of the Czech movement showed how a reformist party leadership could start to lose control to popular forces pressing it to move much faster, and on the other, in a period of mounting tension in Eastern Europe, the Yugoslav leaders presumably wished to avoid unnecessary provocation, or any possible excuse for outside intervention on the grounds that the Yugoslav government was not fully in control of its own citizens. Interestingly one speaker at the LCY Central Committee Ninth Plenum in July linked an attack on the Belgrade philosophers to the Two Thousand Words manifesto in Czechoslovakia 'written and signed by certain members of the Czech intelligentsia, chiefly in a petty bourgeois gibberish' which provided a smoke screen for 'tendencies to suppress the right of a nation to its own elected leadership'.[47] Other speakers at the Plenum commented on the pernicious ideological tendency to downgrade the revolutionary role of the working class and present the intellectuals and students as a revolutionary 'force de frappe'.[48]

In view of the complexities of the internal and international situation in the summer of 1968 it may be glib to reach any easy conclusion about the lessons to be drawn about the limits of dissent allowed by the League. Nevertheless it is reasonable to conclude that the League was not in the last resort any more prepared to tolerate a political movement outside the control of the party than any other ruling communist party. On the other hand, compared with other ruling parties, most notably the Polish which had ruthlessly repressed its own movement of student and intellectual dissent earlier in the year, the liberals in the League were prepared to act with moderation and tact and to make concessions. The promise to promote university reform was kept; and despite the official attacks on the philosophers and party sanctions, no 'administrative measures' were invoked against them until the mid-seventies when they were eventually deprived of their academic teaching posts.

The Croatian Nationalist Movement

The Belgrade student movement challenged the party to apply its declared principles of guidance by persuasion on a relatively small scale. The growth of Croatian nationalism raised the question of the correct party response to a mass popular movement on a much larger scale and — in view of the history of Croatian nationalism — in a much more dangerous way. The evolution of the Croatian nationalist movement has been analysed authoritatively by Dennison Rusinow,[49] and this chapter only attempts to summarize the movement from the standpoint of its significance for the party and the special problems it posed for the reformers.

The first public expression of renewed Croatian nationalism within Yugoslavia occurred in 1967, when a group of 130 Croatian writers and intellectuals, including the eminent writer and friend of Tito, Miroslav Krleža, signed a declaration claiming that Croatian was a separate language, and therefore repudiating the official position (formulated in the Novi Sad agreement of 1954) that Serbo-Croatian was one language with two scripts, and complaining of discrimination against the Croatian language. The Croatian Declaration prompted a riposte from a small number of Serbian intellectuals asserting the rights of Serbs to use their own language and script, including the Serbian minority inside Croatia. The party responded to this display of linguistic nationalism with vehement denunciations and took disciplinary action against communists who had signed both declarations. The communist signatories of the Serbian 'Proposal for Consideration' were treated fairly leniently: nineteen Belgrade party members were punished mainly by a warning or final warning, and Antonije Isaković, who was a Serbian Central Committee member, had to resign his position.[50] Press reports indicated rather harsher measures against the eighty communists who had signed the Croatian Declaration, many of whom were expelled, though some escaped with a final warning. Krleža had to resign from the Croatian Central Committee. The Matica Hrvatska, the Croatian Cultural Association, which had been one of the organizations sponsoring the Language Declaration was obviously under pressure to discipline its leadership: at an extraordinary session in April the Executive Committee of the Matica offered its resignation.[51]

Cultural and economic discontents promoted undercurrents of Croatian nationalism in the late sixties, but the political turning point which set the Croatian party leadership on a course which led them into effective alliance with the nationalist movement was the Žanko affair and the Tenth Plenum of the Croatian party Central Committee. Miloš Žanko, a Croatian Central Committee member and Vice-President of the Federal Assembly, wrote a series of articles in *Borba* in late 1969 in which he expressed his disquiet about the increase in Croatian nationalism evidenced by the activities of the Matica and by the statements of various nationalist spokesmen. Žanko was bitterly attacked by his colleagues for allying himself with 'unitarist' forces, and for trying to undermine the Croatian party leadership by implying that they were unable to deal with rising nationalism. His offence was made more heinous, according to the Croatian party President, by the fact that he had not raised the issue inside the Central Committee but in public, that he had deviated from the official Croatian party policy on nationalism enunciated at the Conference in late 1969, and above all by the fact that he had chosen to publish his articles in the Belgrade based *Borba*, which had been very critical of Croatian developments.[52] In sum Žanko was deemed to have given aid and comfort to the enemies of the republic in Belgrade. Despite the prolonged condemnation of Žanko at the Tenth Plenum, and the decision to remove him as a Croatian representative on the LCY Standing Conference, the Croatian leaders maintained that the real importance of the Plenum was in clarifying policy. At this stage they were charting a course designed to achieve greater decentralization of federal government powers to republics, against federal administrative opposition. It was assumed that meeting legitimate Croatian grievances in the economic and administrative sphere would help defuse the irrational and extremist elements in the nationalist movement, and Bakarić observed that centralist forces inside the Croatian party were much better established and more serious than the long discredited Croat extremists.[53] However reasonable this analysis appeared at the time, the Žanko affair did indicate the intolerant style being adopted to enforce support for this policy. Žanko complained about the breaches of the party statute in the moves made to condemn him, and the penalties he suffered for breaking ranks served as a warning to others to conform. The Tenth Plenum resolutions became a touchstone of party loyalty and right thinking until December 1971.

During 1971 the growing strength of the nationalist movement inside Croatia forced the party leaders to view more seriously the threat posed from that quarter, and the Twentieth Plenum of the Croatian Central Committee in May 1971 attacked moves towards creating a political organization parallel to the League and strongly condemned the views of certain nationalists (some of whom had been cited by Žanko in his ill-fated articles) including Marko Veselica, one of the chief exponents of the nationalist cause, who was later expelled from the League.[54] Bakarić altered the analysis he had made at the Tenth Plenum in the course of 1971, and began to see the nationalist movement headed by the Matica as a more formidable enemy than unitarist forces inside the Croatian party and in Belgrade. He said in the course of a speech that the nationalists had 'posed the question of the party', and started to divide the League into 'progressives' and 'conservatives', implying that the latter did not understand the new movement and that the League needed reconstructing. Bakarić went on to say, in a departure from his normally delphic mode of utterance:

The principal champions of 'reconstruction' are certain circles of

Croatian nationalism. Of course all of them claim that they are in favour of the Tenth Plenum and in favour of the Amendments to the Constitution. . . . In other words, only now has the League of Communists taken up its proper position.

Yes, but do you think that they have enrolled in the League of Communists?

No, they have not! They are founding an opposition party.[55]

It was fortuitously student rebellion that inaugurated the phase in which the nationalist movement in Croatia achieved significant political success, and also precipitated the suppression of the movement. A nationalist group ousted the Communists student leadership at Zagreb University in April 1971; and in November the students went on strike to reinforce nationalist demands on the foreign-currency issue, and disobeyed the requests of the Croatian party leaders to return to their studies. The strike finally convinced Tito that the Croatian leaders could not control the popular nationalist movement which they had encouraged, and he there-fore forced them to resign. The student movement in Croatia, however, was of secondary importance to the role of the Croatian cultural organization, the Matica Hrvastka, which backed the student actions and was emerging as an organized national political movement. Membership of the Matica grew from 2323 to 41 000 during 1971, while the number of branches increased from 30 to 55. The Matica had also specifically broadened its scope in November 1970 to include political and economic as well as cultural questions. It began in 1971 to publish a political weekly, *Hrvatski Tjednik*, which soon reached a circultation of 100 000. During his July visit to Zagreb Tito is reported to have told the Croat Party leaders:

> you have allowed the Matica to transform itself into a political organiza-tion, to such a degree that you will have difficulty in controlling that. It has become stronger than you, you're in no position to curb it.[56]

The Matica had members and influence inside the ruling party, as well as an independent organization and mass base outside it. Leading members of the Matica were also leading party members — at one stage this fact was cited as an argument against undue concern about the activities of the Matica, and prominent nationalists were also prominent in the party-controlled mass organizations. For example the *coup* by nationalist students at Zagreb was applauded by Drago Božić, President of the Croatian Social-ist Alliance, Ivan Šibl, President of the Croatian Veterans' Association and Djuro Despot, a senior member of the Zagreb party. At the Croatian Conference of the League of Communists in July 1971 a notably nationalistic speech — reflecting Matica views — was made by Ivica Vrkić then the President of the Socialist Alliance in Croatia, who championed the cause of Croatian statehood.

The Matica successes in enlisting the support of prominent communists gave them inside information about party matters and the ability to work within the League to isolate their main opponents. The party Commission reporting retrospectively on the evolution of the crisis discovered that a secret meeting of the Dalmation Inter-Communal Conference was told that it would be necessary to arrange a confrontation in the League to clean out individuals opposed to Croatian statehood, and 'to move towards holding an extraordinary congress of the League of Communists of Croatia'. The speakers at this meeting named members of the Croatian Executive Committee who should be removed, including Vladimir Bakarić, who was accused of misinforming Tito about the situation in Croatia. The Zadar party Committee, also sympathetic to the Matica, wrote to the President of the Croatian League requesting disciplinary action against a list of Executive Committee members, who had been calling for party discipline against nationalist excesses. The Zadar party accused them of 'destructive interventions' in Dalmatian politics. The Matica also called publicly in May 1971 for an extraordinary meeting of the Croatian League to expel conservative and unitarist groups, and by the autumn was naming in *Hrvatski Tjednik* those members of the Executive Committee who were 'unitarists'.

The Croatian party was vulnerable to Matica infiltration and relatively weak in the face of the nationalist movement, for a number of reasons. It was by 1971 divided at the centre between the top leadership — Miko Tripalo, Savka Dabčević-Kučar and Pero Pirker — who increasingly supported nationalist demands, and most other members of the Executive Committee, who in varying degrees became alarmed by manifestations of Croatian nationalism during 1971. Rusinow suggests convincingly that the position of the three leaders was weakened by internal opposition in the Croatian party and by their growing isolation when pursuing Croatian demands at the federal level — so that they fell back on cultivating mass popular support for their policies. Since this support was largely based on nationalist aspirations, however, this strategy made them dependent on Matica backing, and therefore made it difficult for them to keep nationalism within the limits they regarded as acceptable.

The three leaders maintained control of the party, despite opposition in the Executive Committee to their policies, because of their control of the communications within the party. For example they gave misleading reports of meetings with Tito to the Central Committee, and refrained from circulating local parties with decisions unfavourable to their own policy, like the August Action Programme adopted by majority vote in the Croatian Executive Committee, and sharply critical of the Matica and extreme Croatian nationalism. In addition, according to their critics, they resorted to 'cadre politics', threats of demotion or political destruction, and 'labelling' of opponents in a neo-Stalinist atmosphere. Thus their power was only broken when Tito intervened from outside.

A number of the arguments the leadership used to justify their tolerance of the nationalist movement drew on the theory of the role of the party which had been officially sponsored since 1966. The Tenth Session of the Croatian Committee in January 1970 held that nationalism had become more vocal due to greater tolerance of dissent, but that the correct response was not to drive such views underground but to argue back and to progress towards more genuine self-management. The three leaders also argued that by adopting reasonable nationalist demands they mobilized mass support while isolating the extreme nationalists, and so achieved the League's goals of promoting popular participation in politics and of guiding this popular movement in the desired direction. After the nationalist takeover at Zagreb University in April 1971 they accepted the loss of communist control of the Student Union and argued that those on the party Executive Committee who were concerned that the new student committee was not communist sponsored were reacting in a conservative and outdated way.

Whether the strategy of the Croatian leaders was really in line with official League policy depends partly on whether Croatian nationalism as interpreted by the Matica was in the long run compatible with Yugoslav socialism — and it is arguable that it was not. The lack of unity within the Croatian party and the pressures from Belgrade also made successful steering of the movement difficult.

It is an interesting paradox that the Croatian party came closer in 1971 to fulfilling the official theory of how the League ought to interpret its role than at any other time, but after the Tenth Plenum the Croatian party also became increasingly intolerant and undemocratic. Even if criticism of the deposed leaders after Karadjordjevo included an element of exaggeration, there was plenty of evidence from the Žanko affair onwards to suggest that the substance of the criticisms was fair and that the triumvirate did manipulate cadre policy and silence critics. The liberal attitude to interpreting the role of the party and the illiberalism inside the party could of course both be explained by the complex pressures upon the leaders and the tricky course they were attempting to steer. But this contradiction undermined the assumption that there was always a necessary relationship between inner party democracy and tolerance of dissent outside the party. The oddities of the situation can partly be explained by the intolerant nature of the nationalist movement itself, which was able increasingly to set the tone. In deciding whether to allow nationalist dissent the Croatian League faced a classical liberal dilemma — whether one should tolerate political forces committed to political intolerance. In making the liberal choice they eventually discredited the theory of liberal reform espoused since 1966.

Notes

1. See *RFE Research Report*, 6 October 1969. See also summary of information about strikes presented by N. Jovanov in a paper to the Yugoslav Sociological Association in 1972 given by Peter Jambrek, *Development and Social Change in Yugoslavia*, Saxon House, Farnborough, 1975, pp. 192–9.
2. *Borba*, 1 February 1967.
3. *Borba*, 14 May 1969.
4. Anton Ravnić, 'Obustava rada radnika u samoupravnom socijalizmu', *Naše Teme*, No. 6, 1971, pp. 1018–19.
5. See *RFE Research Report*, 6 October 1969. See also Nebojša Popov, 'Streiks in der gegenwartigen Jugoslawischen gesellschaft', *Praxis* (International Edition), Nos. 3–4, 1970, which is a translation of his essay in *Socologija,* No. 4, 1969, pp. 605–30. There is a useful survey of the incidence of strikes in Yugoslavia and of the evolution of official trade union and party thinking of the problem in: Marie-Paule Canapa, *Réforme Économique et Socialisme en Yougoslavie*, Armand Colin, Paris, 1970, Chapter 4. She notes that information about the number of strikes was not published in Yugoslavia until 1967, when the LCY took up the issue at federal level.
6. Cited in *RFE Research Report*, 23 October 1969.
7. See Nebojša Popov op. cit.; *RFE Research Report*, 6 October 1969.
8. *Borba*, 14 August 1966.
9. *Komunist*, 27 October 1966.
10. *Komunist*, 21 December 1967.
11. *Politika*, 25 June 1969.
12. *Borba*, 18 November 1969.
13. *Borba*, 16 December 1969.
14. *Borba*, 22 October 1969.
15. *NIN*, 7 March 1971.
16. *Nedeljne Novosti*, 29 December 1968.
17. Jambrek op. cit. p. 199.
18. Gerson S. Sher, Praxis: *Marxist Criticism and Dissent in Socialist Yugoslavia*, Indiana University Press, Bloomington, 1977, p. 209.
19. Duncan Wilson, *Tito's Yugoslavia*, Cambridge University Press, Cambridge, 1979, p. 178.
20. See Chapter 11 and also Dennison Rusinow, *Anatomy of a Student Revolt*, Part 1, American University Field Staff Reports, 1968.
21. *Politika*, 25 October 1970; *RFE Research Report*, 29 October 1970.
22. *Borba*, 23 April 1971.
23. *Borba*, 4 June 1968.
24. *Borba*, 4 June 1968.

25. See special issue of *Student*, 4 June 1968, translated and published in *Review*, No. 7, London 1968.
26. Document 2 in R. V. Layton, 'The student uprising in Belgrade 1968: Documents and commentary', *International Review of History and Political Science*, June 1976, p. 62.
27. See Rusinow, 1968, op. cit.
28. See *Politika*, 8 June 1968, which published the full text 'at the request of a number of faculties'.
29. *Politika*, 8 June 1968.
30. *Borba*, 4 June 1968.
31. Rusinow, 1968, op. cit.
32. *Borba*, 22 June 1968 cited by Rusinow, 1968, op. cit.
33. Svetozar Stojanović, 'The June student movement and social revolution in Yugoslavia', *Praxis* (International Edition), No. 3-4, 1970, p. 400.
34. *Borba*, 6 June 1968.
35. *Borba*, 5 June 1968.
36. *Borba*, 4 June 1968.
37. *Borba*, 5 June 1968.
38. See Rusinow op. cit.
39. Ibid.
40. *Borba*, 5 June 1968.
41. *NIN*, 22 August 1971, reprint of *Delo* interview.
42. *Student,* 4 June 1968, in *Review*, No. 7, 1968.
43. *Borba*, 10 June 1968.
44. *Politika*, 13 July 1968.
45. *Politika*, 11 June 1968.
46. *Borba*, 27 June 1968.
47. *Borba*, 17 July 1968.
48. See Stevan Doronjski, *Borba*, 17 July 1968.
49. See Dennison Rusinow, *Crisis in Croatia*, Parts I-IV, American University Field Staff Reports, 1972, and also Dennison Rusinow, *The Yugoslav Experiment: 1948-1974*, Royal Institute of International Affairs, London 1977, which gives a shorter version of the Croatian events.
50. *Borba*, 22 April 1967.
51. *Borba*, 13 April 1967.
52. *Politika*, 17 and 18 January 1970.
53. *Politika*, 17 January 1970.
54. *Politika*, 15 May 1971.
55. *Borba*, 4 October 1971.
56. Cited in Rusinow, 1972, op. cit. Part III, p. 19.

PART V

IS THE PARTY COMPATIBLE WITH
SELF-MANAGEMENT?

13   The Party in the Enterprise

Problems of the Role of the Party

Self-management in the enterprise has been the cornerstone of the Yugoslav
conception of socialist democracy. It was the first step towards a repudiation of the Soviet model in domestic affairs — announced by Tito early
in 1950 when he promised 'factories to the workers', and was given even
greater emphasis by the party leadership when they renounced the liberal
experiment of the sixties. But one of the declared aims of the party
reforms after 1966 was to create a situation in which party bosses stopped
handing down orders, so that self-management on the shop floor and in
the workers' council could operate freely.

The economic reforms of 1961 and 1965 also raised sharply the question
of the role of the party in the economy. The main emphasis of the
reformers, especially after 1966, was the need to end arbitrary political
intervention in the economy in order to allow the market to work freely.
Conversely they also suggested that transforming the role of the League
depended on implementation of the economic reforms. Stipe Šuvar, for
example. argued that the failure of the party to adopt its new role was
due to its failure to end state control over the economy: 'The League of
Communists declared itself more than 15 years ago for a self-governing
socialist society but self-management barely penetrated or destroyed the
etatist structure of the economy.'[1] This was because the League was still
imbued with an etatist mentality and was closely linked to the state which
controlled the process of investment.

When the party launched its Guidelines on economic and social reform
in the summer of 1968, Mijalko Todorović spoke with some impatience:

The League of Communists cannot reform itself and become the
internal ideological political force of integration in the system of self-
management if it does not quickly free itself from operating from the

position of power. As long as the distribution of a considerable part of
the economic surplus is a matter for an independent centre of political
power [i.e. the government], the League of Communists will also figure
as a factor of power. Therefore its real transformation into an *avant-garde*
ideological political guide and motive force of society directly depends
on the process of self-organization in the economy. . . . The League of
Communists must free itself of illusions about its unimpeachable
authority; it cannot base itself on the glory of the old days, but must
keep asserting its identity as the revolutionary social force.[2]

There was an apparent ambiguity involved in what was required of the
party in the context of economic reform. 'Depoliticisation', an end to
party control, was as much on the agenda as the ending of state control –
the two being interlinked. On the other hand, as Todorović's speech
suggests, there was still a role for the League as an 'internal ideological
political force of integration'. These two concepts of the role of the party
in the economy were compatible because the first required an end to all
central political allocation of investment, whereas the second required
the party at local level to promote the required conditions for an efficient
market economy, in particular the merging of enterprises to create more
viable economic units and ensuring that firms were headed by professionally
competent directors. If vested interests blocked rational economic development, therefore, the commune or enterprise party might be expected to
intervene. Reform spokesmen did justify active involvement by the League
to ensure the correct decisions were adopted on crucial policy issues
relating to the economic reform.

Bakarić commented on how he saw the role of the party in enterprises
in the course of an important policy speech between the Third and Fourth
Plenums in 1966. He said:

> Given the normal operation of the work organization it is quite obvious
> that decisions should be taken by the bodies of self-management set up
> in all work organizations. When this transcends the given frameworks
> and creates difficulties during the transition to the new system – and
> there are still many difficulties of this kind – then we can use other
> methods as well; we can demand discipline on the part of the members
> of the League of Communists who adopt such a line.[3]

This meant, Bakarić elaborated, that party members in an enterprise were
free to make their own decisions so long as they remained within the law
and so long as they were not acting to obstruct necessary economic
developments.

The role of the party in the selection of directors raised some of the issues which bedevilled parliamentary elections. Direct intervention to impose a particular director upon a workers' council, or to depose a director judged competent by his enterprise, did presumably lie outside the new role of the party, especially if the commune party acted arbitrarily. *Borba* in fact published an article in February 1966 highly critical of the way some commune assemblies and 'socio-political organizations' influenced the selection of directors, drawing on examples from Prilep and Ohrid.[4] But in practice selection of the best-qualified director (especially when qualified men were still fairly scarce) was likely to mean explicit support for one individual or pressure to remove an unqualified man.

After Brioni there was some uncertainty as to how far commune or city party intervention in the affairs of enterprises was justifiable within the guidelines of the new role of the party. Prominent party spokesmen were prepared to assert the necessity of the party to intervene to correct abuses or mismanagement inside enterprises. But criticisms were also made of excessive intervention by the commune party.

The Secretary of the Zagreb City Committee of the party took the first position when he explained to *Vjesnik* why his Committee had, on the basis of complaints and requests from workers. investigated the affairs of a number of enterprises. He acknowledged that there had been criticism that the City Committee was the wrong body to deal with these problems, but said that the workers had themselves addressed the party, and commented: 'the League of Communists is a factor of revolutionary change, not a debating club'. He added that in some cases the communists inside enterprises were to blame for this high-level intervention because they had failed to act. He cited the case of Napredak, where the party organization had not objected to the misappropriation of public funds because a majority of members of the party were themselves guilty, and the commune and city committees had threatened to dissolve the basic organization unless it took action.[5]

Tripalo reverted to this question in his report to the LCY Presidium in December 1969, in which he discussed general problems about the role of the party. He noted that the problem of 'interference' by commune party conferences or committees in the work of party organizations in enterprises was often raised, and commented that 'these relations are based on the principles of democratic centralism'. Tripalo went on to note the danger of 'bureaucratic' intervention from outside or bureaucratic defence of 'autonomy' from inside the enterprise. The implication of these remarks — in the context of asserting the continuing responsibility of the League for general policy — appeared to justify some form of involvement by the commune party leadership.[6]

Representatives of economic interests were naturally less enthusiastic about party intervention. *Ekonomska Politika* published a critical article on the role of commune party committees, citing the case of the Belgrade Commune Savski Venac, where the commune party committee had initiated an inspection team to survey the workings of companies and uncover mismanagement or illegalities. The inspection commission comprised executives of the party committee, the Socialist Alliance, the Trade Union Council and the commune government. The article quoted justifications produced by commune officials, who claimed that these commissions did not usurp the functions of enterprise bodies, and also quoted a statement from the commune party secretary claiming that they were only implementing the conclusions of the Presidium of the LCY on the economy made in November 1969. These conclusions specified that commune councils should mediate and undertake other necessary measures to settle problems in workplaces and that commune auditing services, trade unions or communists should initiate enquiries into such problems. The *Ekonomska Politika* writer queried whether the same body should both initiate enquiries and take action on the problems revealed, and whether self-management bodies rather than political forums should not be responsible for taking action.[7]

When looking at the power exerted by the party within enterprises it is necessary to start — as the previous comments indicate — by distinguishing between the influence exerted by the party inside the enterprise and the power of commune party committees and higher party bodies to determine key policy decisions. There is no doubt that the latter could play a decisive role. Up to the mid-sixties the enterprise was to some extent administratively and financially dependent on the commune, which even after the 1965 economic reforms retained a partial responsibility for appointment of directors through an assembly commission. In the case of large enterprises, as Jerovšek notes in his survey of Slovenian communes, the republican government was likely to intervene in the appointment. Moreover, as he also observes, since enterprises were central to the local economy and the commune relied on them for taxes, no communal government could be indifferent to the success or failure of enterprises. It would therefore be surprising if key political officials in the commune, including the party secretary, were not active in the appointment of directors, but party officials sometimes came into conflict with officials or party bodies inside an enterprise.[8] There were also the general political-economic reasons outlined earlier for the party commune committee to concern itself with such issues as 'integration' of enterprises. Some of the research evidence on the role of commune committees supports the view that the party at this level gives considerable attention to economic problems.[9] It is more doubtful whether the average commune party committee or secretary took a detailed part in deciding general enterprise policy where there were no special reasons for the party to intervene.

There is a fair amount of evidence about the role of the party within the enterprise, but it is not easy to interpret: partly because there were almost certainly a variety of power relationships within enterprises, depending on the backwardness or sophistication of the firm, and on local politics and key personalities; and partly because there is some conflict in the evidence. Press stories and official party statements were more inclined to point to party dominance, although press reports also turned up examples of extremely dictatorial behaviour by directors and of open conflict between the director and the party secretary. Academic surveys fairly consistently concluded that the director was the most influential figure in the enterprise with the management board and managerial or technical personnel also figuring high in the rank order of influence. In these studies the League was consistently found to come low in the influence hierarchy, and several studies also found that workers would have preferred the party, along with the trade unions and the workers' council, to have had much more influence on decision-making.

The Party and the Director

When considering the role played by the party inside the enterprise it is necessary to distinguish between the relationship of the party officials to the enterprise director, and the role of the party in relation to the self-managing bodies: the workers' assembly, the workers' council and the management board. The first concerns the balance of power at the top, while the second (though it may affect the power of the party in relation to the director) raises the more fundamental question of whether the operations of the party were compatible with genuine worker self-management.

Press reports and studies of Yugoslav enterprises suggest the existence of two contrasting types of director, and two corresponding modes of achieving the effective dominance of the director over the enterprise. The first kind of director was representative of the unqualified men elevated to key jobs in the early years after the party came to power, and liable to behave in an extremely arbitrary and high-handed fashion, who by the mid-sixties were presumably more often to be found in under-developed areas or backward sectors of industry. The other extreme was represented by sophisticated directors of technically developed and expanding enterprises drawing on Western management techniques to ensure harmonious relations inside the enterprise whilst securing their own power.

The first kind of director appears quite often to have had the support of party officials for his policies or behaviour, but in some cases his arbitrariness brought him into open conflict with the party. Veljko Vlahović mentioned in an interview with *Politika Ekspres* in early 1965 that there were cases of communists in enterprises who had protested about abuses, and had as a result lost their jobs, or been ill treated in various ways by the director.[10] A party member who was a worker in a Belgrade enterprise was cited in an article by a commune party official as saying: 'I dare not talk, although there are things I could talk about, for I'd be transferred at once from the dry to the damp plant. I got this job near the radiator only because I did not talk.'[11] In some cases the party organization used its own disciplinary sanctions on behalf of the director. One example was given in the report of the LCY Control Commission. The director had neglected to inform the self-managing bodies that the Belgrade Regional Economic Court had instituted proceedings against the enterprise, so a communist asked the management board to take action against the director. The basic party organization expelled this communist from the League for 'unfounded allegations aimed at destroying the authority of the director and for attacking the unity of the enterprise'.[12] A survey of trade unionists by Kilibarda suggested the importance in the power structure of enterprises of informal groups who could victimize workers who tried to oppose them. He cites one instance in Enterprise S where the informal group round the director and the party secretary decided to expel one of their critics from the party organization as a 'class and ideological enemy of the party'.[13]

The press reported on interesting and sometimes colourful instances of the director clashing with party officials. A story concerning the director of the Valjevo section of INDKOOP was reported in *Politika* in 1964. Conflict arose over the director's behaviour towards the Belgrade section of the enterprise and apparently began with a dispute over division of funds between the sections. The director, based on Valjevo, had, over a period of two months, arbitrarily moved Belgrade workers from their jobs and suspended or dismissed them — those dismissed for allegedly refusing to report for new duties included three members of the workers' council. The director had also docked the salary of the president of the workers' council (as a punishment for buying breakfast in working hours) and moved all the furniture out of the Belgrade site. A very public confrontation between the director and the workers' council occurred when he locked them out of the Valjevo premises to prevent a scheduled meeting, which he claimed was inquorate due to the dismissal of three members (and the convenient absence of some members from the Valjevo site). The workers' council then met in the street outside the enterprise — while the director looked on from a near-by cafe — and annulled the dismissal of workers. Earlier the INDKOOP party *aktiv*, which was also locked out by the director, had met and agreed to recommend to the workers' council that the director should be relieved of his post.[14]

Disputes between directors and party officials might arise out of personality and power conflicts, but could be sparked off or accentuated by serious policy issues. *Ekonomska Politika* reported on a bitter dispute in a Belgrade enterprise over a proposed merger with another enterprise in the city. The secretary of the basic party organization and the president of the workers' council supported the merger, while the director and the president of the trade union branch strongly opposed it. The dispute led to a marathon party meeting which lasted until 4 a.m., when one participant fainted from exhaustion. The director secured the expulsion of the party secretary and his ally from the League.[15]

At the other end of the scale was the kind of successful manager represented by Emerik Blum, the director of the technically advanced and successful Sarajevo enterprise Energoinvest, which had a good export record, high profit margins and had by 1969 taken over thirty-nine other enterprises. There seems no doubt that Blum was the dominant figure, but he clearly maintained close and co-operative relations with the party inside the enterprise.[16] *Komunist* commented in 1965 on the composition of the Energoinvest *aktiv*, which combined all the top political officials with various expert personnel, some of whom were non-communist.[17] Blum's position inside Energoinvest was presumably enhanced by the fact that he worked closely with the party at higher levels.[18] His standing with his republican party was indicated by the fact he was nominated as a member of the Bosnian group in the Standing Section of the LCY Conference in 1969.[19]

The general impression created by many individual cases — including both unsophisticated and sophisticated styles of management — is that the normal relationship inside the enterprise was for the director to be dominant. Most of the survey evidence seems to confirm this pattern, although more surprisingly it also tends to suggest that the party is seen to play a rather minor role in decision-making in the enterprise.

Various studies by Josip Županov confirm that there is a general tendency to rate the League of Communists inside the enterprise fairly low in the scale of influence. One survey showed that workers regarded the director as the most powerful, and that they listed the professional advisory board and the foreman second and third. The workers' council and the League of Communists were rated either fourth or fifth respectively.[20] Supek, who cites these findings, says his own survey in the mid-sixties tended to confirm them. Since perception of power may be influenced by the formal status of the director, and real limits on power be less visible, Supek checked these perceptions against a 2-year observation of the way decisions were made. This investigation confirmed that directors and representatives of technical services did 'play first fiddle'.[21] Županov also polled the opinions of 60 directors and 170 other leading personnel attending a symposium on business management and asked them to rank the influence of various groups ranging from 1 (the minimum) to 5 (the maximum). The average scores were as follows:[22]

	Directors	Non-directors
Directors	4.30	4.46
Other leading personnel	3.77	3.72
Experts	3.38	3.30
Workers' council	3.42	3.57
Political officials	2.71	2.67
Workers	2.64	2.31

A useful study by Jovo Brekić asked specifically about the influence various groups exerted on cadre policy in enterprises. His findings, based on thirty-nine Croatian enterprises, confirm the general tendency to rate the real influence of the League well below that of the management and technical experts, and to rate the desired influence of the League rather higher. His survey also shows, however, considerable difference in attitudes between occupational strata, and some regional variation which is presumably related to variation between types of industry. The overall view of the respondents was that the director had the most direct influence on cadre policy, followed by the management board and the workers' council. The League of Communists was ranked eighth, after managerial personnel, the personnel section, the workers' council commission and technical experts; the trade unions ranked tenth and the youth organization thirteenth — the last on the list. The generally desired order of influence placed the League third, after the workers' council and management board, the trade unions seventh, the director only eighth and the technical experts and managerial personnel ninth and tenth, respectively. But although all occupational groups list the workers' council first and management board second, views on the desired influence of the League varied considerably: workers ranked it third, managers fifth and clerical staff sixth. The workers also ranked the trade unions fifth, especially those earning low wages, and Brekić notes that the tendency was for those with the lowest education to expect most from the political organizations. The desired influence of the director was rated highest by chairmen of self-management organs and by women (who seemed more inclined than men to accept the prevailing hierarchy in the enterprise). Officials of political organizations would have liked to see the director ninth on this list; political officials and blue-collar workers were in fact more dissatisfied with the actual power structure than any other group.[23]

Brekić's survey suggests several tentative conclusions. One is that the poorest section of workers looked particularly to the party and trade unions because these seemed the organizations most able and most likely to protect their interests, whilst the well-qualified people in good jobs could gain money, status and power through their skills. It is also possible that unskilled workers were more likely to accept at face value the egalitarian and democratic ideology of the party unless directly disillusioned by experience of their local party organization. It should be noted, however, that evidence of a desire by the workers for greater party influence stems from the early or mid-sixties, and that in the late sixties workers may well have become more cynical on this score (as the trade union rank and file discontent suggests), just as they were also becoming more cynical about the value of self-management itself.[24] The second tentative conclusion which might be drawn from Brekić is that the role of the party may tend to decrease in more technically advanced industries where sophisticated management and technical expertise became crucial. Croatian enterprises would in general be among the most advanced in Yugoslavia.

Fortunately the hypothesis that the distribution of power would vary with the level of technology was systematically explored by Rudi Supek in a survey of twelve factories in the metal and chemical industries. He grouped the factories into three levels of technical sophistication: handicraft, mechanical and automated. At the lowest technical level he found that respondents ranked the order of influence as follows: 1 the director, 2 technical personnel, 3 the League of Communists. At the mechanical level the League came first, followed by the workers' council and the director was ranked third. At the automated level, on the other hand, the technical personnel were listed first, the director second and the League only came fifth. Supek was specifically testing the hypothesis that authority would move from the managerial to the technical personnel at higher technical levels. He explains the divergence of factories at the mechanized level from this trend by suggesting that as the workers are most alienated from the work process at this level, there is a greater tendency to seek satisfaction in politics.[25]

The Supek study seems to illustrate a trend often mentioned in connection with the evolution of Yugoslav society in the late sixties and early seventies — the trend towards technocracy. If this is taken to mean the growing importance of specialists in decision-making and the importance of educational qualifications in achieving status and positions of power, in comparison with the primary importance of the party as the channel for promotion and influence, then there is certainly evidence to support this theory of technocracy.[26]

It is also plausible that technical experts would come closer to pure technocratic rule in industry than in the specifically political sphere of the commune or republic. But there is room for considerable doubt about the conclusion that technical experts were in the process of becoming the dominant figures in decision-making in Yugoslav enterprises. One obvious caveat is that much of Yugoslav industry was still a very long way from being automated. But there is a more fundamental objection to pointing to a technocratic trend: that the enterprise has to operate within the wider political system. It is, therefore, doubtful whether the director in his representative role (as opposed to specifically managerial function) will become subordinate to the experts or will cease to be a key figure in important policy decisions. The thesis that the director will remain the major figure in most circumstances, which is supported by the example of Ergoinvest, is put forward by Županov in his study of self-management, who argues that the director, in conjunction with the enterprise political *aktiv*, will remain central in dealing with the commune and republic and that this kind of administrative and political expertise is essential for the enterprise.[27]

The Party and Self-management

It would be premature, however, to conclude that the position of the party in enterprises was weak. There is a reasonable amount of evidence that the party could and did exert influence on the decisions of the self-managing organs, in particular the workers' council.

One obvious method of control, and the one envisaged in theoretical discussions about the role of the party, was to invoke 'democratic centralism' to require obedience to party policy by party members on the workers' councils. But the party could not in many places rely on a majority in the workers' council, which tended to have a lower proportion of party members than other decision-making bodies in the commune, although the actual percentages varied considerably. Discussion at the Serbian party congress in 1965 threw up the example of the Kragujevac district where on average 53 per cent of the members of enterprise self-managing bodies were communists.[28] Tripalo, noting that communists were often in a minority on self-management bodies, said that in Zagreb 31 per cent of all the members of workers' councils were party members.[29] It is arguable that the more influential members of workers' councils were party members. Brekić found in a survey of enterprises in the Croatian town of Varaždin that individuals who were re-elected for a number of terms were more likely to be members of the League.[30] The Brekić findings were published in 1961, but later in the 1960s the practice of rotation presumably reduced the number of long-serving communists on councils. Statistical evidence for 1966 does suggest, however, the existence of an elite on workers' councils and management boards who held posts in the party or other political organizations in the enterprises and often had posts in the commune. Out of 80 200 members of workers' councils (in enterprises with more than 1000 workers but excluding integrated enterprises) 6101 had trade union responsibilities, 3984 held posts in the enterprise party and 4810 had positions in political organizations in the commune. Just over 1000 held three or more political posts (which might include being a member of the commune assembly). At the management-board level about a quarter of the members had one political position in or outside the enterprise and approximately a tenth held two.[31] The figures also suggest that those holding highly qualified technical or administrative posts were often those who also held political positions, and that although 62 per cent of the ordinary members of the workers' councils were workers, only 38 per cent of those with three or more political posts were workers. These figures suggest that the party might be well placed to dominate the management board; it would be less able to dominate the workers' council purely by voting strength, although even when in a minority it would of course have the advantages of acting as an organized group if party discipline was strong.

The most usual method of party control in enterprises or institutions was probably for the relevant committee or group of officials to meet in advance of the workers' council and agree on the line to take. They did not always conduct themselves so discreetly, however. One blatant example of the party overturning a decision made by the workers' council was cited by a member of the technical service of the Skoplje medical faculty. He alleged that 24 hours after the workers' council had rejected a proposal the council was recalled and then adopted this proposal, because the communists on the council had in the interim considered the matter more carefully.[32] Sometimes party committees took unilateral decisions without attempting to present them as the decisions of the self-management bodies. *Borba* criticized the role of 'omnipotent committees', citing among other examples the case of the Rijeka enterprise Transjug, where the party factory committee adopted a unilateral decision to set up a new council of technicians. The article acknowledged that the previous council had been acting arbitrarily, but asked what right the party committee had to dissolve it.[33]

Workers' councils did not always accept party *diktats* meekly, but tended to be at a disadvantage if it came to a fight. An instructive letter to *Komunist* gave a detailed account of flagrant party intervention to depose the director of the Elektromehanika enterprise in Kranj, spirited resistance by the workers' council and the ultimate intervention by the veterans' organization. Following various economic troubles in the enterprise the party factory committee met in September 1965 and without any prior consultation with other bodies demanded changes in the top administration. The secretary of the commune party committee, secretaries of basic party organizations, and representatives of the trade union, youth and veterans' organizations were present at the meeting and publicized its decisions. The management board was at first disposed to resist, but was brought round to comply with the party line. The workers' council, however, openly criticized 'meddling' by 'socio-political organizations', and on a show of hands 70 per cent expressed confidence in the director and refused to accept his offer to resign. The calling of a second meeting and a secret ballot still showed a majority behind the director. The veterans' *aktiv* then intervened and held a special meeting to campaign against the workers' council decision and to call for the resignation of the director. At this point the director was harassed into resigning for good. The workers' council expressed its bitterness at a subsequent meeting which debated a motion, put forward by the president of the council, that socio-political organizations were not responsible for cadre questions and this was the exclusive right of self-management bodies.[34]

Mihaljo Marković indicates the typical measures taken by party officials to pressurize the workers' council:

When the workers' council refuses to make certain decisions which have previously been 'cooked up' in some political committee, the party uses the following procedure: the proposed line will, first, be endorsed by the narrow bodies of experts and political 'activists', then it will be pushed though the mass meeting of the whole collective, where the opportunity for real discussion will hardly be offered; eventually the whole matter will come to the workers' council, which by that time, finds itself under hard psychological pressure from several sides.[35]

One important question which arises is whether there was any significant change in the role of the party inside enterprises after 1966. The decision to abolish factory committees in some industries in the course of the 1967 reorganization of the League is important in this connection, since factory committees appear to have been responsible for some of the more arbitrary acts of party intervention cited in the press, and since rank and file communists criticized factory committees bitterly for their dictatorial style. There is also some evidence that the post of secretary of a party basic organization was becoming, even before 1966, a less clearly dominating position than it had been earlier. A *Politika* article on the difficulties of being secretary of a basic organization observed that 'in the past the secretary belonged to a key group in the enterprise which made every decision and was the centre of all requests'. This was still true in some enterprises in 1965, but conscientious secretaries were aware that their proper job was to promote self-management not usurp it.[36] *Komunist* noted a dearth of candidates for the post of secretary of basic organizations.

On the other hand it seems reasonable to assume that the secretary and other officials of the factory conferences of the party continued to be important figures in an enterprise, though the increasing size of enterprises as a result of mergers would tend to reduce the importance of officials of basic organizations. It also seems that the political *aktiv*, which was an important device for exerting party influence before 1966, remained so afterwards. An article in *Komunist* in 1965 discussing the nature of political *aktivs* criticized the way in which they handed down policies to the party basic organizations. *Komunist* commented on the differing composition of *aktivs*. In the Banjaluka factory Rudi Cajevac, for example, the *aktiv*, which considered every question in advance of the workers' assembly, comprised the key figures in the party, trade union and youth organization. But a Sarajevo railway *aktiv* not only included members of the party factory committee, secretaries of the basic organizations and officials of all the political organizations, but also experts in key positions in the enterprise.[37] *Aktivs* could therefore either be the means of promoting pure party domination, or could co-ordinate the views of political officials and the enterprise experts and administrators. The latter practice was probably more typical, especially as in large and complex enterprises co-ordination became more important. *Komunist* wrote in October 1965

about the development of 'economic-political' *aktivs* to promote co-
ordination between political and specialist organs and to obviate the
tendency for the party factory committee or the enterprise technical
committee to make decisions on their own. But despite the positive role
of these *aktivs* in exchanging views and promoting activity, *Komunist*
observed that they had the undesirable habit of 'often assuming fairly
decisive and firm views which obligate all the organs and organizations'
so that subsequent discussion in the party, trade unions and work units
had a purely formal character.[38] The tendency of party officials and
experts to collude and bypass the formal democratic process was confirmed
in a speech to the 1965 Serbian party congress, which was told that in
certain places the decisions of the workers' council were determined in
advance of the meeting, as the experts would consult with the president
of the workers' council, the secretary of the party and the trade union
president and reach agreement.[39]

There is no doubt that *aktivs* continued to be an important
organizational and political device after the Brioni reforms. Trade unionists
criticizing the lack of workers' control prior to the June 1968 Trade
Unions Congress complained about the standard practice that: 'on the eve
of every important decision a meeting of the presidents of the workers'
council, the trade unions and the party organization is convened in order
to set up guidance for the later decisions of the self-management
bodies'.[40]

Conclusion

Since there appears to be at least some conflict between the survey evidence
and other descriptions of the influence the party has in enterprises, it is
necessary at this stage to try to explain or resolve this contradiction. One
possible reason for the discrepancy is the limitations of the survey method
– a poll of all workers is likely to conclude that the person officially and
most publicly responsible for directing the enterprise holds most power,
unless the party organization had very openly dictated policy. Since,
however, Supek explicitly checked survey results against detailed observation, and since Županov's poll of directors and other leading personnel,
who were in a position to make an informed inside judgement, also rated
directors as the most influential, the weight of evidence does seem
to suggest that normally the director exercised most real as well as
formal power.

Greater room for doubt exists about the accuracy of the low ranking
of the League of Communists in the enterprise. One difficulty concerns

what the respondents understand by the 'League of Communists'. If this is taken to denote the communists as a group or the basic party organizations, then it is plausible that they exercised very little more direct influence than non-communist workers. But if the League is understood in practice to be the party secretary or secretariat, party factory committee, or the top political officials in the enterprise *aktiv*, it is hard to credit that the party at this level exercises less real influence than the workers' council, especially in view of the evidence of political manipulation of the council.[41] Županov's findings, which specified 'political officials' and presumably did allow weight to behind-the-scenes influence, seem to contradict this assertion. One possible explanation is that managerial and technical personnel, and even the workers' council, would exercise more influence over the total number of often technical decisions made, but the political officials might act decisively on certain key issues. The other consideration which might well have influenced Županov's respondents was the tendency in many cases for political officials to work in conjunction with, and perhaps defer to the expertise of, administrative and technical officials. Marković drew on Yugoslav experience at the end of the 1960s when he noted that one of the main obstacles to real 'self-management' was 'the formation of small oligarchic groups, made up of managers, heads of administration, and political functionaries (secretaries of the party organization, trade union, youth organization) which tend to assume full control over the workers' council'.[42]

Two factors might have operated to subordinate the political officials to the director and his aides. One was the increasing complexity of the more developed sector of Yugoslav industry, which would necessarily have enhanced the importance of expertise. The other was an explicitly political consideration. The more the director was responsive to the wishes of the party officials at commune, provincial or republican level, the less he would need to cultivate party representatives inside the enterprise. An interesting comment by a speaker at the Kosovo Provincial Committee meeting in December 1966 suggested how the final authority of the Provincial Committee over the directors of enterprises in the province tended to encourage the director to consolidate his own power inside the enterprise. He noted that in important enterprises the director could not be dismissed without the consent of the Provincial Committee, and that the director therefore relied more on support in the party hierarchy than inside the enterprise. The director also tended to exert personal influence on selection of all key management posts, so that these managers in turn looked to the director rather than to the workers' council and management board to whom they were formally responsible. The result was hierarchic relations throughout the enterprise.[43] The result might also be to subordinate party officials at enterprise level to the director who was in a position to invoke higher party authority against them. Therefore the relative weakness of the party inside the enterprise could be directly related to the comparative importance of party committees at higher levels in selection of directors and in maintaining general oversight of the efficiency of enterprises in their jurisdiction.

These considerations suggest that centralized party organization and discipline strengthened the tendencies to hierarchic and oligarchic rule at various levels, including inside the enterprise. Rank and file communists were often deprived both of their democratic rights within the party and of their rights as workers to have a voice in elections and policy making in the enterprise. The Central Committee criticized cases where communist workers were punished for failing to vote for the manager recommended by the party committee and said this was a violation of workers' self-management rights.[44] A worker at the Proleter factory in Leskovac complained that in the past some party organizations had punished members who expressed personal views contrary to the party line on self-management bodies.[45] In general the post-Ranković discussions tended to confirm the reformers' contention that inner-party democracy was closely linked to realization of the new role of the party. A discussion in the Bor mining area expressed complaints that workers turned up at conferences and were simply told what had been decided by their officials. 'It was said that communists "masterminded this kind of self-management" because this method was applied in the work of party organizations.'[46]

This perception of the typical mode of operation by the party makes it more surprising that workers should say that they would like the League of Communists to wield more influence inside enterprises. But this statement must presumably be interpreted as a wish for the party as a collective body to debate policy options openly and to fulfil their declared guiding and persuasive role. It may also be seen as a desire to counteract the strength of oligarchic tendencies inside the firm, which in principle the League was also committed to unmask and oppose. During the heyday of reform in the 1960s this aspiration would not necessarily have seemed unrealistic, although at enterprise level the aims of the reform do not seem to have taken root in practice. Party officials appear to have remained an essential, though not in many cases predominant, 'factor of power'; while democracy inside the party and self-management in the enterprises were subordinated to oligarchic control.

Notes

1. Stipe Šuvar, 'O uzrocima i pretpostavke reforme S.K.', *Naše Teme*, January 1967, p. 72.
2. *Borba*, 17 July 1968.
3. Vladimir Bakarić, 'The League of Communists today', *Socialist Thought and Practice*, July-September 1966, p. 35.
4. *Borba*, 2 February 1966.
5. *Vjesnik*, 10 November 1968.
6. *Komunist*, 11 December 1969.
7. *Ekonomska Politika*, 14 March 1970.
8. Janez Jerovšek, 'Structures of influence in the commune', *Sociologija: Selected Articles 1959-69*, pp. 115-36. J. Dirlam and J. Plummer, *An Introduction to the Yugoslav Economy*, Charles Merrill, Columbus, Ohio, 1973, p. 51, cite two examples where enterprise officials were in open conflict with higher party organs over the choice of a director or of retention of an existing director.
9. Karen Rosenblum-Čale, *The Communal Assembly in Yugoslavia: Participation, Co-ordination and Development. The case of the Mostar Commune: 1965-69*, PhD. Thesis, London University, 1974, found the party intervenes most often in economic cases.
10. *Politika Ekspres*, 15 February 1965.
11. *Borba*, 23 May 1965.
12. *Borba*, 17 July 1966.
13. Krsto Kilibarda, 'Sindikat u Borbi protiv nesamoupravne moći', *Gledišta*, June-July 1968, pp. 923-34.
14. *Politika*, 29 August 1964.
15. *Ekonomska Politika*, 4 April 1964.
16. Richard P. Farkas, *Yugoslav Economic Development and Political Change*, Praeger, New York, 1975, pp. 63-4.
17. *Komunist*, 22 April 1965.
18. Farkas cites as an example of a similar director Ivan Spika, head of the Industrial and Agricultural Combine (IPK) in Croatia, who also worked through and with the party at commune and republican level; see pp. 61-2.
19. *Borba*, 12 January 1969.
20. J. Županov, 'Some empirical data on the responsibility in working organisations', cited by Rudi Supek, 'Problems and perspectives of worker self-management in Yugoslavia', in M. J. Broekmeyer (ed.), *Yugoslav Workers Self-Management*, D. Reidel, Dordrecht, 1970, p. 232.
21. Supek in Broekmeyer op. cit. p. 234.
22. Josip Županov, 'Is management becoming a profession?', cited by Mitja Kamušić, 'Economic efficiency and workers' self-management' in Broekmeyer op. cit. p. 98.
23. Jovo Brekić, 'Utjecaji u sferi kadrovke politike radnih organizacija', *Naše Teme*, March 1967, pp. 359-78.
24. Veljko Rus, 'Samoupravni egalitarizam i društvena differencijacija', *Praxis*, September-December, 1969, pp. 811-27.
25. Rudi Supek, 'Tehnološke promjene i samoupravna demokracij', *Pregled*, June 1971, citing results published in 1966.
26. See for example S. Verba and G. Shabad, 'Workers' councils and political stratification; the Yugoslav experience', *American Political Science Review*, March 1978.
27. Jospi Županov, 'Samoupravljanje i društvena moć', *Naše Teme*, Zagreb, 1969, pp. 105-17.
28. *Borba*, 25 May 1965.

29. Miko Tripalo, 'Još jedanput o reorganizaciji saveza komunista', *Naše Teme*, January 1968, p. 8.
30. Cited by Jiri Kolaja, *Workers' Councils: The Yugoslav Experience,* Tavistock Publications, London, 1965, pp. 18-19.
31. *Statistički Bilten*, No. 469, November 1967, p. 21.
32. *Politika*, 9 August 1967.
33. *Borba*, 13 August 1966.
34. *Komunist*, 21 April 1966.
35. Mihajlo Marković, *From Affluence to* Praxis, Ann Arbor Paperbacks, The University of Michigan Press, 1974, pp. 236-7.
36. *Politika*, 23 December 1966.
37. *Komunist*, 22 April 1965.
38. *Komunist*, 21 October 1965.
39. *Borba*, 25 May 1965.
40. *Borba*, 22 June 1968.
41. A more specific and perhaps more revealing question was posed by Krsto Kilibarda in his survey of 1576 communists from six different areas, in which he asked how much influence was exerted by individuals (as opposed to organizations or groups). This question elicited varied assessments between factories of the influence of the party secretary, which was clearly related to the extent of the power exercised by other personalities in key organizational posts. Naturally enough, most respondents tended to see the director as the most influential person in the enterprise, with the assistant director, the technical or financial director, the president of the workers' council and the president of the management board also being nominated by some. Comparison between Enterprise T in Kosovska Mitrovica and Enterprise G in Belgrade showed that 3.8 per cent of manual workers and 6.8 per cent of non-manual workers in Enterprise T thought that the League Secretary was the most important person in the enterprise, but nobody at all in Enterprise G nominated their party secretary. He also notes that respondents in leading positions were more likely to rate the influence of the League high and that their perceptions of the real distribution of formal and informal power were probably more accurate. It seems possible that they interpreted the question to give more weight to behind the scenes influence. This survey was conducted by Kilibarda before the Eighth Congress. He cites these findings in his book: *Samoupravljanje i Savez Komunista*, Sociološki Institut, Beograd, 1966 (which is primarily about a survey of the Kraljevo district), pp. 106 and 113.
42. Marković op. cit. p. 235.
43. *Borba*, 14 October 1966.
44. *Komunist*, 19 May 1966.
45. *Borba*, 18 December 1966.
46. *Borba*, 27 July 1966.

Conclusion

A number of central questions about the possibilities of democratic reform run through the detailed discussion of specific issues in this book. It is necessary at this stage to draw these questions together and suggest brief answers to them. The obvious starting point is to ask how far the League managed to achieve the stated goals of the reform: inner party democracy and the abandonment of a commanding for a guiding role. Several elements were involved in the search for a new role — separating the party from power, increasing popular and parliamentary control of government, respecting the autonomy of other political organizations, allowing greater freedom of debate and dissent, and strengthening the independence of the legal process. A radical change in the role of the party was also seen as a prerequisite for the realization of the central ideal of the Yugoslav system, self-management.

A second set of questions concern the reasons for the gap between Yugoslav theory and practice. A number of reasons have already been suggested, and need to be evaluated in relation to each other. One problem is that any radical ideal of participatory democracy runs up against oligarchic tendencies, so the issue is whether the party weakens or actually strengthens these tendencies. Another difficulty is potential conflict between the ideological and the political role of the party and its espousal of democratic ideas and practices throughout society, which leads to a further question about the inherent limits of a one-party system. Finally, it can be argued that many obstacles to reform stemmed from the specific nature of the Yugoslav party and society and the attitudes of key political leaders. How these factors are weighted will determine whether or not the Yugoslav experience in the period 1961–71 seems to hold out promise of more consistent democratic reform in other communist party states, or in Yugoslavia itself in the future.

Assessment of the attempts by the Yugoslav party to implement the declared goals of reform produces a varied picture. A moderate degree of success could be claimed for the movement towards inner party democracy.

Executive bodies did become more accountable to central committees, and even leaving aside the growing power of republican parties, which may be ascribed to nationalist pressure, there was evidence of party organs resisting certain decisions imposed from above, which implied some decentralization in the LCY. There was also undoubtedly an increase in open and critical debate inside the party and greater freedom of individual dissent, while party congresses showed signs of becoming forums for rank and file pressure. The Yugoslav League did in the 1960s wholly abandon the Stalinist model of 'monolithic unity'. But it did not take more than tentative steps towards real choice in party elections, and despite formal encouragement for greater participation at all levels, in practice power at both commune and republican levels seems to have been retained by small groups. During the sixties the party began to establish habits of internal democracy, but this process was cut short before democratic attitudes and practices had been consolidated.

The ability of the party to alter its role in terms of a 'separation from power' was, on the evidence we have, very limited; though there does appear to have been some differentiation of functions between party and government at federal and republican level, and occasional evidence of government acting independently. It is clear that the League made all the major political decisions, took the important initiatives and responded to crises. But it is doubtful whether real separation between party and government is possible whilst the party is committed to overall control of the political process, and debatable how far reformers ever meant the slogan of 'separating the party from power' to be taken seriously. It is therefore more revealing that the League was in practice very loath to relax its grip in areas which seem to promise greater scope for allowing independent activity: over parliamentary deputies, over the elections to the assemblies, and over the Socialist Alliance which has direct responsibility for co-ordinating deputies and overseeing elections. Despite some interesting examples of rebellion, particularly in the elections, the party leaders were unwilling to abandon general control and reacted sharply to disobedience in many cases.

Party domination of the whole governmental process may, however, be compatible with tolerance for autonomy and relative freedom in other political and social spheres. It is of considerable importance to the future of communist party states whether in practice the party can allow independent organization of interests through trade unions or student unions; whether it can tolerate press freedom and open intellectual or cultural debate; whether there are opportunities for dissent; and whether such freedoms are buttressed by respect for judicial independence. The record of the League during the sixties was patchy, but indicated greater sympathy for worker activism than for students or intellectuals. The party sought to keep overall control of the mass organizations through selection of top officials, and by public pressure on recalcitrant bodies, though it did seem to have moved away from treating them purely as transmission belts. Although the League showed some respect for the rights of the press and for freedom of debate and criticism, there were frequent displays of intolerance; and even those party reformers inclined to a liberal attitude to forms of dissent were ambivalent, distrusting 'spontaneity' and all unofficial organization. Judicial independence was upheld in principle during the sixties, and the party tried to avoid direct interference on fairly minor cases, like bans on issues of periodicals, but clearly did intervene in more critical political trials.

It would be unreasonable to judge the success of the Yugoslavs' most central experiment in popular democracy, self-management in economic and social institutions, merely by reference to the sixties. Some of the obstacles to effective popular control in the workplace are inherent in all forms of democracy, such as lack of knowledge, commitment or sense of efficacy. But the purpose of both economic and political reforms was in principle to enhance the reality of self-management by giving greater powers to enterprises, and to end the habit of state and party intervention, so it is relevant to ask whether these measures had the desired results. The problems inherent in espousing a market economy to strengthen self-management, including pressure towards concentration of economic power in the most efficient and expanding enterprises, are of great intrinsic interest, but not central to a concern about the role of the party. At the political level it appears that though the party inside the enterprise may have become less prone to blatant manipulation of the workers' council or management board, the tendency of commune or higher level political officials to oversee enterprises could operate to strengthen the power of the director, normally the dominant figure in the enterprise.

Studies of self-management tended to suggest that a façade of participation disguised a reality of oligarchic control, administrative dominance sometimes being reinforced by technocratic influence. Workers naturally tended to react against this élitism by asserting their desire for real worker control. What is more surprising is the assessment by the workers of the role the party should play, noted in the last chapter, and the expectation that the party would act to strengthen democratic participation. This hope that the party would operate to curb oligarchy was paralleled at a more sophisticated level by Slovene deputies in a survey published in 1969.[1] Although this view implied belief in the seriousness of the commitment to self-management by the party, it also logically required reliance on broad party committees as opposed to inner executives of party officials. The Slovenian deputies made this distinction explicit. They rated the influence of 'leading functionaries' in the republic as excessive, but thought the influence of the Central Committee of the Slovenian party should be greater. In practice the centralization of power within the party and the tendencies towards oligarchy in enterprise management, and in communal republican and federal government circles seem to have overlapped, creating an interlocking élite of party and administrative officials at the various levels. As a result, despite the commitment to self-management, it was possible to argue that in practice a handful of politicians were running the country. This conclusion suggests an important link between the role of the party and inner party democracy.

In assessing the theoretical coherence of the aims of the Yugoslav reformers there is a persuasive case to suggest that inner party democracy is linked to an extension of democracy in the wider society. A party that forbids its rank and file freedom of criticism and debate is unlikely to accord these rights to non-communists. Similarly a party that gives its own members no choice in selection of leaders, and no means of holding these leaders to account, is unlikely to encourage electoral choice and parliamentary power. It is also true that inner party reform is linked to the likelihood of the party renouncing its dominant role for persuasion. A highly centralized and undemocratic party accustomed to handing down orders must acquire a very different attitude before it will let a decision of an assembly or trade union go against the party line. Moreover, as the previous paragraph suggested, oligarchy in the party may reinforce oligarchy in other bodies, thus undermining the ideal of self-management.

Internal party democracy cannot, however, resolve some of the inherent problems of combining a claim to special ideological and political leadership by the party with the principle of giving democratic choice and initiative to all citizens. The party still finds itself in a dilemma when asked to decide whether individual communists can exercise their own judgement contrary to the party line on a workers' council, communal assembly or trade union. If it says 'no' it denies communists their citizen rights, but if it says 'yes' it has undermined the principle of party discipline. In fact a party which did engage in genuine collective decision-making might claim greater legitimacy in demanding disciplined obedience.

One possible approach to the problem of whether the League's two goals of reform — inner party democracy and a new guiding role — are necessarily linked would be to argue that the main problem was that the League did not take the process of inner party democracy far enough.

The leadership always maintained that reform must occur within the framework of democratic centralism in the party, and attacked the idea put forward by various intellectuals that the League should, to make its organization compatible with the broader system of participatory democracy, reorganize itself 'on the basis of self management'. This demand implied a reversal of the centralist principle — Bakarić interpreted it to mean 'that the Central Committee must do what the basic organizations tell it to do'.[2] The other principles inherent in self-management are arguably the right of all to participate and the right to exercise independent judgement, which would logically imply creation of a mass party and a right to dissent from party decisions. Certainly wholesale adoption of self-management principles would have meant abandoning totally the concept of a cadre party and the organization of an orthodox communist party. But it is arguable that the attempt to maintain a modified democratic centralism in the party was one crucial factor undermining liberal reforms and the reality of self-management.

The other basic dilemma involved in the League's interpretation of its role was whether it could allow other political bodies to adopt policies contrary to its own. The concept of a guiding role did not entail repudiation of the basic premise that the party had unique ability to lead Yugoslav society towards communism, it only involved reliance on new methods of persuasion instead of enforcement. But if persuasion failed to work, then the party had to tolerate a policy it believed to be wrong or fall back on enforcement. This potential for crisis was of course one reason for insisting on discipline by party members, who might often be able to avert confrontations between the party and other organs. The real issue here, however, is whether the party can adopt a genuinely guiding role unless it makes more modest claims for its superior wisdom, and can avoid seeing every divergence from the party line as a threat to the future of socialism.

These considerations lead us to the question whether there are inherent limits to democratic reform in a one-party system. It is arguable on the basis of the response of the party to pressures for greater pluralism, and for greater freedom of criticism, that the ban on political opposition must limit the reality of all other freedoms. There are two reasons why it may, both suggested by the Yugoslav experience. First, a party trying to prevent any organized opposition will tend to suppress all moves in that direction, for example a journal which advocates a multi-party system, and all activity outside party control, for example independent parliamentary candidates or spontaneous student protest committees. Secondly, the rapidity with which the Yugoslav League reversed the liberal trend after 1971 strongly suggests the need for well-established institutional checks on the power of the leadership. It is still debatable whether such checks could be provided by greater inner party democracy, by an independent judiciary, parliament and press, and by an active citizenry. The rearguard action waged in Yugoslavia against the imposition of orthodoxy after 1972 suggests that these factors could be significant if sufficiently well established during the period of reform. But the existence of one or more opposition parties can be seen as necessary to reinforce other checks on the abuse of power.

These theoretical considerations suggest that there is considerable tension between the requirements of one-party rule, by a communist party still committed to democratic centralism, and both the participatory and the liberal models of reform. But it is important to ask whether there are specific features of the Yugoslav party and its leadership which militated against a more consistent attempt to move in either direction. Several obvious considerations should be noted here. Firstly, the fact that the party was composed in the 1950s largely of uneducated partisan veterans, who continued to exercise powerful resistance to reform in the 1960s, made the Yugoslav party an unsuitable vehicle for the sophisticated role envisaged for it at the Sixth Congress.

Secondly, the divisions within the party leadership about the desirability and limits of reform, and oscillations in the attitudes of key reformers, resulted in ambiguity and uncertainty. Tito himself was never wholeheartedly in favour of liberalization, and was clearly hostile to academic and cultural freedom. His doubts about restricting the role of the party, voiced openly after 1971, significantly reduced the chances of successful reform under his leadership, and his personal authority was decisive in ensuring the swing away from liberalism in 1972. Kardelj, despite his reputation as one of the chief architects of the reforms, displayed caution in his public statements. The main radical thrust inside the party came from a rather younger group of republican leaders who came to the fore in the sixties; and even some of them, like Marko Nikezić and Latinka Perović in Serbia, became more circumspect after 1968.

Thirdly, the fact that the reforms were initiated from above, and that there was no real movement in favour of reform from below (with some exceptions in the sixties) helps account for the tendency of the leadership to retreat from the full implementation of proposed reforms. The Prague Spring and the Polish Solidarity movement both suggest that strong popular pressure results in much greater radicalism.

By far the most important factor, however, is the role played by nationalism in the reform movement. Nationalist aspirations undoubtedly helped to promote reform in the early 1960s and it is also arguable that

the realities of nationalist politics strengthen federalism at the government level, will ensure collective leadership inside the party, and act as
a restraint on moves towards excessive centralism or abuse of power. But
nationalist demands and attitudes have proved in Yugoslavia to be often
extremely intolerant and illiberal in their consequences. Moreover, the
nationalist rivalries divided the liberal leaders, undermined the achievements of the reform at a number of levels, and most important of all the
nationalists appeared to abuse relaxation of party controls. Therefore
the main Yugoslav argument against the possibility of allowing opposition
parties, that they would inevitably reflect nationalist conflicts, appeared
to be an argument against liberal freedoms in general and against the
policy of reform adopted at the Sixth Congress.

The conclusions to be drawn from studying the Yugoslav model of
socialist democracy are therefore somewhat ambivalent. The findings are
positive enough to suggest the possibility of moving towards effective
democracy in a communist party state, and it is possible that Yugoslavia
in the 1980s will be more favourably placed than in the 1960s for further
experiments in this direction. But as the Czechoslovak reform movement
of 1968 seemed to indicate, before it was brought to an end by Soviet
troops and political pressure, greater success might be possible in a country
with less acute economic and nationalist divisions and a stronger tradition
of political democracy. Whether the more fundamental difficulties of
achieving democracy in a one-party state can be politically resolved is a
question which cannot be definitively answered by looking at Yugoslavia,
though it can be argued that the Yugoslav reform movement of the 1960s
has enabled us to see more clearly where some of the problems lie.

Notes

1. *Politika*, 4 May 1969, summarizes study of 519 deputies in the Slovene
   Assembly by the Centre for Public Opinion in Ljubljana.
2. Vladimir Bakarić, 'The kind of League we need', *Socialist Thought and Practice*,
   October–December 1967.

EPILOGUE

Ten years have elapsed since the Croatian crisis brought the period of liberal reform to an end. In addition Yugoslavia has now experienced over a year of collective leadership since Tito's death in May 1980. Three central issues are briefly examined here: firstly, how much of the reform programme of the sixties was retained after 1972, and how much was abandoned; secondly, what kind of leadership emerged in the seventies; and thirdly, how is that leadership and the Yugoslav political system likely to operate in the future? The first two questions can be answered with reasonable certainty, the third is necessarily speculative.

The Fate of the Reforms

It would be misleading to present 1972 as a total break with the previous period of reform, and it clearly did not mark the end of the Yugoslav experiment in creating a distinctive form of socialism. The thirty years since 1950 have seen various innovations and changes of direction, but there have also been continuities. The consistent thread which links 1950 to 1980 is commitment to the ideal of democratic participation and worker control summed up in the term self-management. Two significant elements of the programme of the 1960s have been retained, perhaps because they reflect economic and political needs. One is the decentralized economic system, largely reliant on market mechanisms, introduced in 1965. Although the proposals for allowing private investment and introducing a free capital market being advocated by the Slovene Prime Minister, Stane Kavčić, in 1971 were ruled out of debate after 1972,[1] and the Tenth Congress condemned the belief that 'socio-economic problems can be solved by the market's automatic operation',[2] there has been no attempt to reimpose a centrally planned and controlled economy. In practice this would be politically hampered by the second legacy of the 1960s: a federal system which drastically limited the powers of the federation in favour of the republics, as set out in the Constitutional Amendments of 1971.

Commitment to the principles of the devolution of power to republics, economic decentralization and self management was reflected in the Constitution of 1974. It confirmed the basic division of powers between the centre and the republics hammered out in 1971, though it slightly enhanced the central powers of the Yugoslav People's Army.[3] The reorganization of the Federal Assembly actually strengthened the federal principle: republics were equally represented in both the Chambers of the new Assembly, and the delegates elected directly by the republican assemblies.[4]

The complicated new system of electing delegates to the assemblies was presented as a means of strengthening self-management, because it increased worker representation and reduced elitism. It was also intended to ensure accountability of assembly delegates to their electors. A further measure to enforce the 'deprofessionalization' of parliamentary politics was a specific requirement that members of assemblies stay in their jobs. The Constitution also addressed itself to curbing technocracy in the economy itself by making work units within enterprises the basic decision-making unit, by limiting the role of managers, and by reorganizing the banking system to prevent control by financial experts. These provisions were expanded in a document as lengthy and complex as the Constitution — the 1976 Law on Associated Labour. This Law codified in detail the self-management powers of basic work units and their rights to make and invest their own profits.[5]

The complex and decentralized nature of the political and economic systems embodied in the 1974 Constitution implied the need for the party to act as a coordinating and directing force. The importance of the League was explicitly recognized in the Constitution, though the Socialist Alliance was formally assigned the main responsibility for the correct working of the electoral and assembly system, and the Trade Unions for the economy. The Tenth LCY Congress of 1974, however, spelled out that the party had a central directing role to play. The Presidium Report to the Congress stated that:

> Since the constitution and work of assemblies on the delegate principle, which include a very large number of working people-delegates, is a complex creative act, the permanent activity of the League of Communists is indispensable.[6]

The Draft Congress Resolution on the Tasks of the LCY in Development of Self-Management specified that:

> Confirming its vanguard role, capacity for action and strength, the League of Communists must, by acting through the Socialist Alliance,

the Confederation of Trade Unions and the delegations, create the
social conditions and relations needed for the effective functioning
of the entire political system.[7]

The theoretical formulations of the League's role embodied in the Congress documents castigated attempts by 'anti-socialist' forces to weaken
the party by turning it into an educational debating club instead of an
'organized force in decision-making'.[8]

The increasing size of the party, 1.7 million members by the Eleventh
Congress in 1978, may reflect the fact that party membership is more
important than in the sixties for career prospects,[9] which in turn is an
indicator of the degree of party dominance in society. Since 1972 party
intervention at all levels has been encouraged rather than condemned.
Nevertheless, the League has maintained its official concern to avoid
identification of the party with the state apparatus, whilst making it
clear that 'isolating the League of Communists from state authority' is
equally wrong. The principle that no one could hold top state and party
posts at the same time was reasserted in 1972 to prevent dual membership of the state Collective Presidency and the LCY Executive Bureau,
but by the Tenth Congress dual membership of the top state and party
bodies was again permitted.[10] The 1974 Statutes did however specify
that no one could hold an 'executive function' in the executive-political
bodies of both state and party. At this stage there was probably more
concern to avoid accumulation of functions and to ensure a collective
leadership below Tito, rather than a real desire to clarify the separation
of party and state.

The Tenth Congress was characterized by its ideological stress on
Leninism, accompanied logically by much greater emphasis than in 1969
on the importance of democratic centralism, which figured prominently
in the Statutes. Despite the Leninist emphasis on discipline, the Statutes
did maintain the right of individuals to resign from the party, first granted
in 1964. The powers of basic organizations were also elaborated in detail.
Most significantly, the right of republican parties to elect representatives
to the central LCY bodies, and the equal representation of republics on
these bodies, was written into the Statutes. This recognition of the role
of republican parties was explained, and to some extent qualified, in the
Congress Resolution on the party's role, which noted: 'the working class
needs a unified revolutionary vanguard . . . such a role could not be
performed by an organization on the lines of a 'federal coalition' of
republican and provincial organizations, or by a centralized 'supra-
republic' organization'.[11] Despite concessions on paper to individual

rights and devolution of powers in the party, the tone of the Tenth Congress – set speeches, no criticism from the floor, and adulation of Tito himself – was much more reminiscent of communist party orthodoxy.

The most decisive swing away from the ethos of the late sixties occurred in the repudiation of liberal freedoms. Immediate moves were made to introduce a more restrictive law on the press in 1972, and despite initital criticism by the press itself, and resistance by the Assembly to rushing the bill through,[12] the Yugoslav newspapers were curbed. The dissident *Praxis* was finally silenced in 1975 by the device of persuading the printers to refuse to print it. Academic freedom was also undermined when the Serbian Assembly passed a law overriding the autonomy of Belgrade University in order to enforce the dismissal of the *Praxis* philosophers. The relative independence of the judiciary came under attack in 1972, as noted in chapter ten, and there have been a series of political trials: against Croatian nationalists, rebellious students and against a group of Cominformists accused of plotting with Moscow. The collective leadership which has succeeded Tito has indicated a degree of nervousness and some tendency towards illiberalism, by making threatening noises against intellectual dissidents and against Djilas, and by initiating further trials of alleged Croatian nationalists.[13] Nevertheless Yugoslavs still enjoy a cultural policy tolerant of western trends, easy access to newspapers, books and films from the west, and a lack of restrictions on travel abroad – which allows the *Praxis* philosophers to give lectures in the west. This relatively open society is a significant heritage from the liberalising trends of the sixties.

The New Leadership

The compromise nature of present Yugoslav domestic policies is reflected in and probably perpetuated by the personalities who came to the fore in 1972, and have stayed in power ever since. In the leadership, as in policies there was a sharp, but by no means complete, break with the previous reform period. The reformers who had triumphed at the Ninth Congress were not themselves a homogeneous group. They were divided in terms of political generations: the cautious liberals with an authority dating back to the pre-war and partisan struggle, like Kardelj and Bakarić, were those who avoided compromising themselves in the crisis period of 1970–71 – though in the case of Bakarić perhaps narrowly. The younger men and women who rose to the top in the 1960s, Tripalo and Dabčević-Kučar from Croatia, Milosavlevski from Macedonia, Nikezić and Perović in Serbia and the Slovene Prime Minister Kavčić, all went too far and were forced to resign after Karadjorjevo, though in Serbia Tito had to wage a hard fought campaign to oust the republican leaders in 1972. The intermediate generation like Todorović and Crvenkovski, who both joined the LCY Central Committee at the Sixth Congress, were eased out more gently between 1972–74. There were also ideological divisions among the 1969 victors which cut across generations. Some of the older generation who retained their positions in 1969 had always appeared to be moderate conservatives in the pre-Brioni conflicts: for example the Macedonian Kolišsevski and the Serb Petar Stambolić, who became more prominent again after 1972. Some of the younger generation appeared to take up more orthodox positions even in the period of maximum liberalism, for example Slovene party President, Franc Popit, the Montenegrin Budislav Šoskić and the Serb Stevan Doronjski, who all stayed at the top after 1972.

The cadre changes in 1972 therefore resulted in a leadership with varying degrees of sympathy or repugnance for the liberal aspects of the previous reforms. The Croatian party leaders selected to deal with the aftermath of the nationalist crisis stood at the liberal end of the spectrum, with no desire to impose an unnecessarily 'firm hand' in their republic, and committed to keeping the gains in republican power granted between 1967–71. Bakarić himself has remained as an elder statesman, and at the time of Tito's death was in charge of an important committee covering internal security. Miloš Minić, who championed the students in 1968, took over as Foreign Minister in 1972, and since he left that post in 1978 has been a member of the party Presidium. Other liberals who have remained to the fore are the Macedonian Kiro Gligorov, an influential exponent of the economic reforms, who became President of the Asembly in 1974, and Sergej Krajgher from Slovenia, who took over the rotating state Presidency chairmanship in 1981. On the other hand both Stambolić and Kolišsevski are members of the state Presidency; the latter was acting as chairman when Tito died, and so became temporarily head of state.

The leadership a year after Tito's death is substantially the same group of men who carried through the policies of 1972. One significant loss was the death in 1979 of Kardelj: the closest to being Tito's heir apparent as the only political survivor, after the disgrace of Djilas and later Ranković, of the pre-war triumvirate round Tito. But a second possible heir to Tito emerged during the seventies, a Slovene and protege of Kardlej, who was Secretary of the Executive Bureau at the end of 1971, and became Tito's right hand man — Stane Dolanc. He was elected Secretary of the LCY again at the Eleventh Congress in 1978, but Tito decided in October 1979 that the principle of rotation which applied to the chairmanship of the Presidium should also apply to the post of Secretary. Since Dolanc continued to be close to Tito, this move does not appear to have been a serious demotion, but rather an assertion of the goal of genuinely collective leadership after Tito's death.

Yugoslavia After Tito

The issue of the leadership is one that arises naturally when trying to assess the future course of politics in Yugoslavia, and the degree of likely stability. The problem of succession loomed especially large in Yugoslavia because of Tito's stature as founding father and effective monarch of his new state for thirty five years. In a state riven by nationalist rivalries, with the consequent threat of foreign manipulation of nationalist discontent or of secession, Tito alone stood above all rivalries as a symbol of Yugoslav unity. When republican leaders were at odds, Tito could impose agreement, and his unique authority and political shrewdness were crucial in resolving crises. There is no doubt that Tito's leadership was a vital factor in establishing the new republic as a viable political unit, asserting its independent international standing and in promoting the experiment in construction of a new model of socialism. But the obverse of his achievements was fear of a future without him, which seems in the 1970s to have led to a certain immobilism in Yugoslav politics and an unhelpful tendency to increase adulation of Tito himself. His death exposes Yugoslavia's political institutions to the test of the strains imposed by Yugoslavia's multi-ethnic society.

One possible solution, which seems the most obvious to commentators accustomed to Kremlin-gazing, would be for a new strong man to emerge. There are however no obvious personalities in Yugoslavia today fitted to play this role. Party leaders have always tended to be identified with their republics, and the trends in party organization since the sixties have strengthened this attitude, so any aspiring heir to Tito is hindered by the likely resistance from other republics. Therefore the possibility of seizing supreme power must depend on having a key role in an institution able to exercise central control. The Secretary of the LCY might potentially be in this position – though in view of the strength of republican organizations, and the republican limits to the power weilded by Ranković before 1966, this is much less certain than in the Soviet Union. The security service suggests itself as a second possible power base, but since the fall of Ranković and the curbing of UDBA's prerogatives, this is highly debatable.[14] The body most often cited as being capable of ensuring the unity of Yugoslavia, and as having stood behind Tito in the nationalist crisis of 1971, is of course the army. There is no doubt that the army is an important force in Yugoslav politics, well represented in the party; and General Nikola Ljubičić has been Minister of Defence since 1967, immune to the principle of rotation of offices. If there were a really serious nationalist crisis, then it is possible the army would back a strong man to reimpose and maintain order. There is not at present any evidence, however, that the army aspires to exercise controlling power. Therefore it seems likely that the republican party bosses will be forced to resolve their disputes by compromise, as Tito envisaged, and to cooperate in a genuinely collective leadership. The virtually confederal nature of the Yugoslav state, and the federal elements in the party organization itself clearly conduce to this kind of solution. So it is possible that Yugoslavia after Tito will, as in many other respects, diverge from the standard communist party pattern, and avoid one man dominance.

The movement from a largely symbolic federalism towards genuine devolution of power to republican units has so far been the Yugoslavs' answer to their most intractable problem: the strength of nationalist passions. In the period 1970–71 it appeared that the attempted solution was simply exacerbating nationalism. Experience in striking republican bargains over the succeeding ten years may have begun to create a tradition of effective federalism, which could lead to stability based on genuine representation of differing republican interests.

No political arrangements can satisfy fanatical nationalism, and nationalist sentiments are always liable to take unreasonable forms, as the extremist wing of the Croatian nationalist movement in 1971 demonstrated. Irrational nationalism, however, is likely to be fuelled by suppression of legitimate national demands, so the still fragile Yugoslav federal compromise is most liable to destruction if the system fails to allow proper representation to justified nationalist grievances. This danger has been vividly illustrated by the wave of Albanian demonstrations and riots sweeping Kosovo in March and April 1981.[15] The Yugoslav authorities have accused Albania of seeking to promote an armed uprising and secession, and have arrested and tried members of alleged seccessionist groups. Whilst the Albanian government may have had a hand in exacerbating the situation in Kosovo, there is a strong case to be made that most Albanians would not be enthusiastic to cast in their lot with the much poorer and more restrictive society of Albania if given greater access to the advantages of Yugoslav society. Kosovo, with its predominantly Albanian population, is a classic case of demographic, economic, social and political factors promoting nationalism: a high birth rate, economic under-development, a background of Serbian prejudice and oppression, and political under-representation. Since 1966 Kosovo has enjoyed a real voice in state and party counsels by virtue of its provincial status, but the demand made by students at the Priština University in 1981 for full republican status for Kosovo is objectively justifiable in terms of the population and territory involved. Achievement of this aspiration is blocked by Serbian opposition to 'losing' Kosovo and by fear of the new republic leaning towards Tirana, so Albanian resentment may become a more potent threat to Yugoslav unity than the historic conflict between Serbs and Croats.

Whilst in terms of practical politics the tensions caused by nationalism and the role of federalism must come first, it is worth remembering that there is a further level of significant decentralization: to local government. The communes do enjoy very real decision-making powers, they can and sometimes do stand out against republican and federal pressures, and they offer genuine avenues for public pressures by citizens through the voters' meetings, local referenda and the communal assembly.[16] Despite a tendency to oligarchic manipulation of these democratic channels, there is also evidence that citizens and their deputies can and do sometimes assert their political rights when vital interests are at stake. The interventionist role adopted by the party since 1972 has clearly not destroyed the vitality of this level of local government.

The decentralization of power in Yugoslavia to both republics and communes does provide a form of pluralism and creates openings for popular pressure to affect policies. There is a real danger, often illustrated in the past thirty years, of local and republican interests being pressed to the detriment of a broader common good. But given the impossibility of a pluralism of parties, and the difficulties of asserting interest group pluralism against the party on the Polish model, acceptance of a regional pluralism may in the long run ensure a degree of genuine democracy and freedom within a stable framework. An optimistic projection for Yugoslavia by the year 2,000 might be that it will have become a socialist Switzerland — enjoying national independence, federalism and participatory democracy.

Notes

1   RFE Research Report, 13 March, 1972 discusses the proposals by Kavčič.
2   The Tenth Congress of the League of Communists of Yugoslavia: Resolutions Belgrade, 1974, p. 27.
3   See Adam Roberts, Nations In Arms, Chatto and Windus London, 1976, p. 179.

4 See Dennison Rusinow, The Yugoslav Experiment 1948-1974, Hurst and Co, London, 1977, pp. 326-32 for a detailed analysis of 1974 Constitution.

5 See Duncan Wilson, Tito's Yugoslavia, Cambridge University Press, Cambridge, 1979, pp. 221-4, on the Law on Associated Labour and for a general survey of political developments up to 1979.

6 The Tenth Congress of the League of Communists of Yugoslavia: Draft Report on the Activities of the League of Communists and Presidency of the LCY Between the Ninth and Tenth Congresses, Belgrade, 1974, p. 106.

7 Resolutions, op. cit., p. 39.

8 Ibid., pp. 5 and 14-15.

9 See for example Praxis philosophers' appeal to Collective Presidency to abolish system requiring job applicants to show 'moral and political fitness' reported in Guardian, 25 January, 1978.

10 In 1972 Crvenkovski was removed from the party Executive Bureau on the grounds that he was in the state Collective Presidency. After the Tenth Congress, which recreated an intermediate Presidium between the Central Committee, all nine members of the state Presidency were elected to the 39 member party Presidium.

11 Resolutions, op. cit., pp. 18-19.

12 See RFE Research Report, 3 March, 1972

13 See Observer, 6 July, 1980; Guardian 11 May, 6 June, 1981.

14 The Minister of the Interior since 1974 has been army general, Franjo Herljević. His appointment could be seen as an ominous merging of police and military power, but it is equally palusible to assume the military have an interst in curbing the security service. Herljević is not a well known political personality.

15 Guardian, 4 April, 2 May, 6 May, 14 May, 16 May, 5 June, 10 June, 11 June 1981.

16 See for example Guardian, 24 April, 1979, on resistance by citizens and Assembly of Zadar to republican and federal pressure for building of a nuclear power plant across the bay. The study by Karen Rosenblum-Čale of the Mostar Commune in 1965-69 throws up examples of citizen activism on issues such as schools and roads, and it is unlikely that at this level there has been a significant change in political practice since 1972. The Zadar case suggests not.

Appendix I Membership of the LCY

Table I *Social Composition of LCY Membership between the Vth and IXth Congresses*

	Total number of members	Peasants %	Workers %	White collar %	Others[1] %	Women %	Youth[2] %
1948[3]	482938	47.8	30.1	13.6	8.5	17.3	
1952	772920	42.8[4]	32.2[5]	18.9	6.1	17.0	
1958	829953	14.7	32.7	34.8	17.8	16.6	23.6
1964	1031634	7.6	36.0	39.0	17.4	17.3	13.6
1969	1111682	7.3	31.2	35.3	26.2	19.1	23.3

1. This category includes army personnel, students, private craftsmen, housewives, and (in the 1960s) the unemployed.
2. Figures for young people are not available for the earlier years. The category of 'youth' comprised those under 26 years of age until 1968, when it was extended to cover everyone under 28.
3. The statistics are calculated from 31 December of the year, not the date of the party congresses.
4. Up to 1953 the figures for peasants were artificially inflated because they were calculated on the basis of occupation at the time of entering the party and not on real occupation. Reclassification in 1953 assigned 90 000 'peasants' to the white-collar category. So the real number of peasants in the party in 1952 was about 240 000 not 330 454, approximately 31 per cent of the membership.
5. Figures for workers were similarly inflated, 45 000 'workers' were reclassified as white collar in 1953. So the real number of workers in the party in 1952 was about 204 000, not 249 110, approximately 26 per cent of the membership.

Table II *Breakdown of White-collar Membership in 1969*

	Numbers	Percentage of total membership
Engineers and technicians	54765	4.9
Workers in health, education, science and culture	132853	11.9
Managerial personnel	67250	6.1
Administrative staffs	138217	12.4
Total	393085	35.3

Note: There was no breakdown of white-collar membership until 1964, when it was based in part on educational qualifications. A clearer occupational breakdown was adopted in 1968.

Table III *LCY Membership by Year of Admission*

Proportion of Partisan and Post-war Generations

Year of admission	1957[1] %	1964 %	1966 %	1968 %	1971 %
Before 1941	0.4	0.3	0.3	0.3	0.3
1941–44	10.3	6.4	6.1	5.4	5.3
1945–48	33.1	19.1	17.9	15.2	15.1
1949–52	33.4	17.9	16.6	13.8	13.0
1953–57	22.5	18.0	16.3	13.5	12.1
1958–62		30.3	26.6	20.9	19.4
1963–67		8.9	16.2	15.8	14.2
1968				15.0	20.6

1. Position on 31 March 1957.
Note: 0.3 per cent this year entered as 'unknown'.

Table IV *National Representation in the LCY*

	Percentages in League 1964 (June)	1971	Percentages in population 1961	1971
Serbs	51.5	49.4	42.1	39.7
Croats	18.6	17.4	23.1	22.1
Slovenes	7.1	6.4	8.5	8.2
Macedonians	6.6	6.2	5.6	5.8
Montenegrins	6.1	6.3	2.8	2.5
Moslems (ethnic group)	3.5	4.6	5.2	8.4
Yugoslavs	1.2	4.0 (approx.)	1.7	1.3
Albanians	2.8	3.4	4.9	6.4
Hungarians (other minor nationalities excluded here)	1.2	1.1	2.7	2.3

Note: In 1961 quite a few Moslems chose to call themselves 'Yugoslavs', but in 1971 they were encouraged to call themselves Moslems. The proportion of 'Yugoslavs' in Bosnia fell from 8.5 per cent to 1.2 per cent (*NIN*, 28 May 1972).

Table V   *Admissions, Expulsions and Resignations*

	Admissions	Expulsions	Resignations[1]	Total number of members
1961	67548	14975		1035003
1962	26725	22655		1018331
1963	39362	15320		1019013
1964	41403	10626	2273	1031634
1965	51398	12878	5762	1046202
1966	39928	13488	7640	1046018
1967	33986	11195	11182	1013500
1968	175293	14235	13363	1146084
1969	49537	11995	10321	1111682
1970	31885	10178	15224	1049184
1971	47606	6813	13625	1025476
1972	58262	12941	11530	1009947

1.   The right of resignation was granted in the 1964 Statute of the LCY adopted in
      December at the Eighth Congress.

Note: Figures are available for some, but not all years for the additional categories of:
(a)   those crossed off the lists of party members for minor faults: 4843 in 1964;
      10 031 in 1969 and over 20 000 each year from 1970-2;
(b)   those who lose themselves from the party records — in 1967 an unusually high
      number, 42 250, had dropped out of the records, and between 1 January 1961
      and 31 December 1969 the party lost a total of 196 173 members (*Borba*,
      8 January 1969, 2 March 1971)
(c)   those who died.

These figures reflect certain policy trends between 1961 and 1972, for example the
tightening of party discipline in 1962 which led to a stricter admissions policy and
a higher expulsion rate; the mass recruitment of young people in 1968; and the
increasing willingness up to 1971 of communists to avail themselves of the right of
resignation, which probably reflected increasing liberalization. It is interesting that
resignations in 1973 dropped to 5694. The figures also confirm a point made in party
and press comment, that the ousting of Ranković in 1966 did not lead to a significant
purge of his supporters at lower levels of the party.

Educational Standards in the LCY

Statistics on educational levels in the party in the period before 1958
are not comprehensive, but there is no doubt that educational standards
rose between 1945 and 1958. At the Fifth Congress in 1948 Ranković
lamented the lack of formal education among the 468,175 party members,
of whom 32,136 (6.8 per cent) had not been to school at all, whilst
258,937 (55.2 per cent) had only received elementary schooling, and

many of these had not finished this basic education. The improving educational standards in the party in the fifties and sixties reflected the successful drive to promote elementary education, especially in rural areas, and
the very rapid expansion of higher education. In addition the changing
social composition of the League meant that by the sixties the highly
qualified sectors of the population were disproportionately well represented in the party, whereas less educated groups like the peasantry were
under-represented.

Table VI   *Educational Standards in LCY 1958–1969*

	1958[1] %	1964[1] %	1969[2] %
Unskilled workers	8.5	7.8	5.8
Semi-skilled workers	11.7	8.7	5.5
Skilled workers	25.0	23.2	19.3
Highly skilled workers	5.2	8.3	7.7
Lower school qualifications	25.0	18.6	22.8
Secondary school qualifications	18.5	20.9	23.3
College diploma	6.1[3]	5.5	7.2
University degree		7.1	8.1

1. The figures for 1958 and 1964 are for those employed in the socialist sector,
    excluding apprentices and members of the armed forces; private peasants, and
    craftsmen, housewives, pensioners and students are therefore omitted.
2. The figures for 1969 cover all members of the LCY except members of the
    armed forces, but maintain the occupational distinction between blue-collar
    workers and the rest of the population.
3. The 1958 statistics give an amalgamated percentage for those with college and
    university qualifications.

Note: Use of the English terms 'lower' (or 'elementary') education and secondary
    education is somewhat misleading. Lower school lasts eight years for children
    between 7 and 15, so 'secondary' schools provide pre-university education
    and some forms of vocational education.

Note on Sources

The main sources for statistics on LCY membership figures are:

Miloš Nikolić, *Savez Komunista Jugoslavije u Uslovima Samoupravljanja*,
Kultura, Beograd, 1967, pp. 746–84, which covers period 1946–66;
Zoran Vidaković, *Promene u Strukturi Jugoslovenskog Društva i Savez
Komunista*, Sedma Sila, Beograd 1967, compares the composition of the
party with that of the general population and includes useful information
on interpretation of categories like 'peasants'; *Borba*, 24 January 1970

ran a special supplement giving exhaustive details about the 1968 figures; Deseti Kongres SKJ: *Statistički Podaci O Savezu Komunista Jugoslavije*, Beograd 1974, covers in great detail the period 1968–73. The Reports of the Central Committee to the 8th and 9th Congresses also include basic figures for the relevant periods between the Congresses.

For expulsions see *Yugoslav Survey*, November 1967 for period 1964–6; *VUS*, 28 August 1968; *Borba*, 24 January 1970; and Deseti Kongres SKJ: *Statistički Podaci*, pp. 94–8.

For resignations see: *Komunist*, 28 April 1966; *Borba*, 3 July 1967; *Borba*, 8 July 1968; *Borba*, 3 July 1969; Deseti Kongres SKJ: *Statistički Podaci*, pp. 133–4. (NB. *Yugoslav Survey,* November 1967 gives figures for proportions of workers who resigned in 1965 and 1966 which appear to be misprints.)

For figures on national representation in LCY see Nikolić, and *Yugoslav Survey*, October 1964 and November 1967; and Deseti Kongres SKJ: *Statistički Podaci*. On census figures see *Yugoslav Survey*, February 1973.

For information on the educational levels of the party in relation to the population see Branko Horvat, *An Essay on Yugoslav Society*, International Arts and Sciences Press, White Plains, New York, 1969. On standards of education in Yugoslav society and educational policy after 1945 see: A. H. Barton, B. Denitch and C. Kadushin (eds), *Opinion-making Elites in Yugoslavia*, Praeger, New York, 1973; Bogdan Denitch, *The Legitimation of a Revolution*, Yale University Press, New Haven, 1976; and *Yugoslav Survey*, No. 1, 1960.

Appendix II   Cadre Policy

The LCY tried to implement four main principles of cadre policy in the 1960s:

(i) 'rotation' — to ensure renewal of party committees at each election and a turnover of party officials (parallel to rotation in parliamentary assemblies and government);

(ii) 'deprofessionalization' — to reduce the number of paid full-time party officials by giving more political posts to amateurs, and to cut down the number of professional politicans by encouraging people after a period of office to return to their original careers;

(iii) 'deaccumulation of functions' — to end the practice, common up to 1964, of one official holding multiple political posts in the party, political organizations and government bodies;

(iv) to improve the social composition of party committees by cutting down the number of professional politicians and increasing the proportion of workers, women and young people.

These principles were all closely linked to the goals of reform. Rotation was intended: (a) to promote inner-party democracy by increasing participation in party leaderships; (b) to oust the partisan generation in favour of a younger, better-educated generation favourable to economic and political reform. Deprofessionalization had three purposes (apart from reducing the party bureaucracy which was seen as intrinsically desirable): (a) to make rotation easier, as professional politicians had a vested interest in hanging on to their jobs; (b) to promote inner party democracy by removing the full-time officials accustomed to making decisions in small circles and issuing orders from above; (c) to encourage the adoption of a new party role, since it was thought permanent officials were more likely to exercise old-style party domination over political life. (See for example a discussion in Slovenia about the importance of making commune party secretaries amateurs in *Komunist*, 14 July 1966.) Deaccumulation of functions which meant separating cadres (a) directly discouraged party dominance over other political bodies and reduced the power of political bosses; (b) chimed with the policy of cutting down the number of professional politicians, who were more likely to accumulate posts. Bringing in a wider range of social groups was made easier by rotation and was intended to strengthen commitment to self-management and the principles of reform.

How Much Success?

The evidence on the workings of cadre policy is rather sketchy and in some cases only covers individual republics or provinces. But it is possible to draw some conclusions on the degree of success or failure.

Rotation

(i) Renewal of party committees.
In this area there was undoubted success. The turnover of membership of committees at local republican and federal elections from 1964 was well above the 25 per cent minimum required in the Eighth Congress Statute.[1]

(ii) Turnover of cadres
The statistics suggest that the requirement in the 1964 Statute that officials should not normally hold the same office for more than two mandate periods was being obeyed, but various official comments suggested that the letter but not the spirit of the Statute was being followed. Political officials tended to exchange top political posts (secretary of the commune party, president of the commune assembly, president of the Socialist Alliance and president of the trade unions) in 'the rotation merry-go-round'. If rotation was not entirely circular, one official usually moved up in the hierarchy, often becoming an assembly deputy.[2]

Deprofessionalization

The available statistics for full-time party workers at all levels of the LCY suggest conflicting trends between republics up to 1965, but an overall slight drop in the number of party bureaucrats at commune level by 1967, and an increase at republican and central levels.[3] A survey of cadre policy in the Vojvodina found a trend towards increasing the number of amateurs holding secondary posts, for example deputy secretaries at commune level and secretaries of basic organizations.[4] A comprehensive survey of the Bosnian party confirmed that professionals continued to hold key posts in the commune and monopolized those at the republican level.[5] There is some evidence from Serbia and from the Vojvodina study that there was some progress in recruiting elected officials from outside the group of professional politicians, but it is not clear if that applied in all republics.

Limiting Accumulation of Posts

At republican and federal levels this policy was implemented fairly thoroughly after 1966, though with some vagueness about where to draw the line and by no means total consistency. (See Chapter 8 for details.) At commune level there is more evidence of the high concentration of posts held by party officials up to 1964 (an average of six per person in a survey of Serbian party officials, and quite commonly seven to nine posts in the case of the most influential members of commune party committees according to a survey of the whole LCY), than there is of later trends.[6] The clearest information comes from the survey of Bosnian cadres at the end of the 1960s, which shows that while amateurs seldom held more than three posts at once, professionals in the commune quite often held five or more (about a third of the sample did). Details are set out in Table I drawn from the Bosnian survey.[7]

Table I   *Number of posts held by respondents at time of survey*

	1	2	3	4	5 or more	Total
Amateurs	44	101	124	82	11	362
Commune professionals	37	68	100	87	152	444
Republican and Federal professionals	22	33	29	15	19	118
Total	103	202	253	184	182	924

Social Composition of Cadres

The available statistics suggest that between 1963 and 1970 the proportion of partisan veterans on commune committees had fallen (15 per cent in 1970), and educational standards seem to have improved. But the proportion of workers and women on commune committees of the LCY fell between 1963 and 1970.[8]

Problems in Implementing the Cadre Policy

The most obvious conclusion from the available evidence is the strength of resistance by middle-level party officials to a real change in cadre policy: hence the 'rotation merry-go-round' and their continued accumulation of posts.

Debate and analysis of the results of applying these principles also suggested certain problems inherent in the principles themselves: for example constant renewal of committees could lead to a lack of continuity and experience; it was doubtful how far the party could go in giving amateurs political responsibility without a loss of efficiency;[9] and in practice the amateurs did not appear to reduce the power or alter the political style of key political officials, but rather constituted a second class of official with inferior power and prestige. Because amateurs could only take on certain kinds of role, they tended to hold the same post for longer periods, or even four or five times with brief breaks, in conflict with the principle of rotation of functions.[10]

Conclusion

Although the reformers achieved a limited success in implementing aspects of their cadre policy, it is doubtful whether this policy promoted the goals of inner-party democracy and a changed role for the League at lower levels of the LCY.

Notes

1. See *Komunist*, 16 July 1964; *Borba*, 7 November 1969; *NIN*, 22 March, 31 May 1970.
2. See *Komunist*, 8 September 1966; *Borba*, 8 October 1966.
3. See *Komunist*, 24 June 1965; Djuro Knežević, *Politički Profesionalizam u Savezu Komunista Jugoslavije*, magistarski rad, Beograd, 1974, p. 100. On the overall growth of full-time staff in the LCY by 1965 see: *Komunist*, 14 October, 28 October 1965; on conflicting trends between republics see: *Komunist*, 14 October 1965.
4. See Djuro Knežević, 'Primena principa rotacija u savezu komunista vojvodine', *Socijalizam*, No. 5, 1971, which draws on materials in his thesis.
5. See Stojan T. Tomić, *Politički Profesionalizam*, Sarajevo, 1972, especially p. 222.
6. See Zvonko Štaubringer, *SKJ izmedju VII i VIII Kongresa*, Sedma Sila, Beograd, 1964, p. 50; also *Komunist*, 27 February 1964; *Politika*, 5 May 1965. *Komunist*, 14 April 1966, suggests attempts were made in both 1964 and 1966 to cut down on accumulation of posts at commune level, but does not document results.
7. Tomić op. cit. p. 224.
8. There is some material on the social composition of committees in: Štaubringer op. cit. pp. 44-9, *Deseti Kongres SKJ: Statistički Podaci O Savezu Komunista Jugoslavije*, Beograd, 1974, pp. 170-5; also in *Komunist*, 23 December 1965; *NIN*, 31 May 1970.
9   See article by district secretary of Leskovac, defending his district against a critical article in *Komunist*, 11 November 1965; the possible advantages of being an amateur official (e.g. easier to delegate jobs to others) discussed by a commune secretary in *Komunist*, 2 June 1966.
10. See Tomić op. cit. pp. 221 and 236.

Appendix III Organization of the Central Committee and other central organs of the LCY: 1964–74

Eighth Congress of the LCY, December 1964

Central Committee of 155 members (elected by Congress)
Control Commission of 25 members (elected by Congress for the first time)
Revision (Auditing) Commission of 15 members (elected by Congress)
Executive Committee of Central Committee, 19 members (elected by Central Committee)
Secretariat of Central Committee: the system initiated in 1958 of having an Executive Committee Secretariat and a separate Organizational-Political Secretariat ended, and one unified Secretariat was created (The Secretariat in this sense is an inner executive organ made up usually of full time party secretaries)

Fifth Plenum of the Central Committee, September 1966, Authorizing Reorganization

Presidium of 35 members created, and members elected.
Executive Committee of 11 members elected and 6 Republican Secretaries co-opted (its membership was quite separate from the membership of the Presidium)
The Secretariat was disbanded

Ninth Congress of the LCY, March 1969

The bodies selected by this Congress were composed on the principle of equal representation for each republic and a lesser representation for the two provinces; candidates were elected in advance by republican and provincial congresses and ratified by the LCY Congress
Presidium (replacing former Central Committee) of 52 members, including 3 members of the LCY Organization in the Yugoslav People's Army

Standing Section of the LCY Conference (to meet annually) of 70 members
Statutory Commission (replacing Control Commission) of 14
Revision (Auditing) Commission of 7, excluding provincial representatives
Executive Bureau (replacing Executive Committee) of 14 members, plus the President, was elected directly by Congress on Tito's recommendation

The Second Conference of the LCY, January 1972
The Executive Bureau was reduced to 8 members

Tenth Congress of the LCY, May 1974
The principle of equal republican representation and proportional provincial representation, and advance selection of candidates at republican and provincial congresses, was maintained.
Central Committee of 166 members, including members of the LCY Organization in the Yugoslav People's Army
Statutory Commission of 24 members
Revision (Auditing) Commission of 15 members
Presidium of Central Committee of 39 members (elected by the Central Committee)
Executive Committee of Presidium of 12 members (elected by Presidium from among its own members)

NB: This summary does not cover the fluctuating and complex structure of the Central Committee's often numerous commissions on policy, ideology and party organization.

Note on elections: in many cases elections by Congresses or Central Committees were a pure formality confirming decisions already made; but there was a move towards greater consultation in selecting candidates and providing a degree of choice between 1966–71. Similarly republican election of candidates to federal bodies allowed for varying degrees of advance consultation with LCY executive organs.

Select Bibliography

This bibliography of books published in the West in English and French is not a comprehensive list of works on Yugoslavia, but focuses primarily on the party and on political developments and reforms since 1948.

Adizes, Ichak. *Industrial Democracy, Yugoslav Style*, Free Press, New York, 1971.

Auty, Phyllis. *Tito*, Penguin Books, Harmondsworth, 1974.

Avakumović, Ivan. *History of the Communist Party of Yugoslavia*, Vol. I, Aberdeen University Press, Aberdeen, 1964.

Barton, A. H., Denitch, B. and Kadushin, C. (eds.). *Opinion-making Élites in Yugoslavia*, Praeger, New York, 1973.

Bićanić, Rudolf. *Economic Policy in Socialist Yugoslavia*, Cambridge University Press, Cambridge, 1973.

Broekmeyer, M. J. (ed.). *Yugoslav Workers' Self-management*, Reidel, Dordrecht, 1970.

Burks, R. V. *The Dynamics of Communism in Eastern Europe,* Princeton University Press, Princeton, 1961.

Campbell, John C. *Tito's Separate Road,* Harper and Row, New York, 1967.

Canapa, M.-P. *Réforme Économique et Socialisme en Yougoslavie,* Colin, Paris, 1970.

Dedijer, Vladimir, *Tito Speaks*, Weidenfeld, London, 1953.

Denitch, Bogdan Denis. *The Legitimation of a Revolution*, Yale University Press, New Haven, 1976.

Dirlam, J. and Plummer, J. *An Introduction to the Yugoslav Economy*, Charles E. Merrill, Columbus, Ohio, 1972.

Djilas, Milovan. *Anatomy of a Moral,* Praeger, New York, 1959; *The New Class,* Allen and Unwin, London 1957; *The Unperfect Society*, Harcourt Brace and World, New York, 1969.

Doder, Dusko. *The Yugoslavs*, Allen and Unwin, London, 1979.

Drulović, Milojko. *Self-management on Trial,* Spokesman Books, Nottingham, 1978.

Farkas, Richard P. *Yugoslav Economic Development and Political Change,* Praeger, New York, 1975.

Farrell, R. Barry. Political leadership in Eastern Europe and the Soviet Union, Butterworths, London, 1970.

Fëjto, François. *A History of the People's Democracies,* Penguin, Harmondsworth, 1974.

Fisher, Jack C. *Yugoslavia – A Multinational State,* Chandler, San Francisco, 1966.

Hoffman, George W. and Neal, Fred Warner. *Yugoslavia and the New Communism,* Twentieth Century Fund, New York, 1962.

Hondius, Fritz W. *The Yugoslav Community of Nations,* Mouton, The Hague, 1968.

Horvat, Branko. *An Essay on Yugoslav Society,* International Arts and Sciences Press, White Plains, New York, 1969.

Ionescu, Ghita. *The Politics of the European Communist States,* Weidenfeld, London, 1967.

Jambrek, Peter. *Development and Social Change in Yugoslavia,* Saxon House, Farnborough, 1975.

Johnson, A. Ross. *The Transformation of Communist Ideology: The Yugoslav Case 1945-53,* MIT Press, Cambridge, Massachusetts, 1972.

Kolaja, Jiri. *Workers' Councils: The Yugoslav Experience,* Tavistock Publications, London, 1965.

Korbel, Josef. *Tito's Communism,* University of Denver Press, Denver, 1951.

Lapenna, Ivo. *State and Law: Soviet and Yugoslav Theory,* Athlone Press, London, 1964.

Lendvai, Paul. *Eagles in Cobwebs,* Macdonald, London, 1970.

Marković, Mihajlo. *From Affluence to Praxis,* Ann Arbor Paperbacks, The University of Michigan Press, Ann Arbor, 1974.

Marković, Mihajlo and Cohen, R. S. *The Rise and Fall of Socialist Humanism,* Spokesman Books, Nottingham, 1975.

Meister, Albert. *Ou Va L'Autogestion Yougoslave?* Editions Anthropos, Paris, 1970.

Milenkovitch, Deborah D. *Plan and Market in Yugoslav Economic Thought,* Yale University Press, New Haven, Connecticut, 1971.

Neal, Fred Warner. *Titoism in Action,* California University Press, Berkeley, 1958.

Pateman, Carole. *Participation and Democratic Theory,* Cambridge University Press, Cambridge, 1970.

Pavlowitch, Stevan K. *Yugoslavia,* Benn, London, 1971.

Robinson, Gertrude Joch. *Tito's Maverick Media*, University of Illinois Press, Urbana, 1977.

Rusinow, Dennison. *The Yugoslav Experiment 1948–1974*, Hurst and Co. for the Royal Institute of International Affairs, London, 1977.

Sher, Gerson S. Praxis, Indiana University Press, Bloomington, Indiana, Praxis, 1977.

Shoup, Paul. *Communism and the Yugoslav National Question*, Columbia University Press, New York, 1968.

Shoup, Paul. 'The League of Communists of Yugoslavia', in Stephen Fischer-Galati (ed.), *The Communist Parties of Eastern Europe*, Columbia University Press, New York, 1979.

Singleton, Fred. *Twentieth Century Yugoslavia*, Macmillan, London, 1976.

The Soviet-Yugoslav Dispute, Royal Institute of International Affairs, London, 1948 (text of the published correspondence).

Stojanović, Svetozar. *Between Ideals and Reality*, Oxford University Press, New York, 1973.

Ulam, Adam B. *Titoism and the Cominform*, Harvard University Press, Cambridge, Massachusetts, 1952.

Vanek, Jan. *The Economics of Workers' Management*, Allen and Unwin, London, 1972.

Vucinich, Wayne S. (ed.). *Contemporary Yugoslavia*, University of California Press, Berkeley, California, 1969.

Wilson, Duncan. *Tito's Yugoslavia*, Cambridge University Press, Cambridge, 1979.

Zaninovich, M. G. *The Development of Socialist Yugoslavia*, Johns Hopkins University Press, Baltimore, Maryland, 1968.

Zukin, Sharon. *Beyond Marx and Tito*, Cambridge University Press, Cambridge, 1975.

Periodicals, Newspapers and Research Reports

Yugoslav Sources

The main periodicals consulted are:

Gledišta
Jugoslovenski Pregled
Naše Teme (Zagreb)
New Yugoslav Law
Praxis (International Edition)
Pregled (Sarajevo)
Review of International Affairs

Socialist Thought and Practice
Socijalizam
Yugoslav Survey
(Published in Belgrade except where stated otherwise)

The main daily and weekly newspapers used are:

Borba
NIN (Nedeljne Informativne Novine)
Politika
Vjesnik (Zagreb)
VUS (Vjesnik u Srijedu) (Zagreb)

The Joint Translation Service, published by the American Embassy in Belgrade, produced daily translations of reports in all the above papers, but also included occasionally translations from: *Ekonomska Politika, Nova Makedonija* and *Oslobodjenje*. In addition the Joint Translation Service included some important articles from the intellectual periodicals (for example *Kniževene Novine*) and the student press.

Western Sources

Radio Free Europe Research Reports provide regular interpretations of developments in Yugoslavia based on the press and on radio and television broadcasts. The newspapers used for occasional coverage are: *Christian Science Monitor, Financial Times, Guardian, Le Monde, New York Times* and *The Times*.

Yugoslav Party Materials

LCY Congresses and Reports

Programme of the Communist Party of Yugoslavia, Belgrade, 1948.
V Kongres KPJ, Beograd, 1949.
Sixth Congress of the Communist Party of Yugoslavia, Beograd, 1953.
Der Sechste Kongress der KPJ, Bonn, 1952.
VII Kongres SKJ, Beograd, 1958.
VII Kongres SKJ: Stenografske Beleške, Beograd, 1958.
The Programme of the League of Communists, International Society for Socialist Studies, London, 1959.
VIIIth Congress of the LCY: Practice and Theory of Socialist Development in Yugoslavia, Beograd, 1965.

Osmi Kongres SKJ: Stenografske Beleške, Beograd, 1965.
Deveti Kongres SKJ: Stenografske Beleške, Beograd, 1970.
Ninth Congress of the League of Communists of Yugoslavia, Belgrade, 1969.
Konferencija SKJ: Aktualni Politički Situacija i Zadaci Savez Komunista, Beograd, 1970.
Deseti Kongres SKJ: Statistički Podaci, Beograd, 1974.
Draft Theses on the Reorganisation and Development of the League of Communists, Belgrade, April 1967.

Republican Party Materials

Kongresi Saveza Komunista Republika, Beograd, 1965.
Peti Kongres Saveza Crne Gore, Beograd, 1968.
Šesti Kongres, SKH: Stenografske Bilješke, Beograd, 1969.
X Sjednica Centralnog Komiteta Saveza Komunista Hrvatske, Zagreb, 1970.
28 Sjednica CK SKH: Izveštaj o Stanju SKH, Zagreb, 1972.
IV Congres SKS: Stenografske Beleške, Beograd, 1960.
Peti Kongres SKS, Beograd, 1965.
Šesti Kongres SKS, Beograd, 1968.
Izveštaji Šestom Kongresu Saveza Komunista Srbije, Beograd, 1968.

Other Sources

Komunist, the weekly paper of the League of Communists covers party meetings at central and republican levels and publicizes issues arising at local levels.
Socialist Thought and Practice and *Yugoslav Survey* both carry reports on LCY Central Committee Plenums, though these are also published separately.

Books and Pamphlets Published in Yugoslavia

Aktuelni Idejno-Politicki Problemi Daljeg Demokatskog Razvoja u Jugoslaviji, Institut za Politički Studije Visoke Škole Politički Nauka, Beograd, 1968.
Bakarić, Vladimir. *Aktuelni Problemi Sadašnje Etape Revolucije*, Stvarnost, Zagreb, 1969.
Bilandžić, Dušan. *Borba za Samoupravni Socijalizam u Jugoslaviji: 1945-1969*, Institut za Istoriju Radničkog Pokreta Hrvatske, Zagreb, 1969.
Bilandžić, Dušan. *Ideje i Praksa Društvenog Razvoja Jugoslavije 1945-1973*, Komunist, Beograd, 1973.

Bilandžić, Dušan. *Some Aspects of the Yugoslav System of Self Government and Worker Management,* Medjunarodna Politika, Beograd, 1968.

Dimković, Borislav. *Seljaštvo i Komunisti na Selu,* Centar za Političke Studije i Društveno-Političko Obrazovanje, Novi Sad, 1973.

Djordević, Jovan, *et al.* (eds.) *Teorija i Praksa Samoupravljanja u Jugoslaviji,* Radnička Štampa, Beograd, 1970.

Djurašković, Djuro. *Devet Kongresa SKJ,* Beogradski Izdavačko-Grafički Zavod, Beograd, 1974.

Djurašković, Djuro (ed.). *Naš Put,* Komunist, Beograd, 1969.

Izbori u Osnovnim Organizacijama Saveza Komunista kao Politički Proces, Radnički Radnički Univerzitet 'Djuro Djaković', Sarajevo, 1966.

Jerovšek, Janez. 'Structure of influence in the commune' in *Sociologija: Selected Articles 1959–1969,* Yugoslav Sociological Association, Belgrade, 1970.

Jugoslavija izmedju VIII i IX Kongresa, 1964–1969, Savezni Zavod za Statistiku, Beograd, 1969.

Kilibarda, Krsto Š. *Samoupravljanje i Savez Komunista,* Sociološki Institut, Beograd, 1966.

Marinković, Radivoje. *Ko Odlučuje u Komuni,* Institut Društvenih Nauka, Beograd, 1971.

Marjanović, Jovan R. *Savez Komunista Kroz Istoriju i Danas,* Centar za Društveno Političko Obrazovanje, Radnički Univerzitet 'Djuro Salaj', Beograd, 1968.

Marks i Savremenost, Prvi Naučni Skup Novi Sad 1964, Institut za Izučavanje Radničkog Pokreta, Beograd, 1964.

Milosavlevski, Slavko. *Revolucija i Anti Revolucija,* Revija, Beograd, 1971.

Morača, Pero. *The League of Communists of Yugoslavia,* Komunist, Belgrade, 1966.

Nikolić, Miloš (ed.). *SKJ u Uslovima Samoupravljanja: Zbornik Tekstova,* Kultura, Beograd, 1967.

Pašić, Najdan. *Političko Organizovanje Samoupravnog Društva,* Komunist, Beograd, 1970.

Pečujlić, Miroslav. *Horizonti Revolucije: Studije iz Političke Sociologije,* Institut za Političke Studije, Beograd, 1970.

Popov, Nebojša. *Partija (SKJ), Politička Vlast i Samoupravljanje,* Radnički Univerzitet 'Djuro Salaj', Beograd, 1966.

Radović, Radovan. *O Društveno-Političkoj Ulozi Saveza Komunista Jugoslavije,* Kultura, Beograd, 1966.

Reforma Saveza Komunista Hrvatska, Centar za Aktualni Politicki Studij, Narodno Sveučiliste 'Medveščak', Zagreb, 1970.

Sadaković, Ćazim. *Partija u Demokratiji*, N.I.P. Oslobodjenje, Sarajevo, 1972.

Šefer, Berislav. *Socijalna Politika i Savez Komunista Jugoslavije*, Radnički Univerzitet 'Djuro Salaj', Beograd, 1973.

SKJ u Uvjetima Samoupravnog Društva, Centar za Aktuelni Politicki Studij, Narodno Sveučiliste 'Medveščak', Zagreb, 1970.

Smiljković, Radoš. *SKJ u Procesu Konstituisanje Samoupravljanja*, N.I.P. Hronometar, Beograd, 1969.

Sokolović, Džemal, *et al. Savez Komunista u Integrisanim Organizacijama*, Studijski Centar Gradske Konferenicje SK B i H, Sarajevo, 1973.

Štaubringer, Zvonko. *SKJ izmedju VII i VIII Kongresa*, Sedma Sila, Beograd, 1964.

Sultanović, Vladimir, *et al. Struktura i Djelovanje Saveza Komunista u Sarajevu*, Studikjski Centar Gradske Konferencije SK B i H, Sarajevo, 1973.

Šuvar, Stipe, *et al. Društvene Promjene i Djelovanje Komunists u Selu*, Agrarni Institut, Zagreb, 1968.

Todorović, Mijalko. *Preobražaj SKJ*, Komunist, Beograd, 1968.

Tomić, Stojan T. *Politički Profesionalizam*, Univerzitet u Sarajevu, Sarajevo, 1972.

Vidaković, Zoran. *Promene u Strukturi Jugoslovenskog Društva i Savez Komunista*, Sedma Sila, Beograd, 1967.

Vukmanović Tempo, Svetozar. *Revolucija Koja Teče*, Memoari, Komunist, Beograd, 1971.

Županov, Josip. *Samoupravljanje i Društevna Moć*, Naše Teme, Zagreb, 1969.

Zvonarević, Mladen. *Javno Mnijenje Gradjana S.R. Hrvatske o Samoupravljanju*, Institut Drustvena Istrazivanja Sveučilista u Zagrebu, Zagreb, 1967.

Theses Consulted

Leslie Benson, *Class, Party and the Market in Yugoslavia, 1945-1968*, PhD Thesis, University of Kent, 1973.

Ramiz Crnišanin, *Socijalna Baza Savez Komunista u Socijalističkoj Republika Srbiji*, Magistarski Rad, Univerzitet u Beogradu, 1972.

Karen Rosenblum-Čale, *The Communal Assembly in Yugoslavia: Participation, Co-ordination and Development: The Case of the Mostar Commune 1965-1969*. PhD Thesis, London University, 1974.

Risto T. Kilibarda, *Socijalna Otvorenost Rukovodstva Savez Komunista Crne Gore,* Magi starski Rad, Fakultet Politički Nauka u Beogradu, 1973.

Djuro Knežević, *Politički Profesionalizam u Savezu Komunista Jugoslavije*, Magistarski Rad, Fakultet Politički Nauka u Beogradu, 1974.

Simo S. Nenezić, *Savremena Sadrzina i Funkcija Demokratskog Centralizma u SKJ*, Magistarski Rad, Univerzitet u Beogradu, 1973.

INDEX

This index covers all the personalities mentioned in the text. Newspapers and journals are indexed where they are part of the narrative or analysis, not where they are simply a source of quotes. General references to the League of Communists (or party) are so ubiquitous that they are not indexed, but specific League bodies, meetings or documents are.